Jim

Best Wishes

Arkadi

ROCK THEN ROLL

The Secrets of Culture-Driven Leadership

Arkadi Kuhlmann

Deak & Company Inc.

Printed in Canada

ISBN-13: 978-0-9869694-0-9 (cloth)

Library and Archives Canada Cataloguing in Publication

Kuhlmann, A. R., 1946-
Rock then roll: the secrets of culture-driven leadership
/ Arkadi Kuhlmann.

ISBN 978-0-9869694-0-9.—ISBN 978-0-9869694-1-6

1. Corporate culture. 2. Leadership. I. Title.

HD58.7.K84 2011   658.4'092   C2011-905190-7

This book is dedicated to the ING Direct
Associates that lead Americans
"Back to Savings" every day.

Table of Contents

CHAPTER 3

Rock then Roll the Market — Not Your Boat

CHAPTER 4

Rock then...What? How to Keep the Rock Rolling

CHAPTER 5

Rock then Roll: A Lifetime Journey?
Or Journey of a Lifetime

FIND OUT MORE ABOUT HOW YOU CAN ROCK THEN ROLL
YOUR BUSINESS AT WWW.ROCKTHENROLLBOOK.COM

BY MICHIEL R. LEENDERS

HOW TO USE THIS BOOK

Early on I tried to persuade Arkadi Kuhlmann to become an academic. Fortunately I failed. Arkadi turned out to be too much a builder of things and less an analyzer of things.

As he explains in his introduction, as CEO of ING Direct he got into the habit of composing daily "CEO messages" to all of his employees, sharing ideas and insights with them. These messages were debated among staff at lunches, breaks and other occasions. Obviously these messages collected here do not follow the typical A to B to C narrative. The messages have been rounded up under five general headings. These chapters are broken down further, but they are not meant to be exclusive or self-contained. Themes and ideas raised in one chapter or section may be revisited in another, but from a slightly different angle. The concept here is that one message tends to inadvertently reinforce another. Introductory chapters rough out the general outlines. But the red meat is in the messages themselves. How do you start?

Probably best to read it straight through quickly and get a feel for the style. Arkadi writes the way he talks: energetic, restless, improvisational—bubbling with ideas. Each chapter ends with a list of "takeaways": the nuggets of quarried gold you carry around with you. Memorize them. Make them a part of your thinking ritual.

After that first read anything goes. Sequence does not matter. Reflection does. This book is about leadership invention. From a leader who tied culture and leadership so tightly together they became inseparable. Focus on the ideas. Do you agree? Why? What surprises you? Do you have a better idea? If not, why not? As Arkadi insists, innovation does not stand still.

Arkadi does not tell you what your goals should be. That is for you to figure out. But he gives lots of ideas on how to get there.

This is a book that is meant to be chewed slowly, and not swallowed. Put the book down repeatedly and think about what you just read. Figure out what these lessons mean for you. Apply them. Use them. Add to them. As he says, leadership is always a work in progress.

Michiel R. Leenders
Professor Emeritus, Richard Ivey School of Business
The University of Western Ontario

WHY *CULTURE-DRIVEN?* WHY *ROCK THEN ROLL?*

Leadership used to be all about authority—top-down and personality-driven. Like a hammer.

Those days are gone. The world is becoming more and more global. The world, as well as business, has become radically decentralized. We have moved from vertically integrated centers of power and centralized authority to localized constellations of horizontally linked networks, where leadership and authority migrates from station to station and from skill to skill. People move around more, feel at home in many places, and communicate from locations around the world as if they were next door. This impacts culture and the way we live.

What does this have to do with business? Or leadership?

The single most dramatic consequence of these seismic shifts has been on how we interpret culture. Not just the culture at large, but the culture of your business and organization. Didn't think your business had a culture? Think again. Not sure what it is? Find out, and fast. Culture is everywhere. If you don't develop an instinct for recognizing the culture you are in—if you cannot develop a leadership approach that makes shaping and nurturing the right culture your priority, the odds are against you succeeding. It's that simple.

To maintain sanity, many of us in business just roll on through. I've done it. We are motivated by the feeling that it's easier to just get along. What's the big deal? We're dong fine. But today's business environment is a twenty-four-hours-a-day, seven-days-a-week butterfly effect writ large: a butterfly beats its wings here and three thousands miles away it causes a tsunami. Every day in business we face a new tsunami. We face challenges from every sector: the environment, the weather, political upheavals, social changes, technology, and social issues that speed up change. Consumer norms or preferences that would previously have taken years to accomplish and become established now occur in mere months. Trends are started overnight and disappear by sundown the next day.

For leadership, and for you as a leader, this cultural shift means a faster assimilation of ideas, more complex approaches to teamwork, and crucial new pressures on building and maintaining credibility—all elements of your survival in an increasingly competitive marketplace. The most effective leadership style today is, therefore, being a rebel *with* a cause.

Why a rebel? Simple. The mentality of a *business as usual* model is finished. Let's face it: the challenges that confront a business today were unthinkable even a few years ago. Every day is a new battle. If you think you can run your business by sticking to one of many versions of appeasement then your chances to win are small. The whole world is your Darth Vader. You have to be willing to fight, and win, every day.

Second chances are a luxury that most leaders cannot afford today. You need to face today's challenges head on, and be a rebel. What has being a rebel in my business meant for me? Just this: I had a cause that I thought was good, that I could commit to, and, above all, that I knew was worth fighting for. A rebel *with* a cause. Win or lose—make sure the journey and the fight have been worthwhile.

By Way of Biographical Introduction

I like to be out front—it is a huge part of who I am. My feeling is, it's hard to Rock then Roll from the back of the line. I have been called a rebel. Sure, whatever. People put tags on things to help them to understand what it is they're looking at when they are unsure.

"What the hell is that? Oh, it's a rebel."

Truth is, I am an outsider. I've always been an outsider. I feel comfortable in my skin being an outsider. That means I have a higher obligation to perform, deliver, and do a job well. Don't get me wrong, there is nothing wrong with being a rebel. I believe that being a rebel means that I'm willing to challenge and take on risks. I'm willing to commit and take on the responsibilities of challenging not only the marketplace but me also, and those around me. In everything I have ever done I feel that I have been true to who I am. This is the best way to be the best leader that you can be: stay true to who you are.

This book invites you to be a rebel leader today. Not tomorrow or next week. Today.

So ask yourself a question: why?

"Why *what*?" you might be wondering. Why do you want to be a leader? Nobody can be a good leader if they don't know why they want to be a leader. It is the most important question you will ever ask yourself. Or better, it will be the most important answer you ever come up with. We will get into more detail about this in Chapter 2.

What the Book Is

Over the years that I have worked and helped to build ING Direct, I'd like to think that I have learned a few things about leadership. What it is and what is isn't. How to build a business that works and how to contribute to a business that doesn't.

The most important lessons I have learned, however, are about how much business and life actually interact. In fact, how they should overlap and complement one another. We all work to live, as the saying goes. We shouldn't live to work.

As a CEO of ING Direct, I was in the habit of beginning each workday by sharing a message with my fellow associates. Some messages were practical and detailed and very specific to our work; some were more abstract or thoughtful, more philosophical or universal. But there was always a common theme, and our founding principles—both guiding and enduring principles—were always the same. Make a difference. Make this day matter.

These daily CEO messages were not meant to coerce or pacify, or to indoctrinate our associates with the party line. I wanted people to think about them—to debate them. Want to disagree? Perfect! Let's do that! In fact, we did. We shared our thoughts on the electronic bulletin board for everyone to read. I have held more than sixty town hall meetings and endless small group meetings and customer dialogues to discuss and debate these messages. I have used job swaps to understand other jobs in the business itself. New hiring classes always debated the principles in a book I co-authored with Bruce Philp, *The Orange Code: How ING Direct Succeeded by Being a Rebel With a Cause*. I am delighted that the book—and the principles on which it is based—are still discussed and debated inside ING Direct.

The messages collected in this book have been culled and winnowed down from more than ten years of experience as CEO of ING Direct. This isn't *The Gospel According to Arkadi Kuhlmann*. I don't want to impress you or convince you. As I say in this book, I'm not out there saving babies or curing cancer. I am in the banking business. So, no, don't read this book if you want to replicate a success story. That isn't what this book is about. I hope it's about thinking differently about the way we do business. About being a rebel. Don't agree! In fact, I hope you disagree with me. I love passion and conflict. I don't want to end the discussion, I want to start one. I want to fire you up to think like a rebel—whatever that is for you. So let me know what you think. No one ever knows so much that they wouldn't benefit from knowing more.

The numbers at the top of each message refer to the order in which they were originally written. We reshuffled them to roughly cohere around some core themes. I have tried to reduce as much repetition as possible and lengthened some entries to clarify or expand on a topic. General principles are covered in section openings. But don't look for a conventional straight-line narrative. Start at the end or the beginning or drop right into the middle. Have you seen the paintings in the pointillist style? Up close they appear as a bunch of colored dots, but as you step back a recognizable scene begins to take shape in the form of a picture.

These aren't answers. These are, I hope, like keys that will open doors to new ways of thinking about leadership. It isn't about what you know; it's about what you *do* with what you know. That is the essence of rebel thinking. Like I say in this book, we all tell stories. This is my story.

What will your story be? Whatever it is, it is for you to create. I hope this book helps you to become a rebel with a cause.

CHAPTER 1

ROCK THEN ROLL CULTURE:

It's What You Create

What is *Culture*-Driven and *How* Does it Rock?

Every business has a narrative. A story.

What's your company's story?

Everyone agrees: a company's culture is important. It's what makes a great company. You can get a sense of it the minute you step through the door. Consider the atmosphere, the architecture, the art, the layout, the offices—even the carpet or the coffee machines. Do you feel the buzz of purposed activity? Or do you see zombie-like employees paralleling the crowd shots from *Night of the Living Dead*? Just as a house or a wine has character, so, too, does a business. How people interact and speak with one another says a lot about their values and what makes the organization they work for hum. It's hard to describe, but everyone can identify it in some way. The key is, it's important.

Differences in culture are most easy to distinguish nationally. Business in Holland is done differently than business in Japan. I can't walk into a factory in Tokyo and expect to behave as the same CEO I am in Wilmington, Washington, or Moscow. Makes sense, right? Different place, different rules.

The same goal, however!

Okay, it's easy enough to accept the fact that people in different countries have different ways of doing things. What about the differences between one business and another? Borders are borders. Whether you find them on a map, in the form of a backyard fence, or in the hallway that divides your office from the one that sits right across from yours. Culture is everywhere.

You need to figure out what culture you are in. How diverse or uniform is it?

A Culture-Driven Landscape

It's not a top-down world anymore. It isn't enough to dictate. Leaders need to react to everyone and everything around them. Most importantly, though, a leader needs to create and nurture the right kind of culture that fits the vision of their business.

Ultimately, culture creates and sustains success. We have plenty of leadership, but not enough leadership based on culture. Culture is the environment, the overall architecture, of the organization we work in—the obvious "what meets the eye" of your business. More important, it is also the sum total of all the people that make up the group. Culture is the values that people embrace. It's the bedrock system of beliefs they talk about and say they will work and fight for or against. Every business has a culture; not every business has the right culture. What I hope comes through in the pages that follow is that your responsibility, as a leader, is to recognize and identify what that culture is—what is working and what isn't—and figure out how to move the culture to where you want it to be and then keeping it going.

Culture Is Active and Not Passive!

Culture will be created either with you or without you. Create the right culture and everyone wins; create the wrong culture and everything implodes. Think of yourself as the chef in a busy kitchen. You need to create a menu of recipes that all of your cooks will not only follow but recipes that they will also *want* to follow. People are not robots. Like any recipe, no two cooks are going to follow the instructions exactly the same way. You as a leader cannot guarantee how it will turn out— you cannot control the outcome. What if someone spontaneously decides to improvise? Creating the right culture does not eliminate risk. It creates an atmosphere of reduced risk where creative energy is channeled and made both more effective and more manageable.

Why do companies have such a difficult time managing culture? First, most have a simple and ironclad mandate to provide returns on capital. The structure is imposed from outside and controls what goes on inside. Be efficient, optimize, and do work. But structure and culture are not identical. Culture is not only the overall structure but originates from *within* and can be resistant to mandates from without. It includes all those individual sets of values that collectively come together to create an atmosphere for work.

Second, work tends to be visible, predictable, and controllable; culture, however, is much less visible, more elusive, and has a tendency to migrate along new and unexpected pathways in very unpredictable ways. It has been my experience that the success or failure of a company can be traced back to a sudden or very perceptible shift in culture. I recall a very large credit card company that was based on a growth model and was very successful in adding new customers and accounts in the affinity marketplace. The CEO needed to meet higher profit numbers demanded by investors, so emphasis was shifted from the growth model to a profits model. The change that resulted was too extreme; it changed the culture. Making profit became the number one goal instead of the customer. Result: customer loyalty slipped and the company dreamed of the old days as it was sold to another bank.

The most direct challenge to company culture, of course, occurs during periods of growth. Many companies lose their way on early successes and think that they are better in some way than the competition. Hubris. No one has the edge on anything for any length of time. You need to constantly be reinventing in order to win your place every day.

Creating the right culture for your business—the way your company works or thinks—is the best process for meeting those challenges. Everyone is better aligned with why the business can succeed and why the ultimate goal can be reached. If the basis on which you want to lead a company is rooted in the culture, then the culture becomes your rock and your foundation from which to lead. It's your watering hole!

Energy and Passion

If a culture has energy and passion then its leadership will have energy and passion, and vice versa. But no system can self-perpetuate indefinitely. Eventually, every culture winds down. You need to learn when the clock needs to be rewound. Thinking about your business as a whole, having and sharing a philosophy about the concept, its products and its services, and being able to communicate, with energetic passion, why it is worthwhile is at that top of the list of things you need to focus on. This passion can start in small steps and does not need to be everything at once. It starts with you; from there it's a continuing and ever-evolving work-in-progress.

Creating the right culture also means that the people you work with need to not only know who you are but also need understand what you are all about. What are your stories? What do you care about? To be and remain authentic and real you will need to prove it over time, and the more consistent you are, the more consistent your message will be, and the better the result. Making culture-driven leadership work for you is thus as much an art as it is a science.

Remember, you as leader are the most important x-factor in the creation-of-culture equation.

Getting the Culture Right

Culture is just as important for the startup of a big corporation and every size business in between. You need a feedback loop between yourself and the rest of your company, especially as the company grows and organizational structures become more complex and remote. In a startup the culture is a blank page. Your responsibility is to fill it up before it is filled in for you, which can happen faster than you think. As your company grows, it gets more complicated. There become simply more and more opportunities for invasive culture to take root, and it is much harder to remove bad habits from a business culture than it is to create and maintain the right habits from the beginning. What is most important is reinforcing the cultural norms that work and eliminating—ruthlessly eliminating—any norms that do not. It is as simple as pulling weeds.

At ING Direct, our culture was based on the Orange Code. Very simply laid out, it is a set of core beliefs that would define and guide us from beginning to end, not only as a company but also as individuals. The Code, and the cultural norms that evolved as a result, became the honey that attracted new associates who shared our vision and the mission. If ING Direct was a nation, the Code would be its constitution. If we were a political organization it would be our manifesto.

The Orange Code wasn't created to control or limit creativity or to regiment behavior. It wasn't a warning sign on the factory wall. Rather, it set out cultural principles like "we will be fair" and "we will constantly learn." The Code wasn't everything, of course. Job skills mattered. Performance mattered. We all wanted to and had to make money.

But we wanted to *do it differently*. The Code took the basics—like having a good job and making money—as a given. What it did was orient each ING Direct associate to a larger goal. Fidelity to the Code mattered. We wanted to change the way our industry operated. We could not do that unless each and every one of us knew what we believed those changes were and why they mattered. It wasn't about conformity. It was about liberating people to change the world by basing change—real change—on principles. That was our culture. It probably isn't the same as the culture at your business. And that is the whole point. At ING Direct we wanted the culture outlined by the Code, not our profits, to drive our business. If we were successful, profits would come, but that was not the primary goal. That was not the mission.

Corporate culture requires constant attention and active involvement. It generates its own momentum—good and bad. A culture will be created one way or another; letting a culture evolve on its own, in your absence, so to speak, is no different than putting a stranger in charge of your business. The preferred alternative is to actively direct and shape it.

The first question you ask yourself is this: can I be a rebel if I have created and maintained a conventional business culture?

Let me help you: no, you can't. You need to adopt and embrace a culture-driven philosophy. Otherwise it's the same box but with a different lid.

The Ten Secrets of Culture-Driven Leadership

1. Every business can be—and is—defined by its culture. The people who work in the business create this culture.

2. A company's culture is what both customers and the public say about it—the way one describes it behind its back.

3. If you do not deliberately influence a brand, it will be created by itself. Company culture fills in the space with symbols, rules, and styles. A company's culture, brand, and people do not operate inside a vacuum.

4. A company's brand is its face to the world, but it's the people that work there that bring it alive with the actions they create. Culture is always personal.

5. Almost every business today is diverse and is a mix of symbols, backgrounds, and values from many parts of the world. The world is now local. No company today can be singularly labeled.

6. To connect with customers and people in your business you must personalize the culture of the business. It's a pure bottom-up and not a top-down flow of ideas and information. As a leader you need to connect with your employees and customers in continuous dialogue. Think horizontal.

7. Leadership is what you do, not where you come from. A successful company culture is always open to new leadership at every level.

8. You must have a clearly defined bias for action.

9. The power a leader taps into is the culture of the company. You are its voice. To be authentic your voice must always be about the vision and the goal of the company.

You must carry the torch and you must be perceived as carrying the torch.

10. There are no universal leadership styles. Leadership today is more of a transitional experience than ever before. Leaders continue to lead because they continue to win every day.

Both the speed and the pace of change are more important for leadership than any other aspect of business activity. Business results are important. But so is luck—being in the right place in the right time. However, luck is not decisive. Making sure your business has the right culture is decisive. What is the right culture? A culture that fits the mission and the business.

How do we know this is true? Everyone has a voice. Everyone wants to be heard. Everything now comes down to a vote. Vote with the ballot box, vote with what you buy, and social media will determine if you are leading tomorrow. News and opinions are constantly flowing about everyday life and events. Leadership and its worth are therefore evaluated every day.

———◦———

CEO Message 43
FOLLOW THE CODE

We would probably all agree that when it comes to leaders, Moses was among the best. But imagine what would have happened had he come down from the mountain without the two tablets.

In business, as in life, we need rules. Not to limit our freedom of action, but to enlarge those freedoms by creating *foundational norms*. Only a fool sets to sea without a compass.

rock then roll culture 17

When we launched ING Direct the first thing we did was put together a business plan to implement the vision. Where do we want to go with this? How are we going to get there? We then established a set of easy to follow, simple, and direct principles that would be our compass in whatever we did and wherever we went. I believed in them; it was necessary that our associates believed in them, too—no exceptions. I still do.

The Principles of the Orange Code

1. We are new here.
2. Our mission is to help people take care of the wealth they make.
3. We will be fair.
4. We will constantly learn.
5. We will change and adapt and dwell only in the present and in the future.
6. We will listen; we will invent; we will simplify.
7. We will never stop asking why or why not?
8. We will create wealth for ourselves, too, but we will do this by creating value.
9. We will tell the truth.
10. We will be for everyone.
11. We aren't conquerors—we are pioneers. We are not here to destroy; we are here to create.
12. We will never be finished.

If you don't have a code, create one. And stick to it. Every mission needs a blueprint, a declaration, a plan, or a manifesto that you can wave and point to as your authority. As a leader, it will be the most important thing you ever do.

CEO Message 119
VALUES, NOT NORMS

The most important thing in any company is to create a culture around values and not behavioral norms.

Norms are easy to identify and easy to describe to anyone: "This is how we do it here."

Values, on the other hand, are aspirations; they function as a compass providing the company with the proper direction and orientation on how to work and how to make decisions for the betterment of both individuals and the company as a whole. Your values—your company's values—need to be clearly set and communicated to everyone to demonstrate the character of your company as it grows. Values cannot, and should not, be changed, they are an absolute. The values create the culture. That culture will drive your business.

CEO Message 69
A CULTURE OF DISCIPLINE OR A DISCIPLINED CULTURE?

Telling everyone what to do is a culture of discipline. A disciplined culture, however, is not merely a semantic inversion. A culture that can be described as focused, rigorous, precise, and, yes, disciplined, starts with and requires a personal commitment towards working that way. In other words, a disciplined culture rewards people with naturally disciplined approaches to work.

It has been my experience that when managers talk about discipline, generally they are talking about disciplining others and not themselves. Do as I say and not as I do. That is culture of discipline talk. The essence of culture-driven leadership is to always be seen as one who leads by example.

Physician, Heal Thyself

Most of us, as managers, favor coaching. However, to be a good coach you need to be able to do the job well yourself. Give credit where it is due, be supportive, and practice what you preach. Simple, but true! Discipline as a component of company culture is a way of demonstrating respect and value for the organization, but it will only be an authentic element of your culture when it is shared and practiced on a day-to-day basis by everyone. Discipline begins with the individual and filters down in the organization; it very seldom goes up. Discipline could be defined as deliberate action moving in a clear way in order to get something done. Do today what needs to be done: same-day processing. Do not leave tonight from work until all calls are answered and all items in the in-box are dealt with. Stick to timelines and deadlines. Be thorough and be complete in everything you do; that is the surest way of avoiding costly mistakes. This is good execution and very action oriented. Discipline is sometimes referred to as execution, but whichever way you describe it, it's all about getting to it and getting it done right.

Make discipline a part of your company culture.

CEO Message 3
MY STORY

I started with ING Direct because I wanted to challenge the status quo. I disliked big banks and the way they did business. As I saw it at the time, at the front lines they were mainly arrogant and looked down at customers. As a customer myself, I always felt that I had to prove or justify why I was allowed to do business with them. I also knew that was not how I felt when I went to, say, my favorite men's clothier. They liked me and my business; they made me feel welcome and appreciated. Why, I thought, can't the banking experience be more like the retail experience? Why was banking culture the way it was? And could I create a different culture for doing the same business? Hey, it's my money. You're not doing me a favor!

Change the thinking; change the culture. Change the culture and the thinking changes along with it.

CEO Message 87
HOW FAR CAN YOU STRETCH THE CULTURE?

A culture is diluted from the center out and, as a result, is more blurred at the edges. It is a fluid thing that needs to be watched and managed.

All companies want to get the most from combining human resources with strategic objectives to build value in a company.

When a company starts up with an entrepreneurial drive, marshalling concepts, creative ideas, passion, and energy, it is easy to create teams, team spirit, and a positive culture. However, as companies grow, more and more is required for structure, such as policies and procedures that seem, on the surface, to take away a lot of the characteristics that make small companies agile and successful. The shoemaker at the corner will help you and give you quick service. That is his culture. The motor vehicle office in town will give you a ticket with a number for a window when it is free. That is their culture. Big companies often create a lot of extra structure in their operations to deal with volume, kind of like layers and layers of scaffolding. That's what a customer sees: your culture cannot be hidden from view.

The bigger the company the more thinly stretched its culture.

A History Lesson

ING Direct started as a very small company and, in a very short period of time, we found ourselves on the verge of morphing into a very large one. The stresses and pressures on our culture were enormous. How would we manage the growth without diluting our culture? Could it be done?

Frankly, it is rarely done. Or rather, it is rarely done effectively.

The culprit is a quite understandable instinct that I call *adding on*: your company begins with one great thing and you succeed beyond your wildest dreams, and then before you know it all critical thinking stops and it's one mad rush to multiply. Another term for it is the *rabbit effect*. The thinking becomes, "Hell, if this works here then we can do it any time, anywhere, any way." Think Krispy Kreme donuts or Blockbuster, Starbucks or Burger King.

How would we be different? How would we grow and maintain the culture that created our success—the culture that our customers liked and depended on? Do customers want this or are other factors at play like regulators or new regulations? As we expanded we continued to split geographically and into smaller and more easily managed units. The thinking was, keep breaking it out and out *horizontally* instead of building it up and adding to layers *vertically*.

Very few business cultures can survive the crushing weight of so much vertical integration intact. Another name for it is *bureaucratization*. Instead, we moved ourselves outwards. More and more teams were created of like-sizes distributed across distances we could manage where everyone knew each other and knew whom they could count on. More important, that kind of distribution never created a crisis of culture. In fact, it was that original culture that continued to keep the growth going!

The rule of thumb for you is, if your company's growth is threatening your culture, you are moving in the wrong direction. The business culture must always drive your growth.

Here is another example of culture-based pressure points.

Most of us are familiar with the problem of having too few employees. For small operations, adding employees and maintaining efficiency is relatively easy. Things get more complicated with growth at a certain magnitude. In management there is a concept known as *factory unit size* that defines maximum capacities for efficiency. Essentially, the maximum for any operation in one location is 250 people. Beyond that, efficiency begins to degrade. Culture dilutes and dissipates.

Growth is important for any business. But for a leader, you need to have an idea of what kind—and what level—of growth is compatible with the skills and interests of everyone in the company. Formulating your own views and strategies on this topic is vital. It is part of the monitoring and the promotion of the right culture. Not every leader is a leader under all conditions—some excel at small operations and some at large. That is why most acquisitions do not work. It's mainly about financial issues and the culture is glossed over, forgotten, or assumed to just work. Obviously, growth itself creates new opportunities, but it can change the rules under which the business operates. I have seen excellent leaders in one capacity migrate to another position only to have their effectiveness neutralized or even reversed.

Nothing can kill morale at a business faster than people finding themselves in the wrong positions. For someone who is outspoken, comfortable taking charge, enjoys running against the grain, or dealing with problems and people one-on-one, a smaller operation may be ideal. A larger operation may need individuals with more diplomatic communication or political skills, and more subtle approaches.

If it's your company, you are going to have to make the hard choices about who fits where and why. If you don't know why, growth will create disastrous pressure and breaking points. The next head on the block could be yours. Learn to say "no" as easily as "yes."

Mission and Vision: Where Are You and Your Business? Who Are You?

For me, a vision—corporate or personal—must be fundamentally good for society; in turn it will also be good for the organization and for the individual. The connection of these three elements—society, organization, and individual—must be identifiable and stand in its own right. Focusing on one while assuming the other two will look after themselves will not go far in today's complex world. A pillar in the Rock then Roll approach is that the vision that animates a company—and to be a real vision it does need to animate the company, a slogan is not enough—needs to have a beneficial or benevolent social component. Obviously this is not true of other approaches. Some businesses are in business to make money. End of. Okay, I get that. It just so happens that I am not interested in that and I have to presume that if you are reading this book that you are not necessarily satisfied with that either. I don't mean that we all need to be Mother Teresa. But your product or service needs to be seen as good and not just profitable. You don't need your employees to believe in your corporate slogan. You do need them to believe in your corporate mission.

Part I: The Culture-Driven Mission

A First Principle

People who work for a paycheck are working for companies without a vision. Create a vision that people can believe in and commit to, and you have created agents of change.

The vision is the goal paraphrased—made articulate, accessible and universal. The mission, in turn, is the means to the goal: how you get to it.

A mission has a specific goal, target, or result in mind. It's usually more short-term, but like a vision for a company a mission is forward-looking and brings to the company story a sense of purpose and passion.

Think of your company's mission as its vision with its feet on the ground.

Collectively then, the mission itself must be inherently good, it must be measurable and it must be concrete. Quality is number one; or, leading Americans back to savings. Both are inherently good and the business results prove the case. The products are recognized as the very best. Americans are saving more.

The goals must be perceived to be achievable. In practice this is not always easy. There are no guaranteed outcomes. Each decision has judgment and risk attached to it. We take risks and assume a lot only to be proven right or wrong later. A vision—and the mission to make your goal a reality—is never a straight line. To make it happen you need to get results. Think of it as a journey or a quest where you have to constantly point the way through uncharted territory.

A Job? Or a Mission?

The most important question to ask yourself about corporate culture is whether you think your employees think they're in a job or on a mission. A visionary leader creates a mission, and inspires employees to feel that way, too.

Remember being a rebel with a cause? You need to create a mission with a cause. It's a shame that the corporate mission statement went out of fashion, though it's easy to see

"Figure out who I am before you say hello." —AK

why it happened. Too many such statements failed at their task. An effective vision has to be one that shakes up the status quo and starts a revolution. No one will ever be inspired by a puddle of ambiguity. Too many corporate mission statements were diluted into dullness by consensus and from being fed through multiple levels of approval, making them utterly ineffective for rallying the troops. Like putting filet mignon through a sausage grinder.

A mission, though, is the best leadership tool you have to work with. In grassroots political organizations it occurs almost spontaneously, without central leadership, because enough people believe in a cause. A team with a purpose beats a team with a process any day! So what makes the difference between a forgettable mission statement and one that turns workers into devotees? There are five key qualities to consider:

First: A mission statement must advocate for someone.

At ING Direct, we set out to champion customers who were being preyed upon by the traditional banking industry. We offered these customers a way to save without the extortionist fees. In short, we empowered our customers to take control of their financial destiny.

Second: The goal in the mission statement should be nearly impossible to achieve.

We never deluded ourselves into thinking we would win every customer to our bank. But the feeling was, and still is, that we might. That was how powerful our commitment to the cause was. Had we created far more modest goals, we probably would have lost interest. Reaching for the goal is the inspiring and satisfying part. It's a journey. The horizon should always remain just beyond reach.

Third: A mission statement should read like poetry.

It should be sonorous and simple, and catchy enough that people won't be able to get it out of their heads. "Ask not what your country can do for you, but what you can do for your country." A president's plea for citizens to dedicate themselves to national service—expressed poetically and memorably.

Fourth: A mission statement should be written with the leader and the most loyal followers in mind.

It does not have to please everyone. It has to matter, however, to the people who are committed and practice it every day.

Fifth: You must come up with the mission statement yourself.

Don't ask the elevator operator or any consultant or advisor to come up with an inspiring mission statement. Declaring the company's purpose is a leadership responsibility, as is creating the culture. Collaborating on your mission statement or delegating the task goes against the very nature of visionary leadership. As leader you must not only embody the company's cause, but also define it.

Part II: The Culture-Driven Vision

A company must have a vision—a long-term projection or far-away idea of what the company can be. A company's culture is how that vision takes shape. It is through the energy and direction of a leader that culture is created.

The story you want your business to tell is not about a set of rules or dogmas or procedures outlined in the company handbook. It isn't about making money. People will always work for money and opportunities for career advancement. That isn't news. *That isn't the story*.

Vision is what animates the mission. It's what gives the mission its life. What really makes a culture click is if its participants can work for a cause and see a future that they can be proud of, one that has made a difference and that individuals feel they were a part of. That is the story.

Make creating and nurturing your company's story the focus of your leadership.

Don't Nail Your Vision to The Wall: Live It!

Every company claims to have a mission; it writes it down and promotes it with lapel pins and brochure statements. Is that a mission? Not to a culture-driven leader. Your challenge is to transform that flat two-dimensional mission statement into a three-dimensional reality—into a story—and manage it in a way that achieves the overall goals and aspirations of the stakeholders in the company. The vision is a living and breathing story that evolves over time, especially during periods of prolonged crisis or difficulty. Everyone will retell a good story. Therefore, you need to be prepared to articulate the vision on an ongoing basis; it needs to permeate all the actions and ideas that are generated throughout your daily work.

For instance, I look at the world around me and ask, what could be done better? Where are the friction points? Every good leader is driven by a desire to do things better and achieve better results. I started in every job I had with a desire to fix something. That approach fueled my vision. The desire to fix and the specifics of my vision, in turn, then become my mission.

A History Lesson

ING Direct really believed that leading Americans back to saving by simplifying financial products was a way for us to reconnect with consumers and be a challenger to the status quo. In economics there is a term for this: disintermediation. It's a process of forceful disruption that leads to creative innovation—like cutting out the middleman. Every good business that has a model to disintermediate the current marketplace and come up with new ways of doing things has to find a new way of connecting with customers.

You rock so I roll? The idea was not to have the same old conversations, but to try a fresh approach—to create a new conversation and a new culture. We looked at the retail model. Our new conversation would be a bank built on the retail model. That conversation would be about making it simple. We would emphasize savings.

Sure, it may sound old fashioned. It was! But we wanted to have a new conversation and this was the point. Customers were familiar with a traditional banking culture. We created a new culture. The mission: "Lead America back to Savings"; our vision: we don't act like a traditional bank because we aren't a traditional bank. Combined, they drove and sustained the alternative conversation we sought with the consumer.

We believed it; they believed it. It was a simple idea. But what a match!

———◁○▷———

CEO Message 28
KEEP IT SIMPLE

No concept is talked about and repeated more but applied less than simplicity.

Keeping it simple. Simple means easy, straightforward, fast; simple saves you time, money, and energy.

You know that making something simple can be very complicated and sometimes daunting. The world around us tends to make things complex and it's a constant struggle to keep things simple. It's common that the more products and services are played with the more complex they become. The last thing that you should do is appoint a product manager—he will spend all his efforts improving and invariably complicating a product. If we are to get our vision accomplished then our mission must be clear, and having a passion about making something simple, celebrating things that are simple, and encouraging things to be simple, is a skill and a goal that needs to be adopted and practiced every day. If the vision is to deal with saving your money, then making it simple is the way to hit the ball out of the park. Our mission at ING Direct was to provide simple financial products for consumers. Nothing more—but nothing less.

CEO Message 259
A TO B AND NOT Z

A culture-driven mission must be straightforward. Intuitively understood. It cannot need or require further explanation—like a reflex. It is a path with actionable steps that gets it done. Now, if you ask most people they will tell you the same thing: they want to simplify things.

But do they? More likely it's just something said. Blowing smoke. Like if the guy who manufactures red tape talks about cutting the red tape. Real simplification is the hard work of tearing everything—every process, procedure, product and *idea* (including especially all your own ideas and biases about how the world works)—down to its essentials. The basics.

The mission also demands that when you simplify you will also standardize and make the products or services easy to understand. It's the basis of customizing. Everyone should be able to fill in the blanks for a simple mission statement.

I think of it as the path I'm on and the goal is the top of the mountain, so to speak. You have to *rock* to get everyone's attention and then you have to *roll* on and deliver. I wanted to make dealing with money really easy so that people felt confident in transacting.

Why So Many Buttons?

I have always had trouble with television remotes. Designed by an engineer and supposedly good for all capabilities, but most people only use three buttons and never touch the other twenty! So design a remote with three buttons and it's very empowering for ninety percent of all users and to hell with the other ten percent. Everyday people are into the here and now! Fast, then faster! I believe that people want to see the movie more than they want to play with the remote! Crazy, right?

Imagine, a remote that actually gets you only where you want to go!

———◄◦►———

Strategy: How to Sell the Rock so You Can Roll

It's been said that more battles have been won by bad generals than by bad strategies: strategy is hugely important.

When a company has a unique customer proposition, which results in competitive advantage, it then has a strategy.

A business strategy is a plan, a set of actions or tactics to achieve a specific goal. It's a game plan on how to succeed and achieve a goal given the constraints in the marketplace. This could involve constraints from competitors, regulators, or any other obstacles that your business could face. What is the plan? How can we win? It is also noteworthy that every strategy is dependent in some way on the people that will execute the plan and implement the strategy that a business wants to use.

You need to focus on your strategy and understand how to use it to achieve your goal. The thinking and the planning are important, but the most important element is the execution. You have to *commit to the strategy* and *personify the strategy and goal*. Simply put, you need to lead and show the way. Rock then Roll is an approach and a style that helps you focus on a continuous change process. What can you avoid doing? What really needs to be done? The style that you adopt and project in culture-driven leadership is not just about the look and the manner—it must be a holistic view of how you handle yourself. Connection to the culture of a business is important. Leading the discussion and the managing direction with a strategy is the first step everyone is looking for: *a reason to follow you.*

The ING Direct vision was simple: lead Americans back to savings. Our mission was to simplify financial products. But what was the strategy? Build commodity-standardized products, make them simple, and sell them in a lower-cost mass-market way to everyday Americans. The vision and mission over the years never changed, but the strategy kept being adjusted in terms of scale, complexity, and trade-offs of evaluating what worked and what did not. Whether to change a strategy or stick with it is the reason businesses have leaders.

The larger the company, the more clear and specific your strategy must be. A small business can afford to be a bit more flexible and less precise and articulate about its strategy. You most likely do not have voting shareholders or boards of directors. As a business grows, however, it becomes increasingly important that you make your strategy explicit and consistent. It's what investors will want to know if they put money into your company.

Large or small, a company, and you as its leader, has to be willing and able to adjust if the economy or the markets suddenly turn against it. The only thing worse than not having a good strategy or having an inconsistent strategy is desperately hanging onto a strategy past its best before date. A Rock then Roll refrain to remember: adapt and improvise.

Warning: do not mix up tactics with strategy. A tactic is a series of specific actions—short-term steps—designed to get you to a specific goal. It's a way of moving the strategy forward. Don't talk about the strategy, just do it. The resulting impact comes from actions and tracking results step-by-step.

Change is hard; implementing ideas and business factors is not easy but it can be exercised. Nothing stays steady and judgments have to be made. Your culture will help define what is possible and what cannot be done. When I was at Deak International, a large precious metal and foreign exchange company, we needed to change strategy and increase profits by focusing more on winning than on too many ideas and project workstreams, most of which were very good but would not have the impact we needed.

I had to make choices on the strategy without changing the vision and the mission, which was to be the best retail distribution company in foreign exchange. We narrowed the geography in which we operated and we changed our tactics: we decided to stay open longer for our retail customers and made it a priority to stake out more unusual and, we hoped, more convenient places to transact business. We accomplished this because the frontline staff could see the resistance to the old methods and saw how this could help us meet our vision and mission. The changes we aligned with our values, and the desire to win in a controlled way fit with how our staff understood our culture, which was rooted in a trading, flexible way to do transactions. Nothing being changed ran counter to these beliefs or the values of the company. The staff liked the "rock" to adjust and then they wanted to "roll" and do some business.

After leadership, strategy is the most misused word in management. When you have a great product or service and it is better than your competitor's market products, then, as a challenger, you will win. Winning is the sum total of many factors and contributions, but a good strategy is a universal fundamental. You cannot win without a good strategy to back up your vision. How do you know if you have a good strategy? Make it simple: Take a step back right now. Ask yourself, How good is my service or product? If they aren't the best, ask yourself how come and what do you need to do to make them the best? Your job as leader is to always be the compass needle pointing due north.

CEO Message 157

IDEAS AND STRATEGY

Think of ideas as raindrops falling from the sky—ideas are plentiful and many of them are good. But there should only be one strategy. Business success is based on the execution of one strategy at a time.

CEO Message 155

STRATEGY, TACTICS, AND EXECUTION

Energy should be spent on execution at two times the rate as on tactics, and three times the rate as on strategy. The awareness and insights to execute well are legendary in the theory that *retail is detail*. Excellent execution can make up for a so-so or an okay strategy, but not the other way around. The thing about execution is, it touches everything. The way you dress, talk, work, and participate is a reflection of your performance.

Get the proportions right.

CEO Message 185

STRATEGY EVOLVES

ING Direct, like all start-ups (especially a disruptive player like we were), must mature its business strategy as the business itself grows. An entry strategy is key, but must be refined and adjusted as the market changes and competitors react. A strategy is not a straight line. The market zigs and you need to zag. A famous philosopher once said, "From the crooked timber of humanity nothing straight is made." The same is true for business.

The vision and mission stay the same, but the strategy can, and should, evolve to meet the needs of every shifting business landscape. What customers perceive about who you are must be adjusted and refreshed over time. The problem many businesses have is confusing mission and vision with strategy, so that adopting a new strategy means changing or abandoning the mission and the vision. Executing an effective strategy is never a straight line.

The Brand: It's What Is Said About You

A brand is the relationship between a company and a customer; the strength of that relationship is measured by reputation.

Branding has become the Holy Grail of the business world. It's hugely important, no argument. But it's easy to get tangled up in the high weeds.

What is branding?

Maybe it's easier to begin with what it isn't. Putting a name, graphic, slogan, or a number of letters on a product, service, building, or a sign is really just labeling. A company's trademark is represented in its logo. It can be direct and simple or complex and evocative.

The letters NBC and the peacock tell us this is the National Broadcasting Company. It's an identifier. On the other hand, it doesn't tell you anything about what kinds of programs they broadcast. It only tells you what the company is, not who they are. It isn't CBS or ABC but that is about all you know. Nike's iconic swoosh logo, however, invokes specific imagery about itself, who it is, and its range of products. Its purely visual logo seems to make it stand out not so much against its competition—say, Adidas or Converse—but outside the world of its competition. So basically, labeling is the process whereby a company defines the products and services it offers or provides, generally differentiating itself from other businesses providing similar products or services. Branding, however, is quite different.

A Brand Must Stand for Something

For a label to be a brand, it has to stand for something. What it stands for is the key energy driver behind the brand attributes. It must generate a real emotional response from a consumer. A child draws a circle with spiky lines coming out of it. She calls it the sun. Okay, the label is the picture. The brand is the sun's heat.

Brand positioning—where your brand falls on the customer receptivity scale in terms of emotional or ideological response and connection—is critical; that connection is a measure of the durability and the development of the marketing activity that contributes to branding. Too much marketing, in my experience, is basically nothing but making noise to interrupt people in the hopes they will eventually listen and buy a product. Good idea, bad execution.

Effective branding is all about creating and sustaining meaningful, emotional relationships between the customer and your product or service. A customer hopefully will feel good about what he bought. It's the key for a repeat purchase. It's important what he says to his friends about the product or service.

An emotional response, then, that is predictable and repeatable, meaning the transaction will create the same response each time, is the template of true brand power. Think of it as marketing with a personal endorsement.

For instance, our mission at ING Direct, as I have said, was to simplify financial products and our vision was to lead Americans back to savings. But would that message resonate beyond the point of sale? Would the brand *carry*? Okay, so what did "leading Americans back to savings" actually mean?

Opening savings accounts? Yes. But the pillars supporting that simple idea were bedrock values like self-reliance, thrift, hard work, financial autonomy, prudence, and a better quality of life.

Our brand was defined as financial empowerment through positive action. Our theme was freedom—a cornerstone of America's great promise of life, liberty, and the pursuit of happiness. It wasn't about logic. It was about making a primal, emotional connection. If you have money then you have choices. Choice is freedom. For ING Direct the magic of the brand was independence and freedom. For Nike's "Just Do It" customer, it is something else.

What is it for your customer? Make your brand synonymous with your culture and vice versa.

CEO Message 209
BE DIFFERENT

Rule number one for effective branding is to make sure your product or service is different from any other. You have to stand out. Whether it's the product, the service the company provides, or even you, you have to stand out. Why? To get anything done you have to be noticed. It is also just as important to make sure the reason you stand out, what gets you noticed, makes a positive connection with your customer. Sounds easy, even obvious, but when it comes to business very little attention is focused on it.

No one needs or wants what is next door. To stand out your product or service needs to be different. These days customers have endless choice. In fact, they expect choice and they will pick what suits them best. Copying a product or service that is already widely available in the market is a short-term gain and adds little to the quality of the market.

It's either choose "me" or "me too."

Get noticed. Be different.

Stand out ... or stand to the side.

CEO Message I
SIMPLICITY BRAND

Keeping it simple sounds simple. But it can be a bitch.

We all talk about it, we all think we know what it means, but how do we make it work? Let's look at the importance of simplicity. Its primary function is to help a customer use a product, make it easy to understand, intuitive to use with no errors. Simplicity also means to do the work with less costs; it's to get the biggest benefit and the most value with the least amount of effort. This is true for the supplier and the user! You ask yourself the questions, "Does what I'm doing today meet the test of simplicity?" "Do we need to change the rules, procedures, steps, or the delivery?" It's hard to identify. It's hard work.

Simplifying things is a struggle but the payoffs are exponential. That's why everyone talks about it but little time or results come out of this battle cry! You and your team need to challenge each other on making it simple—to make the goal of simplicity a part of your conversation and emphasize it as one of your primary duties. Doing things simply is a way to make daily work consistent with the company brand, position, and values.

A sunrise brings a new day, but also drags forward all the unresolved or holdover clutter of yesterday. It's a new start to lead, so shift the agenda and think basic stuff. Today, focus on simplicity—the primary challenge for any business. The biggest challenge for every business, of course, is to be efficient. If you sell a product or a service then you need to do it at a low cost that meets the quality requirements and gives it a price advantage over the competition. Making this challenge explicit and finding creative, smart ways to help a business attain effective leadership can make this happen with energy and, above all, a passion that will infect the business culture.

For instance, at ING Direct part of our business model required that we have customers fill out an application form. We knew the information that was needed to get the job done. But was it simple? We retraced all the steps and all the logic. We looked at how a customer would read the form and how they would fill it in. We tested how fast someone could fill it in without thinking too much. We made it easy. We simplified. Customers even contacted us to tell us how much they liked our application form. Wow.

There are lots of reasons to *add* features to any product or service. For one thing, it's easy. But it's deceitful. Keeping something simple means keeping it authentic and honest. To make a product or service easy-to-use and intuitive is challenging. One has to understand how people use things and how they go about understanding things. Less is more. Make it pure; keep it natural.

A History Lesson

I recall working at Deak International and thinking how we could make foreign exchange simpler. Every hotel, airline, and shop wanted to sell something, but how to deal with foreign currency was a problem. Exchange rates and the logistics of handling cash are not easy. I thought about selling envelopes with fixed amounts that allow you to put a fixed price on the envelope and a bar code to count the number of envelopes. Now anyone could sell foreign exchange and move the transactions along. Fair for customers with small amounts and increased the availability to many more outlets. When changing the game and making things better, it's the win that it's all about.

The mathematician and philosopher Alfred North Whitehead said, "Simplify everything. But don't trust it." Brilliant. Always keep simplifying. Never feel you have completed the task. The culture that preaches simplicity wins every time.

CEO Message 35
ABUSING THE CUSTOMER ABUSES THE BRAND

How many of you can relate to this: you have a question about a product and you call the number that the company provides for customer questions or feedback. What you hear is, "Your call is very important to us. Please hold."

One question: if I am so important, how come I'm on hold?

Part of lousy brand management is forgetting the obvious: your customer has choices.

CEO Message 96
WHAT'S SAID ABOUT YOU IS WHAT'S SAID ABOUT YOUR BRAND

Think of your brand as what people say behind your back. The marketing concept of NPS (net promoter score) tells you the number of promoters of your services versus the number of critics or detractors. Getting more customers to say positive things means delivering good quality at every opportunity.

It's not what you say or profess: it's what you do for your customers that counts.

Interestingly, what is said about your brand is not that much different than what is said about you. That is the nature of culture-driven leadership: in many ways you are the brand. Look at Apple's Steve Jobs.

We cannot control all of what people say about us behind our backs. Let's agree, it happens and it happens a lot. You need to develop sharp radar for workplace intelligence (yeah, what you might call gossip). I wrote earlier that we all need feedback loops. The more visible you are as a CEO the more spontaneous those feedback loops are, but the idea is not necessarily to correct the impression, or debate, or deny. Remember, it's not whether what is said is true or not; what matters is the perception.

Eating Some CEO Crow

Last year, I was told by a senior executive at ING bank that I was difficult to work with. Maybe I should be more accommodating! he suggested to someone else in the company. Now, a few years ago I might have confronted this colleague. Challenged him. Was it true? Was I difficult to work with? I didn't think so. But then, that was *my* perception. His perception was different. Who was right? It doesn't matter! Right or wrong, it was important that I try to shape the perception by preempting any negative with a positive. For instance, in meetings with fellow executives I made a point of leading with that perception as a way of neutralizing the response. "I do not wish to be difficult here," I would say. "As a matter of fact I am totally committed to a good outcome on this credit policy and here is how I think we can all win. I'll do my part."

The point is, I would never know if that complaint about my style was objective criticism or purely personal subjectivity. It doesn't really matter, the perception problem is the same. The key was that I took action. You can too.

Remember the game Whack-a-Mole where the moles keep popping up and you have to hammer them down very fast? That's your program to manage reputation.

CEO Message 37
FIND THE BIAS AND RUN WITH IT

A brand is not always a message you can control. Be in front of your brand. But watch your back.

Years ago when the TV show *Friends* was a huge hit I was in a restaurant in New York. The hostess who escorted us to our table was breathless with excitement. She explained that one of the stars of the show had just been at our table.

"She was so nice!" our hostess gushed.

I was happy for her, of course, but curious. "Well," I asked her, "why wouldn't she be nice?"

Our hostess paused. "Oh I don't know. Just because. You know. She's a star."

What people might think about you, or, more specifically, your brand may not even have anything to do with what you have actually said or done. Your customer may have notions or ideas, unexpressed or powerful biases, for or against you.

CEO Message 52
UNDERSTANDING BRAND

In many ways the brand is meant to differentiate your business from everyone else's. Its real value is long term in regards to getting customers to buy your products and services. Your business has a personal brand.

What are you known for? "We bake bread." Okay, but what kind of bread? How do you bake it? What are you doing that all the other bakers out there aren't doing just as well as you? What makes you special? A personal brand is more than an advertising slogan. Think of advertising as the sign on the outside of the brand; it's what's inside that really counts.

Labeling and advertising are not branding; real branding comes through a customer's experience. It is very hard to get a customer engaged in advertising, letters, newspaper clippings, and billboards. Even events and promotions have limited customer involvement. The real brand experience comes when a customer interacts with the product or service. That transaction is the key to bringing the brand alive

"Your personal brand is what people say about you behind your back." —AK

and creating customer-held perceptions, which, in the end, translate into brand experience. Ideally, that customer's positive experience will translate into a positive commitment to what the company stands for and what it means to them to buy its products. So when you look at the touch points for consumers remember that branding starts with experiencing the products and services.

Every time I meet someone new, the conversation goes like this:

"Hi, I'm so and so. What do you do?"

I tell them.

"Oh, I've heard of your company and I like the orange savings account!"

I'm thrilled that you do.

Still Waiting on That Second Impression?

People like to share positive experiences. It's human nature. I like a movie and I find out that you like the same movie. I naturally want to talk to you about why we like the movie. This critical nexus—the crossroad of positive experiences—is where the most important brand work gets done. Of course, negative experiences can be just as powerful too for consumer unity. Never underestimate the power of brand experience. You'll never have a second chance to make a first impression, right? It's true. Make that positive first impression and your customer is out there spreading the gospel.

Remember that kid no one would hang out with because everyone thought he peed in the pool? As a brand manager, your customers are the pool. Don't pee in the pool!

CEO Message 235
CUSTOMERS DECIDE ... NOT YOU

A company brand is earned and decided by customers for the rest of the marketplace. It always strikes me how misused the branding aspects are dealt with in large companies. A reputation takes years to build and can be destroyed over night. True. A brand takes years to be adopted but can disappear as quickly as a snuffed match. Many leaders wake up one day and find that they had counted on yesterday's momentum and brand value to propel through today only to discover that—poof—it's gone.

Fads need to reinvent themselves in the market and—to stay relevant and valuable—and so does a brand. How do you reinvent a fad? Find a new idea, a new fad, a retro, or a remake. Everything has a lifespan: products, processes, innovations—even ideas. Just when one good idea has run its course there is the idea whose time has come! It's important to always be improving whatever you are working on. Some things last longer than others and some shorter, but everything has a life span. Stay in touch for the exact moment to hit the *new* NEW button.

CEO Message 15
TRUTH

For all of us at ING Direct, our main core value was walking the talk. Our mantra was, "We only say what we will do. You've got to tell the truth."

This specific value has never changed and it never will. It's what sustains the brand. How you present the brand to the customer can change, and it should change. Keeping a brand fresh is a huge but exciting challenge. But what cannot change is the *meaning* of the brand for the customer.

CEO Message 59
FIND THE BRAND GROOVE

Brand culture is about energy, passion, and creativity; to build a brand is to accelerate the growth of the business—like getting into the "groove" of customers wishes! Your culture shakes hands with their culture.

CEO Message 34

GOOD MAY NOT BE GOOD ENOUGH; BETTER IS THE KEY

You cannot build a brand without a good product or service. Get the product or service right; find the value from the customers' point of view.

Unless your products or services are good and better than the competition you don't have a viable business. What is the winning formula of your products? Think of your business being built like Lego blocks. Each product has to be a positive addition to building the brand. I am amazed that even today, after the financial crisis, as balance sheets and profits are being rebuilt, there is so little talk or effort being put out into making products better. It seems that every bank just wants to survive and get back to the perceived normal.

The best secret for a leader in a company is this: create a culture that celebrates better, unique, game-changing products as opposed to more of the same.

CEO Message 36

BRAND PERSONALITY

Find a brand personality (characteristics, habits, etc.) that is the real road map to building a product or service with the customer in tow.

Yes, *personality*!

Is the product important? Is it friendly? Is it outgoing? Is it innovative?

You may have heard that companies share personalities, much like people resemble their dogs, their cars, and the clothes they wear. It's the same for a company. Customers use a few common words to describe your company. So work with that and do not try to change it. You may call it the Seattle

Space Needle but the street may just call it the Needle. Main Street has to like your name or they will change it for you.

In the early days of ING Direct, I often found myself thinking about what type of car or what type of movie I could use to describe the business we were building. Start with a blank sheet of paper. You are thinking about a product, a service, an idea that will sell or, more importantly, will be useful. Someone needs this! We all look to buy something from a company we like, one that we feel an affinity for.

So Who Will You Be?

The better you can articulate this and describe it the better you will succeed at the communication and marketing challenges ahead. You as a leader should fit this personality, as should most of the folks working with you. You will then hear comments like this: "The staff here is really helpful." "It's what makes me come back week after week." Engaged and committed employees must use and buy the products or service that the business sells. Otherwise, what are they saying about the company?

ING Direct was innovative, straightforward, and different than other banks. Those adjectives became our personality traits. We needed to make sure that everything we did tied back into these personality traits. Simple, intuitive, rebellious, fair, and easy to deal with. You can see how this linked-thinking cascades down further. We needed to look more like a retailer—a place that sells—because that made ING Direct very different from every other bank.

Cut as much out as you can that does not fit your company's personality clues.

Case in point: at ING Direct we wanted to be a different kind of bank. So, step one: don't hire conventional bankers.

BRAND TRUTH

Truth is, a company's brand really belongs to the customer. It is the customer who interprets it, talks about it, and defines it. Marketing, especially Internet marketing, which tries to bring a brand to life, can initiate the process but, like all selling, the result is not precise; it's how people talk about it and act upon it. The final verdict on a brand is what people say about that brand when the company is not present. By the way, your personal reputation is also what people say about you when you are not around.

Name a few brands you admire and think of why that is. If you think of Amazon, Netflix, or Southwest Airlines, you know what they are known for and you also know what they do not do. The more distinctive their reputation, the better and more powerful the brand. The truth is short and easy to understand. It's central to good brands.

How Culture Creates Value For Your Brand

Creating value is holistic; it's empowerment, whether the value is products, services, customers, or shareholders. Value has two important dimensions: usefulness and quality. Everything you do has to be useful to a customer and appreciated by the customer for being intrinsic to the product or service. Are the products or services you provide *in themselves* better than what your competitor provides? How is everything you are doing helping to distinguish your product or service?

Value creation is a twenty-four-hours-a-day, seven-days-a-week commitment. It starts with a good idea, but it doesn't end there. If you're lucky you will see sales increase. The risk is interpreting an increase in sales as automatic validation of the choices you made. You can get soft or lazy. A familiar strategy is to fall back on the *more of the same* formula. But sales can be like the tides and by the time they begin to dip it may be too late to tinker with your value-creation strategy.

Minimize the rise and fall of the sales tides by never losing focus. Focus is the key to creating and maintaining positive brand culture. You need to know the real reason why a product or service sells. Don't look outside the culture. Stay true to the vision, the culture-driven vision!

———◦———

CEO Message 237
NOW WHAT?

The value of the brand created has to be reaffirmed on a daily basis. How do we do this? Let's look at the four key steps that each and every one of us can take each day:

1. Focus. Jealously guard the few things that are most important, that you can do the best, and get them done.
2. Simplify. The greatest value in our complex world is to simplify. Draw the shortest direct line between any two points.
3. Measure everything. Without keeping score we cannot ask the questions that will lead to uncovering value. You cannot find a hidden treasure without a map.
4. Culture. Everyone needs to have a shared idea of the brand value and know that this shared vision cannot be compromised.

A culture that strives for value has a distinctive characteristic of discipline. Having a culture that reinforces discipline and puts emphasis on achievement will create its own momentum.

A good leader has to embody these four attributes and live them.

CEO Message 65
WHERE IS YOUR FOCUS?

With values you must focus on content and never on the management process. You look for the best idea and do not care where it comes from or who brought it to the table. It's open and it acknowledges *who* thinks *what*, not *who* says *what* and *when*. This may be too chaotic for many companies and many people. Why do it then? Because the leader's main task is to make something better for the customer. Do this and, trust me, the profits will follow.

Getting the Proportions Right

In every big organization I have worked in, the focus is always the opposite. How much of a profit can we make? How much of a profit do we need to make? And then, how much can be sold?

No surprise that this does not work very well. Most leaders cannot articulate a good answer to the question of, "Why are your customers buying your products?"

Never be confused: customer value drives your business.

CEO Message 202
BRAND EXPERIENCE

All success begins and ends with the brand experience.

As a leader you need to have a mental checklist of how your brand is being used and it needs to be updated constantly. Nothing is more common than success leading to a sense of complacency about what your customers are thinking of buying, what their wants will be tomorrow, and what they will eventually buy.

CEO Message 73
YOU NEED MORE WOW IN YOUR DAY

In my time at ING Direct we received, on average, fifteen thousand calls a day, some days more. Each one is an opportunity to create a "wow!"

What is a "wow!"?

Simple: a virtually priceless opportunity to create customer happiness through first-rate service.

For instance, no automated telephone system. I never allowed our callers to be put on hold. It cost us a fortune not to have our call centers routed off shore, but if you call us, you will get an associate on the end of the line, right away. And most importantly, we insisted on keeping our business structured as simply as possible so that every associate has the power of a CEO to assist you and answer your questions.

It isn't only that we want to process your request. We want to know why you called. Are you having issues or problems? I always insisted our associates ask our callers if there was anything we could do for them that we weren't already doing. This wasn't a kiss off or some fake courtesy, a wham bam, thank you, ma'am! Next? No, I really wanted to know. If it matters to you and we can do it without busting our basic business model, then we'll do it.

Here's the thing: in theory, creating a "wow!" is simple. It is easy to plan it, design the process of implementation, set out the incentives, and focus on it. To do it every day consistently, though, is a tough job.

CEO Message 199
TAKING RISKS

If you want your company to be better than the rest, you need to take a risk and be different. So what do you do?

You need to understand your cost structure, your brand, and your service philosophy; you need to make sure that everyone in the company understands, at a grassroots level, how the customer is using your product or service.

You won't always get it right, but that isn't the point. You can get close, and that is what matters. Always stay as close to your customer experience as you can—be a customer yourself.

But what about your customers who cannot or refuse to be simple? The ones who don't buy into your model or, perhaps, buy only half of it? As I have said elsewhere, it's sometimes better not to have a customer in the first place than to have to waste money and resources retaining a customer for the wrong reasons. I used to tell my associates, always be professional and polite, but firm; firmness is your first line of defense in protecting the brand.

A History Lesson

The problem customer for ING Direct was the one who had trouble with the direct method of using financial products.

The rule of thumb is, no matter how hard you try you cannot make everyone happy.

"I need a paper statement."

We don't do paper statements. That feature was not part of who we were. The reason we could offer outstanding interest rates was because we insisted on low overhead. So, no paper statements. But I know who does provide paper statements.

If your product or service is right, there are always going to be more customers that work well with the way your company operates than customers who don't—so don't waste money and resources chasing the don'ts. The cost and drag on your performance are very real.

CEO Message 321
PURPOSE VS. ENDORSER BRAND?

Brands get built in many ways but also have different jobs to do.

An *endorser brand* creates awareness and supports recognition of what a company stands for and what it hopes to achieve. A *purpose brand* is created to do a job for a customer and solve specific needs that consumers have. It gets known for something and the reputation of the brand is clearly linked to specific performance: "Save your money"; "Let your fingers do the walking." The endorser brand makes no such claim but reports a positive intent. Consumers are clear in understanding the difference.

Google, for instance, came up with "Do no evil." As a company it stands by that endorsement and promises to defend against its defined "evil." Many customers may wish to join Google because of what it stands for. IBM's "Smart thinking" to improve the world is another stake in the ground.

Hugely important: whatever positive identification a company creates with its customers from endorser branding will vanish in an instant if the commitment collapses. So, choose an endorser brand that works hard for your mission and will for the long term, not just the short.

CEO Message 82
WORKING HARD ON THE RIGHT ROAD

How many times have you heard someone say, "I saw that advertisement but I don't know what they sell or do?"

An icon, a color, a slogan can all be evidence of a company; they can be important clues to the recognition of a brand. But nothing on the outside makes up for what is on the inside. A brand needs content—the "what" of what you are known for. The classic mistake is lavishing so much bling on to your product that people forget where it came from. The products can be more famous than the business behind them.

Here is a typical conversation when an ad appears on TV for a new car:

"Wow, awesome!"

"Who makes it?"

"I have no idea."

Your Own Field of Dreams

Many companies fall into the classic trap of advertising the brand and not advertising the product or service. Don't tell me what you are. Instead, tell me what you do and I'll determine who you are! Companies often slip into thinking that if they advertise a certain attribute long and hard enough, eventually everyone will get all the attributes intended.

This very seldom happens.

"Ever feel like you are herding cats?" This was an advertising slogan from KPMG. Okay, what is the product or service? Unfortunately, there is no indication within this slogan. Banks often advertise, "We are here for you!" This states a simple fact but it doesn't tell me what the product or service is that you are telling me about.

It's what I call *build it and they will come* promotion. Do you remember that line from the movie, *Field of Dreams*? Everyone in the town thought the hero was nuts for building a ballpark for no reason. "Build it and they will come." Too many businesses, and the advertisers they hire to brand them, think that if you have a great product or service customers will magically appear to buy it; inevitably, they will (they must!) come.

Fine movie, bad business strategy.

The reason a product or service works is that it hits on a real need or desire. It's an instant customer fit, maybe even a fit that the customer was not fully aware of, but the idea was within reach. No customer decided he or she needed to walk around while listening to music. But the Sony Walkman was invented and customers bought them like crazy. So, was the success Sony's or were people always happy to listen to music no matter where they were?

What did the iPod do? We were presented with pictures of deliriously happy people dancing around while listening to music from a device as small as a credit card. That was the fit—freedom of mobility! It told me exactly what I needed to know *and* in a way that made me feel empowered.

Getting It Right

True success is when a company designs a product or service, engineers it correctly, delivers it the way it's supposed to be delivered, and accurately promotes and advertises it. Think of the Apple iPad. Every step supports the next on the way to a customer's hand. The credibility that is gained by not only delivering what you say you will deliver but also making that product or service remarkable from the customer's perspective is what creates *buzz*—the excitement and energy customers feel when they buy the product, because of the product. The role of advertising is to send a message to consumers, but it is the customer response—the "wow!"—that dictates what the experience is all about.

Job number one is to get the product and the service right. The new idea has to be innovative and the timing has to be ideal: the right idea for the right product, in the right place, at the right time, and for the right price. There is a saying that rings true here: success has many parents, but failure is an orphan. Ultimately, success cannot be predicted.

What F. Scott Fitzgerald said about their being "no second acts" in American life is just as true for business. Amen.

—◇—

The Key to Culture-Driven Longevity: Get Your Customer Right

In the jungle the hungry get fed first. What that means to me in business is simple: I take care of my core customer. When it comes to pleasing and providing for your customer, my zig to the conventional zag has been that we don't give everyone what they want; there's always a little bit of self-selection at play.

For instance, I have learned that people with more than one million dollars in an account need lots of services and lots of help. They've got big financial issues. But people with normal, everyday amounts of money have very standardized needs. The two sets of customers comprise two independent sets of cultures but—at least to me—had always been treated as if they lived in the same culture. The reality of that is not true. A key to getting the customer right is getting the culture right. A culture that is too broadly defined is basically not defined; it ceases to be a culture if it is too inclusive.

The Key to Culture-Driven Longevity: Get Your Customer Right

Be Straight with Customers

Have you ever asked the question, why do you get a different interest rate for a Certificate of Deposit if the CD is six months or twelve months? I'm sure someone would answer, "because there's a longer commitment of time." Well, that's an interesting idea, but is that actually the way it works? No.

Our plan translated into this: sure, we'll take your money. But don't expect anything extra just because your account holds one million dollars and the other guy's holds two hundred bucks and change. You will both get the same, excellent service.

The Customer

Near the end of my tenure at ING Direct in North America we had roughly ten million customers. What that means, especially in the landscape of today's social media presence, is that we had ten million ways every day to either get it right or to get it wrong. Everyone has a voice, an opinion, and a vote. When one unhappy customer makes a negative comment through social media about ING Direct, about something we did, where we went wrong, anything, twenty evangelists for the brand jumped on top of the complaining individual and said, "No, that's your fault. ING Direct is not wrong. ING Direct was right. You're wrong."

On the other hand, if you get it wrong, if you fail to walk the talk, if you break faith with your customer, then what happens? It's not the packaging, the slick ads, the clever advertising campaigns, or any additional bells and whistles that matter—the customer is the keeper of the keys when it comes to your kingdom. Social media is the most powerful branding tool at your disposal; it is also the most lethal. It has never been more important to get your product right and keep it right.

You may not get a second chance.

Advocacy is an important factor in how to get on the right side with customers. It's not just selling a good product or service; it's important to share with the customer your and your company's values—what your company stands for and represents. That is what customers care about and will talk about and recommend to others. It's the key to social media and how the world now connects and interacts. Vote with your time, your money and your ballot box is the new reality. It's instant and it's almost instantaneously viral. Everyone knows everything and being a successful leader requires that you be personal and consistent with your message. You and the message you broadcast via your brand and your culture must penetrate the noise in today's marketplace and resonate with them. Your culture needs to create a positive and self-reinforcing echo.

CEO Message 317
EARLY LESSONS ABOUT GETTING
THE CUSTOMER RIGHT

The Key to
Culture-Driven
Longevity:
Get Your
Customer
Right

My first job as a young boy was to deliver newspapers after school. I may have learned all I needed in life from the experience I got delivering papers every day, six days a week starting at age eleven. After school I rushed home, loaded up the papers on the front and back carrier of my bike, and headed up one side and down the other of each street in the neighborhood. It provided me with good exercise and a sense of accomplishment as the load on my bicycle got lighter and the route shorter as I inched closer to home. This meant no after school activities, but it did mean pocket money and money to help my mom out at home. I learned responsibility to do my job, perseverance to stick with it, and a sense of ownership.

I also learned a lot about customers: picky ones, grumpy ones and, yes, friendly ones. Being charming and helpful with customers worked like magic for my reputation while word of mouth helped me get more customers and resulted in my winning a contest for a transistor radio by signing up the most new accounts that month. The route also taught me a lot about collecting money, even when my customers pretended not to hear my knock on the door. I knocked a bit harder, or maybe I came back later from the other side of the street. The unleashed dogs were a challenge, of course.

The customers that got to know me were mostly friendly and appreciated my good service. Sometimes I got a tip. Usually I got one at Christmas. On my delivery and collection route on Saturdays I would end at Mrs. Ferguson's house. She paid as I tore out her receipt, then she gave me a big, matronly hug. In my customer's bosom I began to appreciate the value of charm and good service.

CEO Message 37
THE CUSTOMER IS ALWAYS RIGHT, RIGHT?

Customers are always right—except when they aren't. Knowing which is which, and when, can be critical.

Customers are *not* always right. But knowing why they are wrong and about what can be hugely important. A great customer will tell us things that flatter us—great to hear! But it's preaching to the choir. A bad or disgruntled customer can tell you a lot about what they like and don't like and how they use a product or service, or how they don't. Deciding whether or not to use a customer's comments to shape the product or service, and exactly how to use this information, is an important task for you as a leader. A leader sets direction and says, "This way!" The way has to be where the customers are going. If things align right, you will win.

How do you know? If you have a business that is done in a specific way and it works, then the customer has to use it the way it is intended. Sometimes a customer may want to use a product or service in a way that may improve its intended use, but not always. A good leader generally has an instinct for those adjustments that falls within the improvement or improved-use category and those that do not. Think of change as having two orientations: vertical and horizontal.

A vertical change takes your further along the path to your goal. A horizontal change, on the other hand, takes you sideways and away from your goal.

Being everything to every customer is a disaster. Knowing whether to change or not, whether to listen to a customer's ideas or not, is a skill that is learned over time and with experience. Like any skill, it is more easily described than defined. But having an understanding of human psychology, especially customer psychology, is an excellent grounding.

A History Lesson

There were many times when building ING Direct that I had to say, "Let's do this now." For instance, a few years back we had an opportunity to buy Sharebuilder, a small unique brokerage firm in Seattle. The fact is, moving into both the investing and brokerage areas was not an obvious choice. I knew we needed to expand our savings products to include brokerage products and I knew that we had to be different than the rest. The timing of the idea was right.

I knew that the transaction would be difficult and that it came with a lot of risk. I was uncertain of the decision and knew it might come across as a strategic move, which, by definition, has an outcome that cannot be easily predicted or seen—similar to a chess move. But I was confident that *I knew what our customers wanted*. This, to me, was a change based on my belief of who our core customer was. It was a vertical change, not a horizontal one.

I decided that this was the way, and it was the right decision. Our customers liked it. Lucky for me the buffalo were there.

Know where the buffalo are and take us there if you want to earn the right to lead. Follow the buffalo, Skywalker!

CEO Message 18
WHAT'S IN A NAME?

A customer buys a product or service once and that is it. The relationship moves in a simple back and forth exchange. If you are lucky, she may come back. If she finds a better price for your product elsewhere then the relationship is broken. If you look at a consumer only as a customer you reduce to a minimum the opportunities for repeat consumption. That raises your costs in the long run by forcing you to invest more in finding new customers.

A consumer is an opportunity for more sales. Keep the relationship alive!

CEO Message 78
NOBODY LIKES BEING SCREWED. SO WHY DO IT?

It's no secret that building a consumer business base is essential.

What might be a secret is this: it is easier and far less costly to keep the customers you have than having to make more investments in a continuous hunt for new customers.

Why, I ask, do so many businesses disrespect their customers? As a veteran of the banking industry, I have nothing but contempt for companies that perpetuate an atmosphere of complexity as a means of fostering consumer confusion. Customers just keep on moving, hoping to find a better deal. If they were switching banks, for instance, because the alternative offered a better deal for the same service, then that would be one thing. But my experience has been that most customers migrate out of frustration. They just want something different, sometimes not even really knowing why, and leave hoping that this time it will be better.

For instance, mortgage rules are scaled and worded so deliberately complex that confused and bewildered consumers feel justified paying ridiculous fees to the banks who arrange them. This is extortion! Have you ever seen a young couple emerge from a typical meeting with a mortgage broker? Do they look happy and confident? Is all this complexity justified?

Hell no.

It's greed. Most companies are focused on short-term shareholder value. Instead of maximizing the total number of loyal customers and recognizing their long-term potential, companies nickel and dime their customers—sometimes to death. And they can do this because most industries, in my case most banks, all conform to the same business practices. So, if you are unhappy with Bank A and leave for Bank B, for instance, you will probably bump into a customer who has just left Bank B for Bank A. And both of you will have the same complaint! Where is the real choice in service here? There isn't one. How are these banks building customer loyalty? They aren't.

Yeah, I Got Gripes

Why are you asked by your credit card company to pay extra for security from identity theft? Shouldn't *they* be providing you security as part of the business experience? It's their product! Have you ever asked why we don't sell syringes to teenagers but we give them credit cards?

How about banks advertising that they will change their priority process manner by charging to your checking account the smallest checks first and then the larger ones? In the past they did it the other way around and then charged you for every item in an overdraft charge. It was unfair, but now they claim to have "seen the light." Well, good—better late than never. But think of the industry mindset that for years deliberately overcharged you and that only recently was shamed into changing that policy, yet has the nerve to advertise it like they had your interests at heart the whole time! *We were always unfair but now due to pressure you should be happy that we are going to be fair.*

Any seller of a good or service has a responsibility not to become an enabler that harms the customer. This is especially true in banking. So at ING Direct we decided that we would have minimal fees. No small print. Why waste creative energy on schemes to squeeze every last penny out of loyal customers and then have to find new ones? It made no sense.

Most important, we knew that a customer that was on his or her way to true financial security was a customer for life. As a leader, you need to think less about attracting new customers and remind yourself what it was you did to get those customers in the first place.

CEO Message 188
ARE YOU BLAMING YOUR CUSTOMER?

At ING Direct our company playbook—our Orange Code—says: "Our mission is to help people take care of the wealth they make."

Good. It's a great message. It still is, and not just for associates of ING Direct. In fact, it seemed to me that if the message we broadcast to our customers was so great then we

ought to be embracing the same message ourselves. Really—
we needed to practice this too.

Knowing how to budget, plan your finances, and be conservative with your credit is important. As is maximizing
savings and living within one's means. We all are different in
how we wish to live but having a quality life starts with common sense. Making sensible assumptions with money and
showing restraint with debt is a big part of setting oneself on
a solid footing. If you want to help others, set a good example.

The Key to
Culture-Driven
Longevity:
Get Your
Customer
Right

We're All Swimming in the Same Pool

As CEO at ING Direct, it was important that we all walked
the talk and set a good example for others.

We all face the same challenges when it comes to money.
Those of us that work in a bank have the same pressures to
manage money as the guy working construction or the phar-
macist at the drugstore.

What does this mean in practical terms?

To me, being an effective CEO is not just about the great
product. It's not about being a one-dimensional leader, either.
I have never been comfortable with one-dimensional commitments from anyone. The "this is who I am at work but this
is who I am outside work" employee never worked for me.

It's been said a million times: business is all about the great
customer experience. But that experience cannot be defined
only in the short term. A terrible debut experience with a
customer is like tripping at the starting line. The race is lost.
But races can be lost in the last turn just as easily as in the
first. As a leader you cannot ignore the long-term implication
of creating and maintaining excellent customer experience.

Customers do not become loyal to you nor will they mutiny as a result of one experience. Customer affection or disaffection is the result of a legacy of experiences. One-time mistakes can be forgiven. A series of them cannot. Don't risk polishing up your resume sooner than you thought.

I made a commitment at the very beginning that ING Direct was going to be a different bank. Part of putting the customer first was drawing a line between what we *could* do as a bank and what we *should* do.

Why Blame the Customer?

Have you ever wondered why so many people get into trouble with their banks? Is it the customer who is always at fault? Or is it the bank that too often dangles shiny toys in front of their customer's eyes and, at the same time, shields them from the dangerous obligations and consequences?

I felt that just because a customer was willing and even eager to sign up for some flashy new deal that should not mean that we as a bank had no responsibility. As a bank, shouldn't we have as much of a responsibility to read the fine print as the customer does? The theory behind the fine print is that the institution knows that you will not spend time reading it.

No fine print! Just don't do it. It's immoral and it's bad business. Would you set your sister up with a friend you could not vouch for?

We All Have a Moral Obligation to Our Customers

Our society is built upon mutual responsibility. As a business it is not enough for us to pretend that our only obligation is to make money. I knew that traditional banking was built on a kind of no-fault morality: "When the customer wins, we win. When the customer loses, we still win. Or, when the customer loses it's somebody else's problem."

As a customer, are you happy with that? Then why do it as the CEO of your company? Business has changed dramatically in the last few years. There is no cone of silence that you can drop over your business, no shield or layers of insulation to protect you from the spotlight. Everything you do and everything you are is out and being feasted on by millions of consumers who can put a torch to your reputation—a reputation it may have taken you years to build—in a matter of minutes. A leader today has to make a commitment to principle. You have to think: we have to be a good customer. We have to be a good company.

The Key to Culture-Driven Longevity: Get Your Customer Right

CEO Message 273
YOU ARE WHAT YOU BUY

Remember: You are what you buy.

A customer wants to belong to a group of people that have the same values, and, above all, the same attitudes. "My kind of people," is how the desire would be expressed in a sound-bite world!

> "Never ever let the bottom line trump the ethical considerations." —AK

At ING Direct, for instance, we worked hard to make savings cool. But the savings message was not incidental to our business—that was our business. It was, and continues to be, who we are. People who liked that idea knew who we were. They knew how to connect with us.

Who are you? How are you helping the customer connect with you? Not *to* you, but *with* you?

No innovation is sustained. The second it hits the market the imitators come pouring down the mountain with your product, only cheaper, or lighter, or whatever. No percentage of market share is ever safe or off limits. How do you prevent customer migration? How do you keep your customer from deserting you for your competitors? Think about this: if all that you offer is a product, then chances are it will be easily replicated. Being a pioneer costs a lot of money and it's risky. Poaching is a much cheaper and far less risky option.

A CEO has to find some reason to keep a customer coming back when the customer doesn't have to. A great CEO is able to do this over and over again. "Never take a customer for granted" is such an old cliché it creaks. But I can't tell you how common it is to hear CEOs talking disrespectfully about their customers. I wonder, who do you think is paying for your shiny new Mercedes?

Relationship Drama

Every business day is a new challenge. You have to be flexible. And it isn't just the market that continues to change, if you've been lucky enough, your business has grown and expanded, which puts tremendous pressure on resources. The natural and almost instinctive response is to compromise. The risk is that a new set of challenges based on new priorities can replace the focus and commitment to the original priorities. It's like the crackling you hear on your phone when you wander too far from the source of the message. We all want to stay ahead of the curve, but that doesn't mean jumping at the latest trend and losing touch with who you are, or, too often, who you were, as a business. Trends tell you where things may be going; they won't tell you who you are or who you should be, and they won't tell you anything about the quality of your relationship to your customer.

If who you are is only about making money, then okay. This message, this book, isn't for you. But what happens when you've made your money? What then? Make a little more?

If your message is about making a difference for your customer—about effecting real change and making lives better—and if you stick to that message the money will be a wonderful fringe benefit, but it won't be the who of who you are.

Less is More

Sound too much like a pep talk? Maybe. But at the end of the day, don't you want to be excited about coming into work the next day? Don't you want to be excited about the possibility of making the world just a little bit better? Making money is great, don't get me wrong. I've made plenty and I never once found myself excited only by the prospect of making more on the way into work.

Man, life's too short.

CEO Message 48
HAPPY CUSTOMERS

Customer satisfaction is my obsession.

The simple fact is, if more businesses make satisfying their customers a priority there would be far fewer problems.

You've heard the pitch before: "At so and so we value our customers." Okay, but what is that message telling you? It's telling you that they want credit for something that should be a given, or that before they didn't value their customers. But now they do, so yay for their team! Most businesses that want to convince you that you are valuable to them as a customer have already lost a lot of customers. So when you hear that pitch your first question should be, why now? Why didn't you value me from the beginning?

My belief as a CEO was always this: don't give a customer a chance to question his or her commitment or loyalty to my business. Don't *tell* them they're important! *Prove* it to them each and every day by what you do and who you are—that way they know.

The Customer-Happiness Cascade

Companies spend millions on market research, customer surveys, and focus groups all designed to figure out what the customer needs and wants. Well, shouldn't you know what the customer wants before you get into business? Why wait until you are already in business to decide how you are gong to meet consumer demand?

The truth of the matter is that in most companies, and certainly it was no different for ING Direct, if we make the customer happy then a whole chain reaction occurs. For instance, every day we had thousands of contacts with customers and potential customers. If we turned each of those opportunities into a positive experience we not only built our brand, but our customers also became our most valuable advertisers. They had a great experience and they can't wait to tell all their friends about it.

A great commercial or ad will get you noticed, but that is it. It's like building a plane with only one wing. Keep your customers by keeping them happy.

Happy customers also make happy employees. If customers are happy then employees feel good about what they have delivered. It's a reinforcement loop that gets stronger and stronger. In today's frenetic and high-pressure business environment, with its intense demands from a long list of stakeholders, it's easy to lose focus, or to focus your attention on the wrong thing. Let's be truthful, it all begins and ends with the customer, and no matter what role we have in the organization, if we can make the right customers happy and take advantage of the thousands of opportunities presented to us every day, success will be guaranteed.

It's easy to frame the issue of customer satisfaction as a formidable roadblock or problem that needs to be solved. Why? Why complicate what is a simple relationship? When is the last time you walked into your business and asked yourself, "If I were a customer what would make me happy?"

CEO Message 19
THINGS THAT BIG COMPANIES DO THAT DRIVE ME NUTS!

I don't know about you, but when I was a teenager the most humiliating event in my life was asking a girl to a dance. It would usually go something like this:

"You want to go to the dance?"

"I'm not sure. *Maybe.*"

The point here is that a customer wants to feel wanted right away, not just until a better customer comes walking along. Here are the top ten things companies do customer-service wise that drive me nuts, and I am sure you have your own list, too.

1. Give me an 800 number that brings me to a machine. It makes me feel very unwanted.

2. Say you will call me back or deliver something immediately and then never do it.

3. Make me chase for what I am promised I will get.

4. Surprise me at the checkout. It says "3 for $20" but now you tell me that was only in the boys' sizes.

5. You just cannot get my name and address right, and you continue to ask for it after I have given it to you a hundred times.

6. Tell me in writing that I am valued, but when I have a question hand me to another world or your version of service support.

7. "I am sorry, Sir, but there is nothing I can do" is just a reminder that the better the before-sale experience, the worse is the after-sales experience. It isn't that there is nothing you can do. It's that there is nothing you are willing to do.

8. Make the customer keep the information and organize the product or service for the company. "Do you have your serial number for your toaster?" No, I'm sorry. But it's your company's warranty so why do you not have it?

9. I'm not credit worthy, rich, and do not have a referral that works for the company. Nice surprise after I have been a customer for five years.

10. It's in the fine print that no one can read but it's now my problem. I should have studied harder, asked more questions and done more work. Truth is, you could have just been fair from the beginning.

MY HANDS ARE TIED—UNTIL THEY AREN'T

When dealing with customers, it is difficult to say no or tell them that something cannot be done. An occupational hazard of contemporary business is our addiction to choice. Finding a creative way of dealing with the disappointment or the unhappiness that a customer might have in not getting something resolved to his or her satisfaction or, indeed, getting something done in the way they would like is certainly a challenge!

Obviously, the further one can cloak the appropriate solution in a way that puts the issue into perspective—and also into a favorable light—is best. We always tend to focus on the "what" and not the "how." But with a bit of diplomacy, skill, tone, and talent, the "what" can be put in a light that would entice the customer to accept it.

The Key to Culture-Driven Longevity: Get Your Customer Right

This can be done by:

1. Putting yourself on the customer's side
2. Being both empathetic to the customer's perspective and efficient
3. Being reasonable and rational, thereby keeping emotion out of the conversation

Don't Promise What You Can't Deliver, or, Don't Deliver What Wasn't Promised

Remember: the easiest and simplest way to deal with unreasonable customer demands is to not make unreasonable promises in the first place.

Deliver what you promise. No more and no less.

MOMENTS OF TRUTH

Any business—large or small—will have customer experiences each and every day. They can be dramatic or subtle; direct or indirect. I call these "moments of truth": moments of truth about the business, the brand, and the culture.

We've heard it already: you never have a second chance to make a first impression. Okay, great. But the real heavy lifting comes after the first impression. What are you doing to reinforce that first impression?

Each email, letter, call, or advertisement counts. Each encounter is an opportunity for you to demonstrate to your customer what you want your business to be. How you do these million and one small things is a measure of how that message is perceived.

The ultimate test for any business is perception. Either grow by a thousand steps, or die by them. A good manager knows what to watch for—the real customer experience. Not how you see it. The way a customer sees it!

Come on, why do you think they choose gorgeous, skinny models to advertise clothes? They don't want you to see yourself as you see yourself. They want you to see yourself *as they want you* to see yourself.

Your Rock then Roll mission is to simplify your products. You have to look at how you can make it simple for your customer, for them to save time and money. Make it short, intuitive, and to the point. Simple words, easy steps. "Follow the Orange Ball on page whichever; step 1, 2 and so on." Think, how would both a younger and older customer do this with no explanation?

If a business designs their product or service so that a customer thinks and experiences it in a natural and easy way then it's a winner. It should be no surprise that few businesses actually get this right. Usually their products or services are a compromise in some way—most for good reasons. Save me money or save me time. You need story. Here's a good one: save me time, make it easy.

CEO Message 129
A THOUSAND TOUCH POINTS

Think about this: every day you touch your customers in a thousand different ways: directly by email, advertising, phone communication, letters, or indirectly by word of mouth or even being out in the world—the supermarket, a baseball game, or a subway car—anywhere there are people, there are customers.

Not too long ago I was out with my wife. After a movie, we stopped at a local bookstore and I was shocked to see a young couple looking at books on home mortgages. I walked up and asked them why in the world they were buying a book on home mortgages.

"It's really complicated," they said. I thought, why the heck should getting a home mortgage be so complicated? The point is that simple—real-life exposure to a real couple was the impulse behind the ING Direct mortgage program. The innovation? Make a mortgage process simple. Because ING Direct wanted to make it simple? No, because *the customer* wanted it to be simple.

It's the customer you need to serve; it's the customer that keeps you in business. I'm still amazed how many managers and leaders decide to ignore that fundamental lesson. Why is this so common? I suspect it's because most leaders and managers get too removed from the day-to-day interaction with customers. If you want to know what is happening in a business then talk to the front line: the sales people. Want to know what's happening in a business? Talk to your customers.

Keeping in touch with what your customer wants is crucial to your staying in business and your staying on top.

CEO Message 267
SAVE ME MONEY OR SAVE ME TIME!

Most managers would be surprised to learn what customers really care about and what they want to spend money on. It's amazing to me how many managers don't see customers as unique individuals who are making discrete choices about how they will spend their money.

Frankly, there is much too much talk about market trends and efforts to reduce consumer choice to causal determinism. Sure, there are some commonplaces out there. Some kinds of consumer preferences are predictable. Like, customers don't want to be lied to or cheated. Mostly, they don't want to be treated like annoying after-thoughts.

This is the kind of predictability consumer managers could exploit if they simply took the time to find out what their customers do!

Bottom Line

Customers care about what—and only what—they already care about. Things like entertainment, sports, socializing with friends. That is where they want to invest their time.

Why make them balance a checkbook if you could provide a hassle free and reliable alternative?

The best thing to do is to get out of a customer's way before you annoy him!

CEO Message 42
CUSTOMER SATISFACTION

It is often said that customer satisfaction is the number one priority for retail businesses. Every touch point a customer has with your business is critical. It is how they judge you and your product. If the touch point experience is happy you have earned their loyalty. If it isn't, you have lost them.

To that end, no detail is too small to monitor in terms of ensuring that the customer experience is positive. As I've said, at ING Direct we made it a priority that no customer who called would ever be put on hold. No routing calls to call centers in Bangladesh. We closely coordinated mail, phone calls, and emails; we monitored complaints and accolades. What is being said about us? And why? How often?

There is no such thing as a customer concern that does not impact you profoundly. Remember: retail is detail.

Most large businesses are deeply layered and we all have very different jobs to do. The larger the company, the more jobs there are and more likely the more highly differentiated and specialized the jobs. So we can't help but create unique perspectives. We all have a bias to our comfort zone, right? We tend to take a holistic organism—the company—and particularize it into discrete fiefdoms or, what I call building silos. How is the view from inside a silo? Limited. Not very wide and mostly up and down. A toxic consequence to your culture-driven business is losing focus on the goal—the endpoint that exists outside the silo—outside your business. It's called your customer. Rock then Roll. The only perspective that really counts is the customer's. What the customer sees and believes.

You cannot afford to manage above the clouds.

CEO Message 130
WHAT IS CUSTOMER SERVICE?

It is direct, short, simple, friendly, honest, one-on-one, and most of all consistent; the same message, the same from everyone, every day. Think of it as the way you would speak to a friendly neighbor if you were in a hurry.

Find day-to-day simple examples of how customers think and act so that everyone in the business understands customers. We are all consumers. What is interesting is how we change from a consumer to an employee once we sit down behind a desk or counter. Our perspective changes almost instantly. You as a customer might have a reasonable complaint. But when that same complaint is taken to you as the employee, what you see is a problem customer. This is a mistake, and we do it all the time.

CEO Message 211
CUSTOMER CONNECTION

Stay close to the customer, understand their challenges, know what they like and don't like.

I can't tell you how many times I have been in meetings with executives and we are all trying to come up with the next million-dollar idea. Well, why the hell are we asking these guys for new ideas? They wouldn't know a customer if she walked in the door. It's our customers who have the next big idea.

And the best part is, they will happily tell you for free. All you have to do is listen.

CEO Message 67
HOW THE DIRECT MODEL CREATED VALUE

Here is a history lesson from ING Direct. See if it helps condition how you may be thinking about your own business.

Our challenge was threefold: to build the right kind of scale, to keep the right kind of focus, and to consistently get this message across to customers so they clearly know who we are, what we stood for, and why the direct model was a great value proposition for them.

That, in turn, would create great shareholder value.

Why was it important for our customers to understand the mechanics of direct model approach? First, this was the cornerstone on which our new banking model would be built. Second, it served as the primary reason why we could say that we were "Leading Americans back to saving." It had to be a linked-fingers connection between who we were and what we said we were doing.

A differentiated business plan rests on the fact that we can provide a better value proposition to customers by having a low-cost model. This low-cost model is benchmarked against other retail financial institutions in the market, whereby operating less distribution costs, less manufacturing costs, and being more efficient in how we manage information and how we reach customers.

This all added up to a cost that is approximately half of what other similar players of similar size would experience. The question was, What do we do with the so-called fifty percent cost-savings? We wanted to differentiate ourselves in

The Key to Culture-Driven Longevity: Get Your Customer Right the market by providing a much better deposit product and a much better mortgage product. We gave most of this value to the consumer.

A History Lesson

The key for ING Direct was having a savings account service that was better than what was offered out there in the marketplace, not only in terms of price but also in terms of features and delivery so that the customer experience would clearly be a better value proposition than what he or she could experience elsewhere. The same exact principle applied when it came to mortgages.

Our mortgage offering came with minimal fees and service charges, offered a much better rate than what was available from our competitors and was immediately perceived as a better value proposition by the consumer. The job, then, was to not only make sure we could execute and deliver on that value proposition, but also to make sure the two hundred basis points, which was the margin, was fairly split between our Orange Mortgage and the Orange Savings Account. This allowed us to adjust the value proposition depending on whether we wished to grow more with savings or with mortgages. But in the end, while we could shift the value proposition back and forth, we could not over do it.

We could not go to a zero proposition in one product alone. The key business objective was to keep it balanced and to continue to explain to consumers that the reason we can do this consistently and in the long run is that our costs are lower than anyone else's. That's one of the reasons why, when we dropped an interest rate, we needed to have that fall back to a simple set of products and lowest possible overhead to preserve value. It is also a reason why we opted not to be a "one-stop shop" for all our consumer's needs. We needed to keep our menu delicious but simple.

That is the ING Direct story. What does it mean for you?

Every Garden Needs Constant Watering

The Key to
Culture-Driven
Longevity:
Get Your
Customer
Right

The what of what your business is all about needs to be stated and restated as often as possible. It's your daily culture-driven business mantra that you and everyone in your business need to be chanting. You may think it's covered but it's not.

Remember: nothing is lost faster than focus. And what is hardest to recover once it's lost? Yes, absolutely: focus.

The game of business is never played on the same field twice. The teams are never the same, either, and neither are the rules. Staff is always turning over and transitioning in and out of departments. Customers come and go. Competitors are always yapping at your heels.

The only constant in the swirling chaos is your message.

I am surprised when I meet a new staff member and find that they are completely ignorant of a critical core element of our product line. I have to stop and remind myself that what is clear and obvious to me seems to not be so for someone new. Simple lesson here is that you cannot take anything for granted. So you as a leader need to keep selling *inside* the business as well as *outside* the business. There will always be someone who has not learned what is second nature to you about what you as a business do.

Here's an experiment. Ask every single employee in your business this simple question: why would I buy our company's product instead of our competitor's?

How many would be able to answer correctly?

CEO Message 275

WHERE'S THE REAL FAILURE HERE?

The marketplace is a minefield.

We tend to focus on the dangers that lay ahead. But sometimes dangers can appear almost from out of nowhere as a result of how your business grows and evolves. Sometimes the danger is not what is out there in your path, but who you are as a business.

A History Lesson

Consider the following example: not too long ago I read an article about a young doctor who was struggling to repay $250,000 in student loans. The parents had cosigned the original loan under the perhaps quite reasonable assumption that becoming a doctor would enable her to pay back the loans without a problem. That assumption has since been proved wildly optimistic. Over the years, taxes, inflation, a more modest than expected income, and penalties had ballooned her debt well beyond its original sum.

The bank, of course, is demanding payment; the young doctor, meanwhile, is struggling to find a better job in a higher grossing segment of the medical profession. Who is the winner here? Who is to blame?

Some might say the blame is with the bank that approved such a large loan. Others might blame the young doctor for taking on a level of debt she had no reasonable hope of repaying. There are countless examples.

Remember the home mortgage crisis? For a time, banks couldn't write mortgages fast enough for prospective homeowners seduced by shockingly low interest rates on home loans. Mortgages make huge profits for banks. Low interest

rates allowed people to realize their dream of home ownership. It was your classic win-win.

Until the economy collapsed. The lesson is this: the relationship between you and your customer must be understood
as mutual—a shared responsibility between supplier and
buyer of a product or service.

The Key to
Culture-Driven
Longevity:
Get Your
Customer
Right

Put Out The Welcome Mat to Your Customer ... And Keep It Out
A business cannot preach to the marketplace or educate consumers on making good decisions. We are not preachers; we
are businesspeople. That seems to be the conventional wisdom. The mantra is, buyer beware.

What I take that to mean is this: I, as a leader of my company, ultimately blame you—the consumer—if you misuse or
abuse my product.

What happened to the win-win? If you and your customer began as partners in this transaction, why are you now
treating him as the enemy?

In my experience, consumers do too little homework
and are not nearly as knowledgeable as they should be about

> "You have to win in each and every
> moment of truth each day with every
> customer." —AK

many of the complex decisions they make. It's true, the total
costs of educating customers—reducing as much as possible
the help they need to make your product or service work well
for them—is considerable.

As a leader in your business, your job should be to make
your product or service more intuitive and as fool proof as

possible. Getting the value proposition right that works for consumers and business today is becoming more complex and challenging.

What do you want the sign out front of your business to read:

"Welcome!" or, "Buyer beware!"?

CEO Message 128
WE ARE DIRECT; THAT'S ING DIRECT

Okay, here's some more history.

At ING Direct our biggest advantage in making us stand out from traditional providers in the financial service marketplace was that we operated directly. By operating directly, we cut out the middleman and saved you, the customer, money. Second, we kept services to a minimum and that meant we could offer higher rates.

So the deal was this: by adopting the practices of a retail business instead of a traditional financial institution, by being simple, focused, and direct, our plans all added up to more value.

That was a retail appeal that consumers understood and were familiar with, and it became a key driver in that we repeated and emphasized it in everything we did.

It still does.

The message is: this is *how* we do it and *why* it's good, and it's the only way we do it. Stay focused and stay on point. Someone will always try to convince you to do something else. Or to do differently what you are already doing very well.

Best advice is, ignore it. If you do not try something different, make something happen, get a hit, then nothing changes. Conventional wisdom is just another name for the status quo. It's that long single file of people that when you ask them why they are standing there, they point to the sign on the wall. "Line here."

' "If it was not for bad management, no new businesses would be started." Dilbert! Wise advice!

CEO Message 252
WHICH IS IT?

In my experience, most banks look at the value of a customer before they actually look at the customer. It is an analysis based on the potential profitability of the customer to the bank. That is one way to look at it: the customer as a unit exchange. Not right for a culture-driven company, in my book. The other approach—the positive culture-driven approach—is, "How does the value of our service improve for a customer?"

But it's not a chicken and egg issue. Using the customer value approach you are sure to get the basic business model right for the long term.

CEO Message 150
THE CAFÉ STORY

The ING Direct Café experiment was a way of keeping excitement alive, and making our marketing a paying attraction with customers. Our cafés became merchandising and selling platforms, so that within that geographic footprint of the café, our marketplace thinks of ING Direct as being at home. As a new bank with a retail spin, we needed to create excitement from the retail level. We had come up with great product ideas with individual retail variations that created variety and interest around the core theme of our focus and direction for our savings and mortgages. The cafés were a perfect venue for showcasing that innovation. Why tell people you are different from your competitor if you look exactly the same?

Clearly, we needed to demonstrate the value proposition of our products through our retail activities in the cafés. The cafés told consumers on Main Street that working with ING Direct was as easy as enjoying a cup of coffee. You can get coffee in a Styrofoam cup at your bank and drink it standing in line waiting for an available teller. Or you can sit at our café with friends, talk, and do some banking. As we grew, we never wanted to lose sight of this differentiation.

The customer disconnect problem

In business there is always the very real chance to become alienated or disconnected from customers. The feedback that we obtained from the daily interaction with customers in the café, I believed, was the life blood of ING Direct's on-going thinking about strategy: to always stay ahead of consumer trends and attitudes, to always be in touch with consumer expectations as well as to always be alert to consumer response to our marketing and sales efforts.

Some good ideas came from customers. Admittedly, a few seemed like a real challenge but we dug deep and found a way to make it happen. All businesses grow on innovation. Where does it come from?

For ING Direct a source of innovation was the cafés. For you it will be something else. Find them and try them. Be curious. This is a characteristic of any good leader. Have a dose of curiosity and be a bit critical in the things you look at. This may make the difference for success. A really good place to start looking for innovation is with your customer.

It's Your Bottom Line

You can spend millions on consumer research. Or, you can buy a customer a cup of coffee. It's your choice and your budget.

---◄○►---

Creating Rock then Roll Culture: The takeaways

- Culture is storytelling.
- A leader's most important responsibility is creating and sustaining the right culture.
- The right culture is based on values, not norms.
- Culture is diluted from the center out—from the top of the organization out.
- Keep it simple. It doesn't matter what *it* is.
- Strategy is what makes your vision tangible. Strategy can change; the vision can't. Leaders with fuzzy visions walk into walls.
- Business is like dating. It's best to figure out what your customer wants before you get into bed with them.
- Deliver what you say you will deliver. No more, no less.
- Make the ten secrets your daily leadership mantra.

CHAPTER 2

CULTURE-DRIVEN LEADERSHIP:

The Essence of Rock then Roll

The Leadership Style You Choose Makes a Difference

A Question about Leadership

Business schools spend a lot of time training students to become leaders, teaching skills and knowledge aimed at turning smart, young people into effective leaders. Company training programs continue the process.

In my experience, however, one question is never asked. Why?

That's right. You may remember I wrote in the Introduction that we would discuss this question in more detail. I know you *want to be* a leader. People tell me that every day. What I want to know is, *why?*

There are three reasons why people are driven to become leaders. First: to be a success. The fancy cars, the big houses, the private jets, and all that. Second: a need to belong. And third: the person has a higher goal or vision. This person wants to change the world. Most leaders probably have a bit of all three mixed in. But there is always one reason that predominates. It's who they are. It is what drives them.

If you don't know your *why*, figure it out. It will make your approach to your own leadership style a lot easier and much more effective. Why you want to be a leader goes a long way in defining the kind of culture you will create for your business. It's an absolutely critical aspect of your leadership profile.

Leadership today is far more complex than even a few years back. The demands are more numerous and the challenges have multiplied exponentially. Successful leadership depends on positive culture. To build teams, to work effectively, and to communicate well, a culture has to exist in a group or a business where it is understood by everyone. The success of a leader then depends on how he or she fits to the culture. So is it the culture that demands a certain type of leader or is it the leader that shapes the culture to a great extent?

This is all-important. But many of the most valuable qualities a leader can have are never taught in a classroom.

They can be learned, but only from life. Emotional maturity, authenticity, and a strong character are all essential to good leadership of a culture-driven company. So is a close alliance between the leader's own passion, the company's mission, and the corporate culture in which it all transpires.

The Culture

We talked about culture in the last chapter. But culture and leadership are so intimately linked and intertwined that it might help to talk about it some more.

Basically, there are two kinds of culture: *self-directed culture* and *other-directed culture*. Self-directed culture is the sum total of what you do to create, maintain, and extend your brand, mission, vision, etc.—the culture. But a culture can also be driven by forces outside your control, i.e., other-directed.

Other-directed influences can include people's attitudes, values, and, most important, experiences, prejudices, conventions, and biases—anything that is alien or external to the culture you create. The most profound method for creating and promulgating a self-directed culture is by selecting the right people to share and help shape the culture.

A good leader needs to able to seamlessly migrate between one and the other. No business is ever going to be completely self-directed or other-directed.

As I have said, for me as leader at ING Direct it was creating a bedrock set of principles—the Orange Code—and then hiring people who could completely commit to those principles.

The companies with a real innovative or game-changing culture are the ones built on principles and values and they make that the central theme of everything they do. Throwing a brick through a shop window is not the act of a rebel. Coming up with a new way of doing things that makes the world a better place—and doing it against the odds—is being a rebel.

Remember: it is not about conformity; it's about consistency.

Leading The Cause

The folklore in leadership has always idolized the individual who becomes larger than life. From the heroes of Ancient Greece to the corporate raiders of the 1980s, we mythologize leaders who appear to be lone wolves or outsiders. Today, though, a new type of leadership is evolving—and it's just as effective as the old kind.

Things have changed in recent decades. We all know about the information revolution. Now it's possible to be in touch with anyone, anywhere, anytime. This has had a profound impact on leadership. No one boss can be the central conduit for information about a particular company, because employees across the world are talking to colleagues and customers all the time.

No one boss has all the answers, because the Internet has given us instant access to experts on any subject. The way we look at leaders has changed, and who we follow has become ever more situational. In fact, one of the reasons it seems so challenging to find successful political leaders today may be that the cultural dimensions of society have become too complex and diverse.

The great information highway has also brought us vivid images of every scandal and embarrassment that embroils our leaders from the political, corporate, and entertainment realms. The result is that society has become more cynical, and much less tolerant and admiring of its leaders. That's not necessarily fair; most leaders today genuinely try to get things done for good, and even altruistic, reasons. They are nonetheless often perceived as motivated solely—or mostly—by money, materialism, and self-interest. That perception is something leaders have to deal with, by redoubling their efforts to shake of the stigma and earn trust. No one is above it all. No leader can escape this reality.

The
Leadership
Style You
Choose
Makes a
Difference

To have an impact in this new environment, the leader today must be closely aligned with the culture where he or she hopes to lead. That culture might be specific to one corporation, or it could be much broader, reflecting the language and nationality, or ages and interests of employees. The leader who parachutes in from the outside is a thing of the past.

One accepted concept of the corporation sees it as a moneymaking machine. But when employers and employees alike see the company that way, no one is very happy or productive. When everyone is just putting in hours for a paycheck, one has to ask, ultimately, what is the point? Who gets what share of the profit? A successful company must have a cause that is bigger and broader than the organization itself. A successful leader must truly believe in a vision and a mission that defines itself as a cause. He or she must be closely identified with it. Walk the talk is the leading criteria. The best leaders are those whose authority then comes from a genuine, inspiring sense of purpose.

The Leadership Criteria

An effective leader of a culture-driven organization will be recognizable by several traits. When others try to describe him or her, they think of the vision first. The leader is thought of more as a person devoted to a cause than a manager in a company. He or she evangelizes the values of the organization in a way that is explicit rather than implicit, and his or her personal commitment to success is obvious and verbalized frequently. The culture-driven leader constantly demonstrates passion and energy for the work to be done and is not alone. Leadership itself in a culture driven company is copied and emulated by many at all levels of the company.

The Rebel Perspective

I've always thought about how to make things better and I've always had a desire not to follow the status quo but, rather, to break it down. And if you're an outsider—if you're a rebel like me by attitude (maybe not totally by design but certainly by attitude)—you look at every situation and say, how could I make it better? I am tormented by this. No matter what I do in my life, whether I go to restaurant, I drive a car, I use a tool, I do my banking, the thought that always goes through my mind is, why can't this be better? Why can't this be easier? Why can't this be faster?

My emotional thought at the end of the day is always, okay, if I could fix everything and make it all faster and better, what would I do with my spare time? You know what I came up with? I just want to hug people. I want to love my kids, I want to spend quality time with my neighbors, I want to enjoy the good things in life. Wow, wouldn't that be great. If I could get away from all the drudgery and make it quick and fast, then maybe I could enjoy other things in life more. How's that for a platform?

I'm totally engaged, all the time. That is the distillation of my profile as a leader. I truly like people and I am totally engaged in whatever I do. That is why I choose carefully what I do. If you're emotionally engaged, if you're intellectually engaged, and if you're financially committed, you're either going to succeed big or fall flat on your face. That is the risk. For the rebel there is no comfortable default to the middle. It is also the thrill. I have fallen flat on my face a few times. The good thing about that, though, is that when I die, my last thoughts are going be, I gave it one hell of a good run. So, I'm not rusting out. I'm burning it out and anybody who wants to be a leader should be on the side of burning it out.

Style You
Choose
Makes a
Difference

Magic

A leader can't make everything appear too mechanical. To drive the passion of your company, you have to create some mystery around you. You need to appear, in some small humble way, as different than those that look to you. They want to follow but need a reason. It has to work like pixie dust.

By the way: Do I know why I wanted to be a leader? Absolutely. And I'll tell you at the end of this chapter. But by then maybe you will have figured it out?

―◁◦▷―

The Ten Rules of Rock then Roll Leadership

You can't swim if there is no water in the pool. Here are ten principles to think about how you *rock* and then you *roll*.

I. You must possess a calling. The leader must have a sense of purpose that is in sync with the company's corporate vision.

culture-driven leadership 97

At ING Direct, our calling was to lead Americans back to saving.

2. You must have the guts to make the calling personal. It must come from a real place. Otherwise, the authenticity is missing and no one sees the walk the talk type process. The leader can't be an invention of the marketing department or a speaker for the mission. The leader has to be the author of the mission and personally feel a passion for it.

3. You must have a powerful enemy. If there's no one to fight with, there's no job for the white knight. For ING Direct, the enemy was the credit card companies pushing spending and buying at any cost with no restraints. Retail banking is in need of a broader purpose. Having an enemy is neither a shortcut to create a business opportunity nor is it a mere strategic convenience. Having a dark force to fight against creates a highly effective leadership goal. The idea of an enemy transforms competitors into dragons to be slain by all employees. You believe that you are one of the "good guys." For workers, that makes coming to work every day more heroic and more of an adventure.

4. You must possess an inner circle. Picking this core team is one of your most fundamental responsibilities. Unfortunately, it's not an easy process to find and select people that would join a mission. The normal recruitment process does not work nor does the personal address book of friends work either. So you have to network and search out the right people. Many are in very unusual places and circumstances. Character and motivation are the two qualities that separate loyal, enthusiastic workers from mere jobs. Lots of people can put together an impressive curriculum vitae. Often, though, the best hire is someone who has experienced failure and has something to prove to themselves and the world.

5. You must face the possibility of failure. Working in a constant state of impending crisis is not for the faint of heart. It can, however, create a company-wide feeling of being potential prey to an outside force. Without the risk of failure, everyone will grow complacent, and corporate ego becomes the silent killer. A sense of crisis keeps the enterprise in an energetic, startup frame of mind.

6. You should have a clear vision of what you want to get done. Make sure you can easily communicate the vision. Make sure it's a big enough of an idea to make a difference.

Everyone has an idea. Everyone wants to say something. Really, what you need is a vision. A picture that you think will make the world a better place. To rock, you have to shake things up and make it worthwhile. Why? Because you will need to be committed. You will pay an emotional price because it will work or it will fail and so will you. Now that's not bad or crazy; it's just the way it is. You have what it takes you just have to dig for it. Look at it this way. You have one shot at life—so take it. And Rock.

7. Work out a plan of attack. Heat in the kitchen alone won't do it! You have to create action with your plan. Being active also means you have a better shot at luck. You always need some luck. A plan is also never about the short term; it is always long term. Focus on the long term.

You have to make your own luck. The more you work at it the more chance you have of making something happen. Once you have a vision of what you want to do then think about a game plan. How are you going to do it? It takes many steps but with a clear view of what you want to achieve and how you're going to do it then you have the right ingredients. Keep going.

8. **Sell the vision to anyone and everyone. Be persuasive.** You are the champion and you need to personalize it and make it yours. Now you have to sell. No idea just happens. It's never been done. Every success and every great leader has slogged through many days and obstacles to get there. You have to be determined. Let's face it, there is no shortcut. Remember that victory is sweetest when it's really yours. Yes, roll on.

9. **Validate that the vision and the plan are in line with what society thinks is good.** Be realistic and listen to feedback and adjust.

To believe in something means you have to defend it. After committing to selling you have to stand up and defend it. It's true grit. Latch onto an example or metaphor that helps you prove your idea. Sure, you have to weigh the odds and see if it has a chance; it will never be certain. But that does not mean that you cannot take a shot and go for it. You never want to regret that you never tried. Amen.

10. **Never ever deviate from the vision or the plan no matter how tempting or logical it may seem.** Single-minded determination is key to success. If you go down, you go down fighting. The battle will always have been worth it. It makes you better for the next challenge.

Most single or individual ideas ultimately are absorbed by a process of consensus or when other ideas enter the mix—everybody with their hands in the air! Think about it. Single-purpose ideas win out and make leadership real and, best of all, admired. Stay focused and don't sell out. The key is single-minded focus. Rock then Roll and never stop.

Those are the ten principles. Think of them as the water in your business or corporate pool. It's time to jump in!

---<o>---

CEO Message 113
DO YOU HAVE THE FIRE?

As I said earlier, business schools spend a lot of time training people to become leaders. What cannot be taught, however, is having the desire, drive and willingness to take the lead. You have to have the personality that wants to lead—the impulse to take responsibility and risk both failure and disappointment. That cannot be taught, either.

What you *can* learn is how to manage yourself and a situation better, and that is probably why you are probably reading this book. Your reasons may be personal. Mine were.

Some Personal History

I was a happy graduate philosophy student when my fiancée walked into an exam I was taking to tell me the marriage was off. She had thought about my prospects and decided I was low potential. That was that. It was a tough lesson, one I have never forgotten, and it taught me something about loyalty. Anyway, I decided I was going to make a million dollars and prove her wrong.

Do I recommend revenge as motivational tool?

Well, it worked for me! The point is that you need your own fire. You need a cause that burns in your belly, that keeps you sharp and focused.

But that is only the beginning. For me, revenge was a powerful aphrodisiac. But it wasn't the end of the story. It was only the beginning.

A Simple Question

Everybody wants to succeed. It's a given. It is also a given that not everyone will succeed. I lecture often and mostly to business students. What surprises me consistently are the answers I get to some simple questions. Like, I know you want to be successful. But what is your notion of success? What is it you want to be successful doing? What inspires you? What motivates you? Is there a cause or a principle you would sacrifice everything for?

True leaders have answers to these questions.

CEO Message 6
WHAT MAKES A GREAT CEO?

Every time I am asked to lecture to a business group or get interviewed by a newspaper, or magazine, or TV reporter, I am asked, "What is the most important quality for a great CEO?"

Well, being able to think on your feet. That might not sound that impressive or have the hefty feel of a Golden Rule, but it is true and, frankly, a quality that distinguishes okay managers or CEOs from great ones.

What I want to tell you is this: if you didn't grow up as a street kid, you'd better start thinking like one. The world is a rough place and business has its share of brutal situations. The fact is, most people want to see you fail. It's the law of the jungle. Fact two is that you will be loved and you will be hated. If you are a CEO you are everyone's target. You are always right there in the crosshairs. So, how do you handle the pressure? Think fast on you feet.

The other thing is, you have to learn how to think in two and three dimensions. Be aware of what is going on. Read the signs, the tea leaves. Remember, *think towards the horizon*. Don't be that nervous driver who is always looking in the rearview mirror. The only reason you're going to be a leader is because people are going to follow you, and they're only going to follow you if they have confidence in you. If you're leading a charge you can't stop to look at a map. Know where you're going and how to get there!

The leader who earns confidence and respect is the one who sees further than everyone else—the one who sees the goal even when nobody else can, but who can also convince you that you see it too!

First one with the hand up and the right answer gets the win!

CEO message 94
THE LEADERSHIP GENE

Are leaders born or are they made? Is there a leadership gene?

It's hard to know. I can only extrapolate from my own experience, but it may be a bit of both. What I do know is, whether or not they are made, they can be made a lot better. For me, I have a natural instinct for stepping up. I really like whatever the problem is. I like to get close to the fire—I just naturally gravitate to it.

Do you? If you have the inclination to lead then you can sharpen this ability and learn how to use it. Think of it as an athletic skill. If you don't have it, on the other hand, be a smart and good follower. All of us follow at some time or another. Every leader has her moments. Find out what you are best at and do it well.

I was interviewing a candidate for a management position once and I asked why he thought he would be a good leader?

His answer was that routine kind of thing that focused on job experience and personality traits—that "what I want for Christmas" stuff. Things he wanted to be but not what he actually was.

"Have you ever mentored anyone?" I asked. "Have you ever coached anyone in anything?"

Pause. "Uh, no. Not really."

My point is, step up. How can you be a leader if you have never led anyone in your life?

CEO Message 340
WHO IS BEING SERVED?

Ask yourself about what you are doing: is it serving the shareholder's interest or the consumer's interest?

When I began with ING Direct, my idea was to take the opposite approach from full-service, traditional banks and their complicated products, programs, and addiction to fees and service charges. My thinking was to create an *alternative conversation*. By this I mean among all the usual things bankers talked about—consumer here, buy there, charge here—I'm, instead, saying, "Why don't you *save* something?" Our motto was, "Get people back to saving."

Right, saving money as a radical innovation? Doesn't that, in fact, sound like a really conservative virtue?

I thought that was good for people, and I thought that was good for society. I still do. Yet that approach was radical to other bankers. They were horrified—absolutely dumbstruck. What, no platinum, gold or silver packages with high-value coupons? No paper monthly statements? No complicated mortgage packages?

Nope. None of that. Just savings accounts and excellent interest rates. Nothing we were doing followed the traditional format. We deliberately and directly positioned ourselves out front as the bank who would be a strong advocate for the consumer. That was our conversation. That was not the conversation our competitors were having.

So, what is your alternative conversation?

CEO Message 103
SIX SIMPLE QUESTIONS TO ASK

Most businesses have this challenge. You are looking for new ideas and insights.

Remember that old idea of the suggestion box? What I remember most about it is that no one at the top paid any attention to it. How come? Where do we think new ideas come from?

Every day in my journey I walk through the door and imagine I am heading to the suggestion box. What is my contribution? How am I, as a leader, moving this business forward?

It all starts with an idea and you have to hunt for it. It's the "Aha!" moment. There are big moments but also many small ones. You have to recognize them and focus on them. A useful shorthand for thinking about culture-driven leadership is to approach everything you do with a list of questions. Consider the five Ws: Who? Why? When? Where? What? And a sixth question—How?

CEO Message 83
IF THE SHOE FITS, GREAT. BUT WHAT IF IT DOESN'T?

Every situation demands a leadership style that fits the challenge.

Are you—as a leader—in the right situation? Does what you are being asked to do mesh with your ideas, goals, and ambitions? More important, is your skill set appropriate to the job at hand? I may have strengths in the analytic area, but if my primary responsibility is communicating then I am headed for trouble. There is nothing wrong with saying, for instance, that for this particular task I am not the right leader.

I think of myself as a builder, a development-oriented leader; running a big and complex organization is not well-suited to my leadership skills or style. Admitting upfront and from the get-go that a certain position is not the right fit for you could be the best choice you will ever make. Having a successful marriage, for example, depends on picking the right partner to begin with. So it's not just a job, it's also knowing that it's the right situation you can run with.

CEO Message 114
EVERYTHING COUNTS

A leader's performance is like a chalkboard with no eraser.

It took me a long time to let go of the past and realize that in life you cannot start over. You cannot start over in a job, either. You cannot start over once you lead. The results are real, tangible, and never forgotten. Do everything deliberately and with purpose. You will make mistakes; we all do. But you will have given your best.

You can only go forward.

CEO Message 17
GET OUT OF YOUR IVORY TOWER

At least a few times a month, more often when I could, I would sit down to take calls from our ING Direct customers. It's something I liked to do. It kept me connected to the concerns of my customers. It also helped me to get insight into what kinds of problems or issues my associates might face.

The leader who parachutes in from the outside is a thing of the past. A rule of Rock then Roll is that a leader who is inseparable from—synonymous with—a company's culture is likely to be much more effective. To be the leader you need to be seen as the leader *leading the way*. It is not enough to

> "Leading is like writing on a blackboard that cannot be erased." —AK

slap the nameplate on the door; you need to be the tugboat in the busy harbor nudging and steering and keeping all your ships in line, on time, and on message. You cannot do that by standing on the top of the ladder.

If I wanted my team to do the best job they could for me, it helped to know what it was exactly they did. To be honest, I have been in situations where executives or managers have only learned an employee's name or occupation at his retirement party.

How is that leadership?

Second Hand May Work for Clothes ... but Not for CEOs

Listen, unless you get a first-hand feel for what work gets done in different departments and what individual employees are going through, you won't have credibility when it comes to forming opinions about strategy. CEOs have to make a huge effort to stay connected to employees and customers.

Your job is to build bridges, not burn bridges. Your job is to break down hierarchies and all the friction they create. You will hear this again and again: walk the talk.

CEO Message 65
POWER CORRUPTS

Don't confuse power with effective leadership. Power is a tool. It's conditional. When used properly it can create positive results. It can help build and sustain the right culture. When used improperly it creates disaster.

There is a famous story that when Stalin was asked about the Pope's worldwide power and influence, the Soviet dictator scoffed, "How many battalions has he?"

Power is attractive. Let's be honest, it's much better to have it than not to have it. Power allows you to compel compliance. But it does not create loyalty. These days, loyalty is much harder to come by and much more important to reinforce. As a leader, one of the most important lessons you can learn is how to use your leadership position to inspire your team and not just dictate.

A Balance
"My way or the highway."

No, I don't think so. That authoritarian top-down style of management went out of style and is not coming back. Look, people don't pop out of cookie cutters. No matter what business you are in and no matter how big or small, there will be disagreements, different views, and sometimes quite passionate collisions or confrontations. If you have passionate and creative people on your team it is a given. It's that friction that creates the sparks that generate the heat your business needs. A certain amount of tension is necessary to keep ideas alive. No sparks, no fire. But people need confidence that when all is said and done it will all turn out right. Companies need confidence.

Nothing is more toxic to a company's culture than doubt. My primary job as a leader is simple: eliminate doubt in every situation. You will read this again and again. It doesn't mean that doubt does not exist. It means that doubt cannot be a component of your leadership composition. It's easy to say, very hard to do. If all it took was a big smile and a slap on the back and making promises I couldn't keep, then every used car salesman would be a CEO. The market is an infallible and ruthless speed trap for bull. You try bluffing your way through doubt and you'll be annihilated.

So, yes, encourage free debate and seek out and welcome input. But at the end of the day you need to create a consensus. Don't find yourself herding cats instead of herding cattle. Communicate that decision to your team and make it stick. You must have that bias to action.

Decision made, discussion over.

CEO Message 193
YOU LIKE ME!

It's no secret that one of the things I think is most important for a leader is to like the people he works with. Of course, this is not always possible. What is possible—what is necessary—is that everyone respect you as a leader.

What is the dividing line between being liked and being respected?

In my experience, the respected leader is the one who directs attention away from himself and towards the goal. I

"The number one responsibility of a leader is to eliminate doubt." —AK

would rather have an associate worry about letting his fellow associates down than fearing my displeasure. You should worry about letting the team down, not the coach.

The desire to win, however, comes from the coach.

CEO Message 201
FIND AN ENEMY

At the beginning, as in any business, we marketed and sold ING Direct like crazy to everyone that would listen. But probably the most important thing we did was to immediately and completely position ourselves as the enemy of the traditional banks and banking of yesterday.

Nothing I can say will be more important to remember than this: you need an enemy. They can be real or imagined, but you need one. It's a bedrock Rock then Rule principle and from a day-to-day perspective it may be the most important. Nothing over the long run keeps a company more focused than having a shared and primal belief in a powerful enemy. Us versus Them. Good versus Evil.

For me, the traditional banking establishment—with its exploitative and consumer-unfriendly profile and practices—

was my mortal enemy. They didn't like me and I didn't like them. They wanted to destroy me. Bring it on. Give it your best shot. We branded ourselves as the defender of the consumer.

We didn't ask the banks to let us in. We didn't ask them if we could play with them. We came out with fists flying. We had our own game. Our game; our rules. Don't like it? Too bad. I couldn't care less if they liked me because our consumers liked us.

The position you take with your business is like those awkward moments at a wedding reception when guests wander into dinner and hunt around for place cards telling them where to sit.

Do you want your industry to tell you where to sit? Or do you sit where you get the best view? To my mind, the outstanding leader is the one who has already decided where he is going to sit, and sits there.

CEO Message 313
WHEN WISDOM COUNTS

Pablo Picasso said that, "One starts to get young at the age of sixty, and then it's too late."

I am not so sure that, at least in business, it is ever too late.

One of the things I have learned is that your style has to mature and evolve. Nothing would be more soul-destroying than approaching each and every problem or challenge in exactly the same way. If all you have is a hammer then every problem is a nail, as the saying goes. As a leader you have to know how to learn from experience. The faster, the better. A huge part of that is trusting that adaptation is a good way of actually maintaining your competitive edge. As a leader you need to challenge others around you, but they need to see you challenging yourself too.

A Personal Digression

So what have I learned? I am more deliberate now than I was ten or fifteen years ago. Shooting down an open road at a hundred miles an hour on a custom Harley is a rush that can't be beat. It's distilled sensation. Powerful. What I don't waste time with now are the distractions—the white noise that can dilute a room of focus. As a result, I'm able to handle frustration better now than I used to. I can tolerate much more chaos. Early on I had a short fuse and not much patience. The bar was set pretty low. At a meeting I would fidget until I had heard enough. "Okay, that is enough." End.

I still don't like wasting time. Today I'm willing to let you sort of stir around because I'm more sensitive to your need to be critical and make a contribution with a point. We all have our own paths, right? Some people wander. They think in a way that mimics a leisurely stroll. Others are direct to the goal types. Which is better? It depends what you're after. I never support anyone, colleague or associate, free-associating or blue-skying just for the hell of it. Just to be heard. Time is precious, man!

Youth and arrogance are allies. With age and experience comes the knowledge that there can be many paths that lead to the goal. Today, I am more focused—more invested—on the goal than the path.

CEO Message 365
MAKE EXCELLENT HABITS OBVIOUS

If you choose to lead and seize the moment, make the opportunity work for you. Then you need to act. Walk the talk. If you think about it, good leadership is doing what you are asking others to do and follow. You will have to set the example and act. Think about your willingness to follow through and do the hard work. You can do it.

CEO Message 289
IF YOU FEEL LUCKY, GO TO VEGAS

There were a hundred decisions I made every day. Those decisions had to be more right than wrong. There is no such thing as getting it right by luck, at least not over time. The scales always adjust. As a leader, I needed to make good decisions not once in a while, but all the time. I needed the people around me to make good decisions, too. I needed them to think broadly and to be open to new approaches. I needed them to continue to educate themselves, to expand their base of knowledge.

A Stopped Watch Is Right Twice a Day

People who are too narrowly educated can be lucky and get it right some of the time, but they won't have the broad base built on knowledge and perspective to be right most of the time.

CEO Message 9
WHAT'S DRIVING YOU?

Leaders need to engage in demand-driven thinking. Demand-driven thinking makes the customer experience the first priority.

Intuition As Your Edge; or, Is There an Inner Artist in You?

One of the smartest investments a leader can make—in business or in life in general—is to remain open and intuitive when it comes to new ideas or new ways of looking at things. What can be the first casualty of success? Instinct. The thing "what brung us here."

One of the biggest mistakes for a leader is not to listen to your gut and go with it.

Intuition, a hunch, that feeling in your neck is generally right. It may not have surfaced in that brain as a conscious thought yet, but the mind is processing a response and that response is generally right.

The decisions I have regretted most were the ones where I ignored my instincts and thought or rationalized my way to a decision. Trusting your instinct is most important with calls on people. An important Rock then Roll rule is having that trusted inner circle. Why? It's simple: staying on message is hard work. Being a leader is really hard work because you are on all the time: 24/7. Everyone is always looking to you for everything all the time. Who you have around is as much about getting things done as it is being able to trust that the culture you are creating is being translated outward with as much clarity as possible. The worst moment in my professional life was finding out I had been betrayed by a very trusted colleague. I was devastated. It still pains me.

Create an enemy, right? Make sure that enemy is out there, though, and not inside. Nothing is more important to your culture than its level of trust. You need to be able to trust everyone. You have to feel right about the people you work with. If you have the passion and you have the right cause, trust makes it happen.

Out of Shape and Out of the Game

Success makes us soft. It makes us think that we know what we are doing even when we haven't done it.

Complacency is natural. It's no fun always steering a boat that is bounding over choppy waters. Success can be like a sunny day with calm breezes. It's nice, but you know it won't last. A huge part of Rock then Roll is developing a sense for your business climate—developing techniques for forecasting. Not something that should be confused with thinking outside the box. To me, that is just putting a slightly bigger box over the same box. Rock then Roll is more basic—more raw. It means completely rethinking everything you are doing even while you're doing it. It means being an explorer in your business—an explorer in your own creative mind!

Be an artist!

———◄○►———

CEO Message 237
WE ALL PLAY ROLES. WHAT ROLE DO YOU PLAY?

It may seem an esoteric or irrelevant question when it comes to leadership, but there is an important link between the artist and the effective business leader.

Think about an actor and what he does. He plays a role. The difference between a good actor and a bad actor is how authentically he plays the role. Why does this matter? Because we all have roles we can play. At work I am playing the role of CEO of savings. At home I am playing the role of father to my children.

Okay, so we're all playing roles. Just play your role to the fullest. Don't get the roles mixed up. And don't make excuses. Making role changes require a bit of conscious effort. When your son or daughter says to you, "Hey, Dad, I'm not one of your employees!" you know you are in trouble with roles.

Be authentic.

Next, anyone who thinks about art and the universe thinks about the classical form of the drama. There is a beginning, a middle, and an end to everything, whether it is a

"Don't like who you are? Then pretend to be someone else and be good at it." —AK

conversation, a meeting, or the company itself. Artists know that; they are comfortable with the dramatic form. And in the other sense, they bring the drama.

CEO Message 79
YOU ARE THE PRODUCT

If I'm selling you a product—a car or a pen—I try to sell you the functional, qualitative features of it. Yet, principally, I try to sell you the meaning, the brand of it. I try to convince you that there are emotional aspects that will make you love your pen—the color, the shape, and what it says about you. Everything people buy is a way to find a positive expression. Make the product or service *you*.

Business people generally understand how to project a product's functional qualities. It's a comfort level. Artists understand intuitively the qualitative or emotional content of their subject. They see past function to form. The problem is that function is less flexible and less intuitive than form. How can I use a phone differently if they are all designed exactly the same?

Rock then Roll. You zig and I zag. Where do bankers go to find out what is going on in their business? Yeah, conventions sponsored by the banking industry! Bankers meeting other bankers and all talking the same talk.

Why not think like an artist? Try looking for unexpected insights into your business in unexpected or unusual places. If we manufacture phones, why not drop by a flower show to find out what they are doing?

That is what's missing. We need more people who look beyond a particular industry. We need more creative artists.

CEO Message 83
WE DON'T READ ENOUGH

You've heard the expression, "Every picture tells a story"? Well, every face tells a million stories. I can basically tell eighty percent of your story just from looking at you.

We love stories. It's in our make up. We listen to our own stories, too. We fall in love with our own stories. But we seldom know the real story. We love all kinds of stories, in particular war stories of lives of accomplishments and wins. It happens in all walks of life and business is no different.

One of the most important stories you will ever tell as a leader is the answer to the question, "Who am I?"

And the Award for Best Actor Goes To ...

If you walk into a room and you aren't telling me a story about who I see, I don't see you as a leader. And if what I read is the wrong story? Then I don't trust you.

Look, I walk into a room of suits and I'm wearing an open-necked shirt and cowboy boots. "Who the hell does this guy think he is?" someone might ask. Okay, exactly. Who the hell *does* this guy think he is? Right off that bat, I am saying this: what I do and how I do it is a hell of a lot more important than what I am wearing when I am doing it. You may hate cowboy boots. Fair enough. But what you are probably also thinking is this: if he can dress like that in front of a crowd of industry executives, he probably has something different to say. Maybe he's worth listening to.

And, at the end of the day who are you going to remember?

Sell the vision to everyone, right? You are the leader. You are the vision. You are the culture of your culture-driven business. There is nothing about you that should be circumstantial or contingent.

A great leader is the total package. It's not about fooling people. It's about telling people who you are. Find your story.

CEO Message 266
CONTROLLING? OR CREATING?

Business people—people who have classical business training—think about ways to control what already exists. It's like finding new ways to tame the same lion. They keep talking about what customers will buy but often do not consider creative ways to find out what it actually is that customers want. How those wants evolve over time. In what circumstances are they relevant?

Artists think about creating things, not controlling things. Is there an artist in you?

CEO Message 117
YOU HAVE THE POWER

As a manager or CEO, you must understand the strength of personality.

People tend to rely too much upon hierarchical power and authority and they totally underestimate personal power that comes from presence, confidence, and personal authority. Rising to the occasion and having your presence felt is very effective. Natural power is personal power.

A company's culture is what people think it is.

Hierarchical power reveals nothing but what is already obvious is structure. The power you need to embrace is the power that originates from the culture you create. The power that comes from hierarchy can move in only one direction: down. You cannot make your leadership about exercising or showing off your authority; it is about creating a culture where discipline, hard work, commitment, and all the other values embodied in the culture-driven leadership pantheon are understood, valued and shared by everyone.

———◆———

Personal Brand: Sometimes It *Is* All About You

Companies have a brand; a reputation, what they are known for. People are no different. I became known as the bad boy of banking—the rebel that set out to shake up a traditional industry. I wear cowboy boots and drive a Harley. What are you known for? I don't mean your company. I mean *you*. What are *you* known for?

What do you *want* to be known for? If you do not actively work on this it will happen for you automatically. Trick is, you can direct it and shape it. Your actions, your views, and how you look are important, but your principles, your values are what stand out in every interaction. In a company culture, your personal brand will be the main criteria for you fitting in.

Do it consciously.

Be Where You Need to Be—and Stay There

As I have said, I like to be close to the fire. So when I started out I emphasized the things about me that stood out, but without threatening everyone and everything. I learned something very important: power is like joining an exclusive club. Sometimes it becomes more about keeping people out than letting people in. Power likes to preserve itself and its exclusivity. The decision makers I mingled with thought of me as a mercenary outsider—a hired gun who rides to town to clean up the mess. I had talents but I was no challenge or threat to their authority. "Hey we can use his creative ideas but he can never be one of us!"

I am not making that up. I actually heard that in a hallway by accident. Right then and there I knew that, one, I should make no assumptions about ever being accepted and, two, I made damned sure I would trade well for my work. Thank you, Big Company. *Useful outsider* worked well for me. How about you?

—◁○▷—

CEO Message 13
PRIMAL THERAPY

I focus on primary things—primary emotions such as fear, greed, love. I don't have problems speaking words like evil and good. Create an enemy! We are always told that life is more complicated than black and white. Well, it is my belief that in a culture-driven business it *is* that simple: black and white. These can be metaphors, and metaphors are always useful.

You need to create metaphors for your business. Why are you in the game? What are you trying to do? Make it real, man! Give your bull dogs something to bite into and rumble with!

CEO Message 231
THE REBEL MANIFESTO

I feel a lot more comfortable as the underdog and challenger.

I don't come from the status quo. I believe that in the twenty-first century we need to find a new way to look at things. When it comes down to it, I'm promoting evolution. I don't belong to the elite. I belong to that group of people who find themselves in the curious position of making a difference by agitation.

You don't need to be an underdog. Maybe you aren't comfortable with that role? Okay, I get that. But what role are you comfortable with, that makes you the inspiration that will win others over to your cause? Remember, this isn't about being a better leader; it's about being a leader in a culture-driven business. To be that kind of leader you need to champion a cause. Find that cause and be that cause in everything you do. Think of it this way: anyone who champions a cause is an underdog.

CEO Message 20
IF YOU ARE NOT MOVING YOU ARE STANDING STILL

Learn this and you've learned it all: when it comes to leading a team, your job as leader isn't to keep people happy. Your job is to generate disequilibrium and keep team members productively uncomfortable.

Of course, there are two huge disclaimers: disequilibrium is not the same thing as disruption. And productively uncomfortable is not the same thing as angry or frustrated. If we find ourselves standing on an uneven surface we tend to find our balance, right? Apply the same principle to your business. Level is everyone's favorite surface. It's safest. Build in a step and suddenly everyone is more aware of where they are standing. It eliminates complacency and reinforces intuition and creativity. The same is true of being productively uncomfortable. It all comes down to challenging your team to exceed their expectations. So how do you know if it is a

"The secret ingredient of success is pixie dust." —AK

good challenge or a bad challenge? There is no rule book. Resentment and anger tends to emerge as a consequence of tasks that seem disengaged or remote from the mission. Always make sure the path to the goal is understood. It may be too high, but that is fine, as long as we can see it. Hey, reach for the stars! We don't really think we can do it. But that is the metaphor! Where would we be if no dreamer ever reached for the stars?

We Are Our Routines

We all crave routine and predictability. Fact is, to keep things moving you have to keep changing things. I have always been asked, "Why the change?" Or have been told, "Don't fix what's not broken." Purposeful work needs an evolving story that shows progress. Nothing in life stays the same. It's good to think about managing in the same way. So what are you going to change today so things don't get stale? How are you going to explain it? What is the next page in this story you are working on?

CEO Message 45
THE VALUE OF HUMILITY

I believe that one of the most valuable qualities a leader can have is humility. Another is vulnerability. I do a lot of things well. But what I don't do well I need someone else to do well. Being up front about that allows me to surround myself with people who complement my skills set.

A really good leader seeks to complement, not to confront or to create conflict. This is a primary difference in leadership today: the old military arrangement that dominated business culture for decades—where authority very clearly moved from the top down and the troops at the bottom were expected to obey—has been turned on its head. The workforce today has never been more diverse. As a leader, you need to do more to appeal to a person's aspirations. You need to be far more accommodating. A culture-driven environment treats diversity and variety as a huge plus. Instead of imposing a "we all look exactly the same" military-style discipline on the troops the culture-driven leader focuses less on structures of authority and much more on norms of behavior. How do we work together? How do we all fit together and how do our varied skill sets complement one another?

Don't be paranoid about the skill sets of others. As a leader, you need to be confident enough in your strengths to allow others to flourish. At the end of the day, you all look good.

And isn't that the point?

CEO Message 38
YOU CAN'T FAKE REAL

My philosophy of leadership is to be authentic in the way you deal with people. And that means if you're going to walk the talk, do it! The second thing is, you can't lead if you can't follow. Third, you need to create a mission. It is never about you. It is always about the mission. And people will follow you if you are prepared to get a mission done, something with a goal that is a little bit beyond the reach of all of us. It's not easy to be passionate and detached at the same time.

That's what leadership is about, Charlie Brown.

CEO Message 233
ALAN ALDA MEETS GORDON GEKKO

Probably nothing is more cliché than the portrait of the CEO as the egotistical, ass-kicking, take-no-prisoners bully who rages, thunders, and delights in intimidating everyone he encounters into meek submission.

Classically trained business people are molded on the leader as authoritarian prototype. I'm the boss and I know what is best. I have the authority from the shareholders and the board of directors. There is also the accountability issue to confront. The structure of discipline—traditionally—is top to bottom. Think about it: when authority always moves from the top down, what ever rises from the bottom up? Resentment? Anger? Hostility?

Rock then Roll leadership is all about allowing talent and creativity to filter up. Think of talent as having its own natural buoyancy. Let it work for you; don't work against it.

But just for the heck of it, let's pull a new costume out of the wardrobe closet and see how it fits: what would you think if I suggested that you as a CEO be less authoritarian? More relaxed and down to earth. Right, images of a touchy-feely Alan Alda-type CEO with a guitar and a campfire and off-key renditions of *Kumbaya*. Not exactly the image of power and resolve you want to project.

I hear you. The fact is none of us are perfect. When we are doing what we do best, for instance, there is a practical advantage to acknowledging that there are gaps in my expertise. If I am exactly myself and I'm prepared to be vulnerable, then you actually have a very good chance of making a true, authentic judgment of who I am. If I am prepared to be completely authentic with you, I am inviting—sort of demanding—that you be the same.

And that is the best chance you have of being the best you can be.

CEO Message 53
GUYS? LISTEN UP....

Indulge me a minute.

Women wonder, "Why do these thirty-year-old men I meet have great jobs but will not commit to a relationship?"

It's because they are still boys. They might have the attributes of a man physically, but they're not there mentally or emotionally. One reason may be that our culture no longer enforces the ritualistic rite of passage. In many cultures a boy was required to endure an often painful and emotionally harrowing ritual in order to transition into manhood. We are missing that. There are no rites of passage. We would have more good managers if people coming into business were more mature.

A core belief of mine is that only a mature person can be both committed to a cause *and* disciplined enough to make it happen. Yeah, save the whales! A great cause. But while the kid on the corner with the Greenpeace clipboard has the passion, he probably does not have the discipline to make it happen. You need both: passion and discipline. Results, right?

Results Matter

Nobody pays a CEO a salary because they have a great resume, or a killer handicap in golf. Not even because they graduated with honors from a great business school. They pay them to get the results. In leading a business the pressures are relentless. Remember, fate is the wheel, right? It never stops spinning. One minute it's up and things are sweet, and the next minute it's down and a disaster. The thing is, your salary is a down payment against fate, against outcome. Every time the wheel spins the CEO has to make a decision. That is what the pay is for. Will it be the right decision that produces the positive outcome? Or will it be the wrong decision?

It's a demanding scorecard: the more mature you are the better your business decisions will be and so the better your commercial outcomes are likely to be.

At the end of the day, there is no way to escape the score. It always feels much better to win!

History Doesn't Lie

Caesar's legions either won in Gaul or they lost in Gaul. We can go back and dissect till the cows come home. They should have done this or they should have done that. But we're not going to escape the eventual outcome. The legions triumphed. Gaul was subdued; Caesar won.

———◁◦▷———

A Culture-Driven Scorecard: the Value of Principles

Earlier I wrote that one of the biggest mistakes we make as leaders is discounting the value of intuition. The other biggest mistake? Not having a commitment to principles. Intuition and principle. On what basis does a leader make a decision: rules, policy, practice, or conviction?

The only choice is to always rely on your principles. You may have to challenge a policy or rule, but know that these always change with time. When in doubt, trust your own principles. In the end, it's what you will have to live with.

Start with principles. Then come values, followed by knowledge. What you should never do is look at principles last. A simple example is good and evil. Remember I laid out the principles of Rock then Roll? One of the rules was: *create an enemy*. That is bad and this is good. Just ask yourself the question, "Is the likely result of the decision I am making good or bad? What do I *value* here?" Don't have one foot in one circle and the other foot in another. Good or bad, man. No in-betweens. Decide. When you have both feet well inside the circle marked *good*, then, and only then, do you follow through. It's not straightforward and it can be complicated and—frankly—gut wrenching. But always make sure your decisions are grounded on principle. It's the best way.

Listen to your voice. Over the course of time you will find that a commitment to principles and a strong set of principles and values has been a better compass than any skill you will ever learn. A bedrock set of principles needs to be the basis of every decision you make and every plan you propose. Put simply, without principles you cannot have intuition. Think of intuition as your internal compass. Your principles are the needle that constantly points due north.

Principles are the basis for action.

Intuition is the will to act.

Rock then Roll.

———◀○▶———

CEO Message 90
HOW GOOD ARE YOU?

I am asked constantly what is unusual about the way I run my company. What is my secret?

I am a believer in commitment. I don't expect people to commit to me just because I come into a company with a fancy suit or a nice car. I want your trust. I want your investment in me as a leader and a commitment to the goals of the company. After all, if I want the best from you I need to know that you are getting the best from me.

So, I ask my employees, "Would you vote for me to serve with you another year?"

An Employee-Based Litmus Test for Leadership? Why Not?

The first time I tried this my directors nearly fainted. I think the board thought I had lost my mind. But I wanted everyone who worked with me to know that I had no intention of leading them if they could not commit to me. It wasn't a popularity contest. That is the huge difference. Yes, I generally want to like the people I work with and to be liked by them. But mostly, I needed to know they respected me. Respected what I was trying to do, and how well I was doing it.

So, why not let them be the judges?

One, it let them know I didn't take my job for granted. Two, it made both me and my performance accountable to them and not to directors behind closed doors.

Look, you are called upon to make tough decisions. Some of those decisions are going to be unpopular for the short-term. Culture-driven leadership is not a popularity contest. It is about sticking to principles. If your decisions are right then time will validate.

You have to walk the talk, right? If a pillar of culture-driven leadership is recognizing the value of all contributions to the company's success, shouldn't the hardworking people who are making all those contributions have some real say—especially about who leads them? Power to the people, man! Rock then Roll!

CEO Message 126
STICK TO YOUR PRINCIPLES

At ING Direct we used to get a lot of criticism from industry observers and critics for what was considered our bank's "weak returns."

Sure, it was a fact that our return on equity was lower than that of traditional banks. But it was just as much a fact that we were not a traditional bank and had never set out to play by their rules, so why were we being judged by the conventional metrics? We were building a franchise. The goal was making money for the *longer* term.

The truth is, I have more ways of making money than God has angels. If someone came to me and said, "You need to make your bank deliver twenty-five percent on equity," I could do that. What I could not do is deliver that return *and* deliver on our core operating principles. I had to make a decision about my priorities. Was I more concerned with making more money or an amount that the market demanded or about keeping my commitment to our customers?

I find it interesting that so often my commitment to principles is received skeptically. It can't be real. They think it's a strategy: timely, improvised, but not long-term.

Principles *are* a kind of strategy—but for the long-term. My principles keep me grounded. No leader can be right one hundred percent of the time. But an important corollary to the Rock then Roll rule of committing to a vision is this: if you are going to fail, at least fail for the right reason. Put simply, the x's and y's of many business decision equations are easy to bring to account. But a pillar of culture-driven leadership is that making the right business decision is not the same as making the right decision. One accounts only the balance sheet; the other measures your commitment to principles.

Committing yourself to a set of rock-solid principles—and that includes the priorities you set from the beginning—means that you will win a lot more than you will fail.

If sticking to principles meant upsetting the gatekeepers of conventional wisdom, so be it. For me, it was an easy decision.

As a leader, you have to decide: who do you work for? Does the idea that I could have been making more money keep me up at nights? No, it does not. Do I rest easy because I know I have kept my commitment to my customers?

You bet I do.

———◇———

Certainty versus Doubt: The Leadership Mantra

The primary responsibility of a leader is to eliminate doubt. Yes, you have read that before. You will read it again. It is that important. Look at areas of doubt and figure out how you are going to address them. It's you at the head of the wagon train, Pilgrim. What are you going to do?

CEO Message 183
WHEN THERE IS DOUBT
By definition, the leader is called upon to make the call.

We are all familiar with this scenario: in the course of a meeting on some routine a problem arises. There is much discussion. Questions are posed and ultimately you are looked to for a decision. You have two options. One, you postpone your decision. You want to collect more information, conduct some research and analyze all your options; set some priorities and organize your thoughts in a way that limits risk and, not incidentally, makes you look good in front of colleagues or your boss. Advice that, from time to time, works.

Or, two, you decide. The secret of really effective decision-making is inherent in the term: decision-making is *making a*

"If there is doubt, then there is no doubt." —AK

decision. As quickly as possible and as decisively as possible. Too often, deferring a decision is merely inviting speculation that you lack commitment to the outcome. "Listen to the force, Luke!" Remember, the first thing you learn in management is that you will never have all the facts. The second: you are dealing with people, not robots. Often the best strategy is to move fast. Intuition—both trusting intuition and acting on it—puts the roll into the rock.

When the moment comes to make a choice, don't delay.

CEO Message 200
A TALE OF TWO MANAGERS

There is the rational leader and the intuitive one.

Which is better? There is no answer to that. Circumstances dictate. However, coming to terms with the distinction helps you manage resources more effectively. Some people are good at one kind of situation and others at another. Some tennis players are geniuses on grass and terrible on clay. And vice versa.

Which one are you?

Generally, the risk for the rational manager is their need to know more—to wait until the problem has been fully quantified and the direction for action explicated. The risk for the intuitive manager is their not knowing enough before acting and possibly running up against conventional wisdom. Of course, that might reveal something more about the impulsive manager than the intuitive manager. How come there are so few impulsive leaders? They don't last. They can't. Never confuse the *impulsive* gesture with the *intuitive* one.

You should work on both—the rational and the intuitive—but in the end you have to decide. Culture-driven business mantra: *a leader has to have a bias to action.* You won't always be right. There are no right and wrong in all decisions. In my experience, more harm has come from waiting too long to make the right decision than acknowledging a bias to action and making the wrong decision in a timely manner. Make no mistake—action has consequence and the wrong decision can be fatal. But you need to learn the difference between a decision that turns out wrong and the wrong decision. One is outside your control; the other is in your control. Everyone has the ability to be rational. Not everyone is willing to trust intuition. You need to learn to trust it, and to know when you have the advantage. There is a responsibility to move forward. It's your call. Learn what your default approach is and look for situations where you can use one bias or the other. In the end, winning comes from getting it right more times than not. So improve your odds: use both.

CEO Message 12
IS THAT A FACT?

There are facts you can't live without, and facts you can.

A good manager delays a decision until she has all the facts.

A great leader finds out what she needs to know and acts.

CEO Message 127
SILENCE IS...?

If you were to say half of what you usually say and just think the other half to yourself, would things work out better? Your best communication tool often is silence. Using it well just requires good timing and practice. Earlier we looked at personal versus hierarchical power. Silence is a good example of the positive benefits and the valuable effects of personal power.

A remarkably effective—but too seldom used—tool today is the strategic and judicious use of silence as a motivator. First, silence is not *no*. It carries no harsh reprimand or tone of disapproval. Second, silence can induce a team member to voluntarily reconsider or rethink a position. Third, it can be an effective strategy for creating a sense of neutrality between contentious viewpoints.

The key here is the word strategic. The use of silence must be prescriptive, not reactive. You have to be seen as an "active" listener. Silence is not a disengagement from conversation. In fact, it is exactly the opposite. It is making direct eye contact with the person in front of you and it is compelling *reflection*. It is a way of encouraging the person to deepen their insight or to think through a problem in a more thorough and meaningful way.

Applied incorrectly, silence is misinterpreted as indifference, criticism, or a failure of insight. Silence, as they say, speaks volumes. But silence as a leadership technique is less effective if no one has a sense for your thinking—an appreciation and understanding for how you approach decisions in general. Silence needs to be the reinforcement of a leadership state of mind that you have communicated to the team and that they understand implicitly.

CEO Message 74
ELIMINATING DOUBT VERSUS DOUBT AS A CREATIVE SOURCE

I have said that a primary responsibility of a leader is to eliminate doubt. But the key to eliminating doubt is, somewhat counter-intuitively, the capacity to acknowledge doubt as a creative premise for business and life.

"When we are not sure," wrote novelist Graham Greene, "we are alive." What Greene is saying is that uncertainty is a source of creation. What a leader does not want to do is smother that creative source by pretending to a certainty she cannot have. Eliminating doubt is not the same thing as arrogance.

Input versus Output
Arrogance might be thought of as coming up with one-dimensional solutions for a three-dimensional problem. Leaders who are confident are not afraid of complexity.

The doubt we want to eliminate is the uncertainty of your commitment to the objective or the goal, or concerns about your method.

Yes, get lots of input before making a decision; try to get good advice, quality information, and, if possible, opposing views on the issue. Good management is about delivering short and long-term results, and it is filled with contradictions and always has layers of quantitative and qualitative aspects to it. Making a decision requires judgment and vision. Ignoring conventional advice and listening to your own inner voice will serve you best over the long term.

Ask questions; get advice. Not bad. Be critical. Just don't feel like you have to take it. Always best to hold your own counsel.

CEO Message 149
TREES FALLING IN THE FOREST

"If a tree falls in the forest and no one is there to hear it, does it make a sound?"

Sure, it's a philosophical chestnut. But if you want to succeed in business, you need to think of intuition as those trees in the forest. You need to learn how to listen to that voice inside your head that says, "This will work."

When we see a customer complaint or comment about our products or services, we must remember that they are often the tips of the iceberg. They usually are an early warning signal and you need to make it a priority to quickly determine if this is a single instance or a broader problem. Most managers fall into the trap of "break and fix," and then pride themselves on how responsive they are.

However, a business that is performing well is proactively oriented; it responds to the earliest warning signals and tries to stay ahead of things as much as possible. With this in mind, many things can be accomplished by being agile and flexible.

Think of doubt as incentive.

So the next time you encounter a situation that causes you to have doubt, look at your feet. Where do you stand? Remember: principles and intuition. Do you need to change direction? Do it. But don't shuffle your feet. If there is doubt, there is no doubt.

———◦►———

Walking the Talk: Commitment is a 24/7 Principle

Commitment is not a part-time job.

At the entrance to the ING Direct headquarters in Wilmington there is a white line on the ground at the front door. Some people walked right over without a thought. I would see these people and think, "If you don't see that white line then you're not someone I want to do business with, or someone I want on our team."

That white line is a powerful symbol. The message is that once you crossed it you made a commitment. A commitment that you fully embrace and support the corporate values that embody ING Direct and that you are committed to personally promoting those values.

Look, we all want to be successful. But being successful is not a commitment: it's a consequence. There are lots of things that separate human beings from other species. But one of them is that we can be aspirational. We want things. We dream things. A dog never dreams that one day he might be a cat, right?

Visionary? Or Loser?

Some of us dream of the impossible. If we succeed they call us visionaries. If we fail they call us losers.

Since we have aspirations we also have intuitions, often quite powerful ones, that we could fail. No one, no matter how visionary, is immune. We are also hedgers. We make risk-assessment calculations in our heads. Some of us are more low-bar enthusiasts who believe we can succeed only when the risk is low. These are the nervous types who tend to jump ship at the first sign of stormy weather. But if you are the type that dreams big then the risk for failure is bigger, too. To be successful—to beat the odds—requires incredible teamwork. Successful teamwork requires a personal commitment from each team member.

Commitment is a decision you make not only with you head, but also with your heart. My mantra is that the purity of a commitment is what makes the difference between us giving our very best or us just going through the motions. So if there isn't a white line in front of your door at work, make one. Make sure you and every member of your team and business knows which side of line they're on.

Remember the oath of the Three Musketeers? "All for one and one for all!"

———◁◦▷———

CEO Message 301
GETTING NOTICED
Walking the talk can feel like walking the plank.

I know.

Years ago in New York, Nicholas Deak, the chairman and founder of Deak International, asked me, "What can you do for our company?"

I said, "Grow the business and beat the competition."

He asked, "What do you need to do this?"

"Capital and time," I said. He then looked at me over the rim of his glasses and said, "Anyone can make money with money. I need someone who can make money without it!"

"Well," I said, "if I could do that then I could work for myself!"

"Fair enough," he said. "You have the job."

Now, most business leaders I know can relate to this story. They'd have their own comparable moment and they would relate. Okay, of course I know what the lesson of this story was for me. But what do you think it means?

Leadership starts with a blank page. Step up and stand your ground. Get noticed.

CEO Message 146
THINGS GET DONE

It was Isaac Newton who discovered that an apple doesn't just fall from the tree. A force—gravity—is actually at play that *makes* it fall. Cause and effect.

Same in business. In business, things just don't happen. Someone decides something will get done and it gets done. There is a force behind every action and event. Most of us have a great idea at one time or another. Some of us have lots of great ideas. But the apple doesn't fall just because it is there. To make the apple fall in your business you need not only the idea but also the will—the energy and determination—to make it happen. It is a powerful combination and a powerful tool in any situation.

I can't tell you how many times I have seen an opportunity lost for no good reason other than a failure of will or not enough energy. For most people it's unfortunate; for a leader it's fatal.

"Walk the talk or don't talk at all." —AK

Don't *let* it happen. *Make* it happen. *Develop the bias to action.*

Learn how to do that and the only question becomes, "What is worth doing?" As a leader you decide if the battle will be worth the price to be paid in lives to achieve the goal.

It's your call. It's expected of you.

CEO Message 160
A LEADER IS ALWAYS UNDER A MICROSCOPE

Most leaders express opinions; good leaders speak with conviction. Opinions by their nature are exploratory; convictions are based on values, which by their nature are proactive.

Do not confuse "I believe" with conviction. "I know" is a much better start. It's a huge, and hugely important, part of selling the vision. You have to make it personal. Have a clear vision of what you want done and have a plan of attack. No prisoners, man! Sell it!

Why is this so important? Let's face it, we live in a hypercritical age. Everyone makes instant judgments about everything. We don't reflect; we react. The details of cultural and business and political life, the trivial and profound and everything in between, are broadcast all day, every day on everything to everyone, everywhere. We have become an on-line real-time world. Everything you say or do is instantly mirrored in cyberspace for all to judge. Being critiqued is difficult under the best of circumstances. Today we live in a less discrete world and the drumbeat of criticism can be relentless. Being constantly judged is difficult to endure—especially when the sniping is uncensored and often grossly unfair.

Everyone out there is waiting for you to fail. Today you have to do ten out of ten things right to be recognized as a good leader.

CEO Message 164
NEWSFLASH: LEADERSHIP IS DIFFICULT

Admit it. To take risks, to be self-critical, to commit to improve, and to continue to learn all takes courage. It makes you vulnerable, puts you in touch with your limits. But the best reason for doing it? It will tell you who you are—and that truth is empowering.

How do you do it?

Here's a tip: Look at yourself in the mirror in the morning. That is your best conversation. It allows you to face the morning sun straight on.

I have often been asked why leadership is so difficult. Well, it is. And it seems that every day it gets harder. First, you have to trust people. That is hugely difficult to do. We talk elsewhere about situational loyalty. As a CEO I was on a mission. It is hard enough to find even a few people to share the commitment to that mission, much less finding thousands. If you don't have Jesus then you better have some disciples— your trusted inner circle. But even Jesus had his Judas. People are in business for all kinds of different reasons. You have to be able to trust people.

The other hard thing is that you have set the example. Walk the talk, right? But as a CEO I could not walk the talk every now and then. I had to do it all the time. All the time! You set the example. You are the culture, right?

A leader cannot be put on a pedestal. You have to be where the culture is. Look at Steven Jobs and Bill Gates. They write the computer code! You need to always relate the culture back to the mission.

CEO Message 170
ARE YOU A LEADER?

What ultimately will distinguish you as a leader comes down to this: do people think you are "for real"?

Trust, loyalty, and authenticity are all part of the mix. Your natural character and personality, therefore, should be easily seen. It's that personal power, right? You create the culture by being who you are and then you draw on the power that is created to sustain the culture. Authenticity cannot be faked. It can't be employed selectively or on occasion. If I'm fried chicken and you order meat loaf, when I show up on your plate, you'll know, right? Who do I think I'm fooling? Don't hide what or who you are or pretend to be something else. Let the real you shine through. It's more powerful than you think.

Everyone has a natural style. Use yours to your advantage.

CEO Message 54
IT'S NOT THE *WHAT*; IT'S THE *HOW*

Effective leaders know that many times they must ask others to do difficult or unpleasant tasks; the most effective leaders measure the tone and how they set the direction of the request that appeals to the rational response.

An emotional response tends to be defensive and in response to a perceived threat. Defensive action separates the person from the desired goal. An appeal that produces a rational decision preserves that commitment.

If you as leader show you understand how difficult or unpleasant a situation is and you feel it on a personal level, and you share their concerns across the board, you'll achieve your result more easily. In developing the skills we use for dealing with difficult situations, let's focus on the *how* as much as on the *what*. It's *how* culture gets built.

It is ironic that we talk a lot about the *what* but the success of most decisions rests on the *how*. It's a good topic to work on.

If I Had a Hammer

Think about it: you tell someone with no carpentry skills or knowledge to put up a fence. That's the *what*. But without a hammer and nails they don't have the *how*. That creates tension and resentment. It's also a huge distraction from achieving the goal and increases the likelihood that even if the task is done it could be done wrong. If you focus forward on the *how* of how the work needs to get done, however, everyone will pick up on that focus—everyone will become immediately invested in the process—and there will be a lot less friction generated.

I know managers who trust everyone to trundle off to figure it out for themselves. Trusting initiative is hugely important. Initiative is an important component of innovation. But you need a leader in the room to clearly define the problem or task that needs to be solved and the outline for achieving it. "Let's do this and here is how I think we should handle it." That way, at the very least, you know that the task will get done. If someone comes back and says, "I can take two steps off this process and here's how ..." Well, that's innovation.

Of course results are the bottom line. But routinely overlooked by too many managers is the critical question: how it gets accomplished. The *how* of the process also speaks to the way everyone works together as a team. If the coordination is good, desired results are achieved with efficiency. It makes success reliable and repeatable, and further strengthens the team's ability and capacity to perform.

You've got the tools!

CEO Message 109
GETTING BETTER

Is your job your goal? Or is your job your starting point?

The most admired leaders I've met are the ones who continually profess to be learning, are open to new ideas, and, most of all, demonstrate the importance of working on getting better. *Leaders come from anywhere.* If you don't keep learning you won't know what the emerging ideas are that are going to transform your business—not the leaders who will emerge as the champions of those new ideas.

Getting better is an on-going challenge, which holds true for athletes, actors, and most other professions. You should make it your rule to continue to focus with enthusiasm on ways you can improve, and direct your energy towards that improvement. Don't make it just about your improvement, either. Building the right culture means making self-improvement a company-wide objective. Support and encourage one another to improve, because at the end of the day it is the journey that is most important; when looking at the journey, you will always receive what you have put into it. Making you a better manager is a wonderful reward. An easy way to remember this is that life is a journey. The reward is the journey itself.

You know the saying: today is the first day of the rest of your life. If you focus on today and make *today* your reward, then if you get another day that is great. A bonus. You need not expect more.

It sounds easy. It isn't. But you can train yourself to live more in the here and now. For any effective leader this is one of the best sources of energy and passion.

CEO Message 57
DO WHAT IS RIGHT

"Even when you report to the ultimate authority," writes Michael Useem in *Leading Up*, "it is your solemn duty and in this case a sacred one, to give your best counsel, render your best judgment and persist in the expression of both, whether such upward leadership is specifically sought or not."

—◦—

So What Kind of Leader am I?

I began this chapter on leadership with a simple question: Why?

Why do you want to become a leader? I said there were only three reasons: to be a success, to feel like you belong, or because you have a higher calling or purpose.

What was my reason? I wanted to belong to something. I was an immigrant kid. I had a hard time fitting in. No one could spell my name. I even had a teacher who asked if she could call me Archie instead of Arkadi. I said no. I became the classic outsider. But I like feeling that I belong. It's why working with people I like is really important to me. Does Donald Trump like who he works with? I have no idea. My guess is, it isn't that important to him.

What is important to you? It will make all the difference.

—◦—

How to Be the Rock then Roll Leader: The takeaways

- You must be indistinguishable from the culture.
- You must have: a calling; the willingness to make it personal; an enemy; the trust of an inner circle; the risk of failure. Have a vision; a plan of attack; sell it; validate it and never deviate.
- You must have the answers to the abstract questions. Eliminate doubt.
- The view from the top floor is always nice. But all the action is on the street.
- You can get lucky once. You can't stay lucky.
- You need a story.
- Your job is to generate disequilibrium and make people creatively uncomfortable.
- Management theory won't change the score on the scoreboard.

- Know what you need to know and decide. The rest is gravy.
- Principled decisions are the easiest to defend.
- Commitment only comes in one color.

How to
Be the Rock
then Roll
Leader:
The takeaways

CHAPTER 3

ROCK THEN ROLL THE MARKET—

Not Your Boat

Conflict and Chaos: Like It or Not You Are In It

What do you think of your market? Is it a fixed point on a ruler or is it like a cluster of stars you see at night—something way out there and out of reach?

From where I stand, the market is not a fixed point. It isn't the sum total of all those numbers and graphs on those endless printouts you pore over in an attempt to quantify a qualitative problem. It isn't even a fixed place. It's the roller coaster sum total of everything we do and think and see and experience. Remember what a wise old philosopher said: you can never set foot in the same river twice. Nothing stays the same; everything is changing all the time and in constant flux.

Conflict and Chaos

It's all around us. All the time. Some leaders build up levees against a rising tide. Their management approach is basic: whatever currently exists needs to be protected at all costs. Innovators, true leaders, are the ones who find advantage and opportunity in channeling the river's power.

As we will see later in this chapter, innovation can be the light-bulb moment that illuminates and dispels the chaos—the rare flash of genius that transforms both life and society as we know it. But innovation is not always about knocking down walls or scaling impossible heights. Meaningful transformations can, and usually do, occur much closer to the ground. Close to the conflict. Sometimes what goes on that's new is inside the walls. There are two kinds of chaos: one is naturally occurring and external to your business and is the source of opportunity and innovation. The second is man-made and internal and is destructive to your business' culture.

The word *chaos* comes from the Greek word for form-less matter, it does not have a shape that lasts through time, and it is not predictable. Chaos is all the random, patternless, haphazard stuff in our universe.

When I am up in a plane looking down at the world from 33,000 feet, however, I am astounded at how amazingly organized everything is—just as it should be. Yet when I am at ground level I see every imperfection and problem; perhaps it is perspective.

The question you need to ask yourself is simple: are you the leader of a fundamentally sound business in a chaotic world? Or, are you a fundamentally chaotic business? The philosophy of culture-driven leadership is that the former is highly desirable, while the second is ... not.

A good leader should not be afraid of chaos from without: the naturally occurring chaos. Do not try to control it. Instead, welcome the dynamic aspects of chaos as tools with which you can shape and achieve the goals of your business.

Think of chaos as the cask in which a company's vision is fermented. Crisis is inevitable. The primary benefit of creating a culture-driven business is its flexibility against chaos. No business can avoid confronting unexpected disaster. The question any leader faces at that juncture is simple: "What now?"

Indeed. "What now?" It's a question that cripples many traditional business structures. They have no answer. But to a culture-driven business the answer is direct: stay true to the mission.

No business deliberately makes bad decisions. We try to eliminate doubt by turning over as many qualitative factors as we can into quantitative ones. And yet doubt persists. Will things get better or worse? No one knows. We consult our projections and tables of figures like tea leaves. Have we done the right thing?

Ultimately, though, is that even the right question?

To be a culture-driven leader means learning how to be ruthlessly objective about the information at hand and having a bias to act. It has been my experience that traditional leaders have the most difficult time dealing with chaos in direct proportion to how far they have disengaged from the mission that animates the company. To be always guided by a commitment

"Zig when everyone zags." —AK

to the mission means to be objective about dealing with chaos. "I don't know what to do because I don't know what I want."

If you, as leader, know what you want—by which a culture-driven leader means having a commitment to principles and a mission—you have already found the narrow edge of the wedge.

What would Lincoln have accomplished had there been no Civil War? But what would Lincoln have been as a leader had he been ambivalent about the cause he had championed? For Lincoln, war was an opportunity to change society for the better. It was his statement of culture-driven leadership!

If you have built the right business culture, what you will find is chaos that occurs naturally is an opportunity. You will meet the challenge head on and more than likely prevail. On the other hand, if you have built a poor business culture—the culture that breeds chaos from within—the results could be fatal. More than likely you will be so swept up in managing endless but avoidable internal breakdowns that you won't see the storm clouds gathering on the horizon until it is too late. Think of your business as the area of calm within the eye of the hurricane. Nobody can prevent naturally occurring chaos. But creating the right culture for your business is the best preemptive strike against chaos permanently destabilizing or swamping your business.

Can you rock all the time? Not any more than you can dance all the time. You want to create an attitude that looks for chances to rock:

- Stand out
- Be different
- Find the moment to make a difference

Opportunities come in two sizes: big and small. What is often overlooked or unappreciated is how personal the search for opportunity is. The world is getting more chaotic and that means developing a sixth sense for opportunity will be even more important. As a culture-driven leader you have you own style. Make developing your curiosity a part of your leadership profile. This will help you navigate the chaos.

I can't think of one business that doesn't claim it is always on the hunt to improve. But what is missing consistently is any real commitment to improving. Interesting idea! Let's have a meeting and study it! Six months later that interesting idea has been put on the back burner. A year later it has been forgotten.

Man-made chaos, remember? Probably more harm is done to culture from failing to adapt to change as from resisting change—from having the right solution and not implementing than implementing the wrong solution.

Staying with something—a strategy, plan, or a procedure—for too long or not long enough is a familiar problem. A sudden gust of wind blows and we panic and give up on it. Alternatively, a mild breeze turns into a tornado but we refuse to relax our grip. Events, in this case, unfold and make decisions for us. The essence of the culture-driven approach is to be purposeful how you think about it. Ask yourself, will this really work or make a real difference? Why are you hanging on? Is it for the right reasons? Or is it because you have no response?

If you are clear about the culture you are in, then you are purposeful and directing your own circumstances.

You are really rolling.

———◁○▷———

CEO Message 105
CHAOS VERSUS UNCERTAINTY

Your main responsibility is to take uncertainty out of any situation.

The key here is this: be certain about what is causing doubt. Figure out why it is there and take steps to remove it. Your job is to take issues off the table. Break it down. Focus on responding to the solution instead of responding to the problem. Every action requires an action to remove doubt.

Take a familiar everyday example: a friend tells you they hate their boyfriend or wife or whatever and they want to split up or get a divorce. You ask them, what happened? What's the trouble? How long has this been a problem? On and on. All these questions are ways of breaking down the statement to get at the cause. Once you have the cause you are on track to a solution. Maybe it turns out that the real problem is he watches too much sports on TV or she spends too much time with her friends. So then maybe they don't really want to split up? The point is you have taken the uncertainty out of the equation.

You need to communicate clearly what to do and how to get there. No situation will ever be completely free of chaos.

A certain amount of uncertainty is a given. Find a way to feel comfortable with chaos. It takes practice! Managing to keep your head when all others around you are losing theirs! Incorporating uncertainty into your leadership mindset takes getting used to—especially if you prefer controlled situations and neatly predictable outcomes. Instead of wasting valuable time and energy fighting to control uncertainty, think about eliminating points of doubt. Sort out facts objectively and continue to apply intuition. Do your homework. Think it through. Remember: break it down to take issues off the table. The competition is facing the same issues you are. Ignore them. Sort out your plan of action.

CEO Message 28
MANAGING CHAOS

Monday morning for me is a good example of internal chaos, and another feet-on-the-ground reminder of why a culture-driven leader has to be "on" all the time. I have way too many items to deal with and not enough time. So instead of controlling everything, I prioritize: I look for the impact-items and do them one at a time, I do not multi-task, work faster or cut corners. A lot of things get left but it's important that what I do, I do well.

You have to think of everything you do as opportunities for mentoring everyone around you. It is your job as leader to create leadership skills in everyone in your business. That mentoring begins with you. Even the tiniest and most mundane task needs to be addressed in a direct and disciplined way. You are always teaching! Always mentoring!

CEO Message 4
MISSED DEADLINES ARE MORALE KILLERS

Deadlines are everywhere.

And because the world has become so much more competitive it seems that deadlines are becoming more of a challenge too.

A law of nature: we have to meet deadlines. There is just no escaping it.

Whether this is setting up a release on the new application, meeting a publishing deadline, or answering a call within the company-proscribed goal of twenty seconds. It has never been more important, then, that deadlines be accurately established. Never casually establish a deadline and never casually miss a deadline.

A deadline is your lifeline.

If a deadline has to be re-set, make sure it is re-set with other parts of the business in mind. The losses of missed deadlines are not geometric but exponential. One day here is not one day there; it's one day here and five days there. And then two weeks down there and on and on. There is nothing more positive for employee morale than to know that a deadline has been met, a project has been successfully completed and the business has moved forward. What a great sense of satisfaction!

On the other hand, morale crashes when the system fails.

Remember the Rock then Roll rule: have a clear vision of what you want done. A huge factor of knowing what you want done is your knowing exactly when it will get done.

Nobody can deposit promises, okay?

If you are responsible for a deadline or have leadership on a project or a specific delivery and for some reason that deadline cannot be met, you have a real obligation to not only explain it but also find a way to lessen the impact on your colleagues and co-workers. It is extremely frustrating to waste time and resources on missed deadlines—especially the costly necessity of dealing with the consequences. We are the culture. If we don't work together we end up working against each other.

A true measure of your leadership is the commitment and respect you have, and that you demand from your team, for meeting deadlines. Meeting deadlines is a sign of respect that you have for the company vision. Never deviate from the mission.

Establish realistic deadlines that everyone understands. If it needs to be adjusted, do it quickly and move on.

CEO Message 30
ROCK THEN ROLL TWO-MINUTE DRILL

We all love it when a project works out. Let's party! On the other hand, we tend to want to sweep failures aside and just forget about them.

It's best to keep moving. Celebrate victories *or* failures for two minutes and then go to the next challenge. Spending too much time on victories or unhappiness over failures and set-backs will not help. Everyone needs to see the next chance to do something well and your job is to keep the drive going forward.

Leaders can often be found looking over their shoulders. You should always be looking ahead. Focus yourself and every-one around you on tomorrow and the challenges ahead—new challenges and new deadlines. How? Keep asking questions directed at tomorrow and very little on the ones focused on today. These need to be done as well but can very well be delegated. You are not alone. If you do not let go of today every question of how things went will take your focus off tomorrow and distract you. It's all about the road ahead.

CEO Message 5
PRODUCTIVITY

ING Direct had the happy problem of undergoing rapid—almost quantum—growth. Of course, it was not all sunshine and rose petals.

We took a lot of heat on controlling expenses. There was all this growth and a lot of money was being spent and it appeared there might be no limit.

The truth, of course—as it often is—was the exact opposite.

At the end of the day we needed to bring expenses in line with *or better* than industry averages. For ING Direct that amounted to less than one cent out of every dollar of deposits. Not much wiggle room there, my friend.

The point is, we did it. So must you.

To run a high volume, low margin business, cost control takes on a huge priority. Spending in the right places and not wasting money on flashy but low-return efforts or unnecessary and self-indulgent expenditures is paramount in meeting growth goals as well as eventual profit goals. Productivity is achieved in little steps. I found that if a lot of expenses were embedded in the bank and not really yielding good revenue or growth impact, it would be very painful to restructure them later.

Cost savings are also not about being cheap. Anybody can be cheap. There is no art to slashing a budget. Maintaining good quality is the answer to efficiency in keeping a program extremely focused on what is needed to achieve.

For ING Direct, for example, to provide good value to our customers and meet the requirements of all the stakeholders involved, the only thing we could really achieve was good cost performance because that was the only enduring quality to making ING Direct a short, as well as a long, time winner.

Here's some grandmotherly advice for CEOs: spend money at work the way you spend it at home. Your personal spending is an example that all others see. My grandmother used to reuse teabags. I'll never forget that. It wasn't because she was cheap; she was thrifty. She and those of her generation understood the value of a dollar. Believe it or not, everyone knows whether you are generous, foolish, or cheap with your spending. It translates into your business dealings as well. It makes a big difference.

If you design a business model to be a low cost company then *all* your focus should be on measuring and getting costs down to make that reality a success.

CEO Message 235
FOCUS ON THE PRESSURE POINT

Every business model has a weak spot or vulnerability. You need to know what it is. You must manage the pressure point because that is exactly where a breach is likely to occur.

The ING Direct retail business model, for instance, was not easily understood and many have managed it in the wrong way.

For example, when the Internet craze arrived, most banks took their branch operating procedures, mainly ones for manual transactions, and just copied them onto their electronic forms. They were cumbersome and slow for users.

No one thought that the user experience needed to be different and that the way people wanted to work with the Internet was different that manual in-person work.

The difference was critical to the way we wanted ING Direct to do business.

We sold market-priced mortgages that were funded by customer deposits. The cost of funding those deposits was high and the bank needed to sustain itself for revenue on that narrow interest margin. That was less than half of a traditional bank's revenue. Traditional banks struggle to get growth. Our unique approach got ING Direct the growth but not the revenue. Our problem was that the business model created a unique set of pressure points around revenue.

We managed sales volume very efficiently to offset shortfalls in revenue. Switching the focus from sales volume to revenue meant we had to find more marginal space by getting better with pricing for all customers. The value proposition had to get a little less valuable but in a positive way. This is a classic problem for all businesses that need to pass on price increases in a fair way.

What is your company's weak point or vulnerability?

If you don't know, find out. And make it a habit to constantly know. The world is changing way too fast to pretend you can survive by sitting comfortably on the sidelines. Think of it this way: put a bull's-eye on your business. Find that enemy, right? Think of the guy out there with you in the crosshairs. What are you doing to defend yourself?

Our weak point was our ability to wrestle costs down to a low-enough level to meet growth and the profit numbers. For an outfit like Netflix the challenge was shifting from mailing movie discs to live streaming. Sometimes change is fatal. Not too long ago a company like Tower Records dominated the retail music industry. Not any more. How has Blockbuster fared? Some companies confront major shifts and have the flexibility and capacity to change. Many others cannot, or will not, either because they fail to recognize the need for change or take action too late. There is no such thing as an early warning system for business failure. You may as well invest in a crystal ball or a Ouija board. You should know—you should be able to sense—when things are not going well. Don't we all have that sense in general? Same in business. You can sense disruption. The difference is, we don't think about business the way we do about individuals.

What is the most critical challenge your business is facing? Many leaders will not know. You should. You have to have the answer. You have to be able to sell within the culture of the company. Raise the red flag!

CEO Message 90
PROACTIVE

The famous Artic explorer Roald Amundsun had this to say about his meticulous pre-expedition preparations: "Adventure is the result of poor planning."

Most managers are confronted by many daily problems, the root of which is often found in not getting things lined up early enough, getting behind in issues or situations, and not having done enough advance work; in many cases, just not being proactive.

Being proactive means anticipating events and outcomes— forecasting the chaos. This is just as true on a personal level as

it is on a broader business level. It means having an awareness of how various issues and actions will be interpreted by
people around you. Being on the ball, being on top of things,
and having social radar are learned skills and can be practiced effectively to create a preemptive solution to problems
and reduce the stress in the work place—all in ways that
reflect well on the organization. Questions like, where do
you want your company to be in two years? What are some
revolutionary changes in the offing that will impact my business? Will that innovation in *that* business come to have an
impact down the road for my business? Finding time every
day to think and plan about what's happening today and in
the weeks ahead is well worth the time.

Think long term: look to the horizon. It is my way of imposing some order on chaos and uncertainty, and it is amazing how few leaders actively work on it.

CEO Message 91
PROACTIVE PART II

My having become known as a rebel is due largely to being
proactive. For instance, I consciously decide what outfit
I need to wear every day. I am thinking deliberately about
the image I want to emphasize. How will it make me feel?
And how will it help me act? What impression do I wish to
achieve? How will it be received? It became a part of my personal branding message. Remember, if you don't plan the
brand, the brand will plan you.

All leaders that you can name have a distinguishing feature. Billionaire Warren Buffet? Drives an old car. It says he
is thrifty. Old fashioned. Not easily fooled. Donald Trump?
Bad hair. "You're fired!" The Donald. Flashy. An unapologetic

and tireless self-promoter. Arkadi Kuhlmann? Wears cowboy boots and rides a Harley. The Bad Boy of Banking. A rebel who revolutionized the banking industry.

You need a distinguishing feature, too.

It's the unexpected. The unknown. Everyone has a basic stereotype to which they conform. The trick is to dress it up and be conscious of what it is and make it work for you. It's not for everyone. Dealing with uncertainty is not everyone's cup of tea. For a good leader it sharpens his or her attention.

The personal style you develop as a leader is the clue to what you want people to know about you that makes you stand out from the crowd.

The Boy Scouts' motto is, "Be prepared." An effective leader's motto is, "Think ahead but be ready to react." All the pre-game practice in the world is useless if you—as quarterback—aren't willing to throw the touchdown pass.

CEO Message 214
LAYERING A CAKE, NOT YOUR MESSAGE

The toughest job in leadership is staying on course, especially when the winds of dissent start to blow.

Both the commander at the helm of his ship and the general in command of his army have someone second-guessing them. The Rock then Roll rule says you have to have an inner circle. Absolutely, but in every inner circle there is also your biggest potential enemy. Remember the plots from the classics you studied with their webs of dark intrigue, deceit, and deception? They are all being played out still. Trust me!

Remember Caesar? Hector? Achilles? Robin Hood? Luke Skywalker! A boardroom is a battlefield. The corpses are real. It's no fiction.

Remember, your job is to take uncertainty out of every critical situation. You have to fill the gap. It is your voice that says, "It will be alright. We are on the right course." That takes patience, awareness, and conviction.

CEO Message 204
BOWLING LANES?

Everyone at any business or company has run into the "that's not my job" defense, or "that's their job," or, "I asked them to do it" excuse.

Silos are created when volume of work, specialized skills, and work complexity all reach a critical threshold. From CEOs to receptionists, we all wish to have things straightforward or simple. The reality is, by making it simple for the customer, which is always the objective, the risk is failing to understand that simplifying at one end can create complexity at the other.

In business we cannot work the way teams bowl. In reality, there is only one lane to the customer. So, what can we do to fix this dilemma? The answer is this: look at work in the larger context. Follow the impact of what you do throughout the organization and remember that you and your team are all directed at the same goal.

There is a new idea, bowling without lanes. It sure will help you focus on what others are doing around you.

CEO Message 343
CONSUMER ATTITUDES ARE CHANGING

"Our products are sold not bought!" You know what? I have heard this I don't know how many times and every time I do

I run like hell. It's the hard sell that screams at you that you need this or that product whether you need it or not.

It's a big excuse for thinking that business knows what's best for a customer; that all they need is a motivated salesman to educate the consumer. Well, most consumers are pretty smart. I have rarely come upon a customer who has had a happy "hard sell" consumer experience. In fact, it is usually the opposite.

The conventional theory of the marketplace as cooperative and self-regulating is disappearing step by step. Money, products, information and knowledge all flow people-to-people like water and electricity. It's virtually impossible to stay ahead of all the information available. The marketplace evolution! And the pace of that change is being dictated by consumers and how they manage information.

These trends bring tremendous challenges to business. One of the most crucial being, when it comes to a new idea, new product, or service, is it better to be first or to be smart?

ING Direct was trying to shape a new attitude between consumers and financial products both in the way financial products were bought and the way customers interacted with them. For us, being first was probably more important *right off the bat*. We were one new company with a radically new way of doing business pitted against a gigantic but extremely traditional industry that viewed us, if they viewed us at all, as irrelevant.

First always has en edge coming out of the gate. It never lasts, but it gets more recognition. What do you reach for? A tissue? Or Kleenex? But being first also means that you could be the easiest target to pick off. Timing may or may not be a factor that you can control. One of our culture-driven secrets stated that luck and timing are factors. But more important is that the quality of your product or service is completely and unalterably under your control. If you are not the best horse in the race it probably does not matter how much of a lead you are staked. In the end, best always outruns better.

Einstein said it best: God is in the details.

It's as true for business as it is for the universe. Simplify everything. All the time. Simplify every process. Fine-tune every product.

Be the genius. Get the details right and your Rock will really Roll.

————◁◦▷————

Innovation versus Stagnation: Rock or Be Rolled Over

Remember those old movie westerns where some old prospector would be on a railroad track on one of those wheeled-carts that had to be pumped up and down? When I hear the expression "thinking outside the box," I think of that guy. He's working really hard on something that has only two directions that are really basically the same: this way and that way.

Nothing should be more obvious than the fact that what we call the market is a volatile place. We waste a huge amount of energy improvising strategies or theories to deal with or minimize that volatility. We try to create conditions that immunize our business from the battering that is inevitable. Sure, it's a reasonable thing to do. It's instinct. CEOs are mother bears protecting their cubs. But the problem is spending more time on preservation than on inspiration and innovation.

Innovation is the oxygen of the business world. Nothing can be done without it.

But innovation always begins, and cannot occur without, a simple question: "Why not?"

Why not rock?

Genius Is Not Required

People look at the genius of Thomas Edison and say, "Wow, that guy was amazing." But what I wonder is, if you think Edison was so amazing how come you don't spend more time thinking like he did? Look, when you come right down to it, Edison wasn't doing much more than we all do when we come upon a product, or service, or tool that doesn't work the way it's supposed to.

We think, "Why doesn't this work right?"

Edison and Einstein and others like them asked the same questions, but all the time and about everything. Why? Why not? Only, they wouldn't take no for an answer.

Rock then roll. In my experience the preferred path to genius—the more reliable road to meaningful innovation—is learning how to look at things in a different way.

Memory Lane Moment in a New Car

Once I decided I wanted to buy a Mercedes.

Now, I'm a committed saver and I don't do flash but I had the money and I felt I deserved it. A great car: excellent quality, terrific resale value, etc. So I walk into the dealership. See a car I like. Only one problem: "I don't want air conditioning. I hate air conditioning." I'm just a guy that loves to have the windows open, fresh air. "Can I order one without air conditioning?" I ask.

The dealer says no. I couldn't. That wasn't how they operated, he said. It's a package. You have to have it all.

"Well, that's a problem for me, I really don't want that."

He said, "Well, I have a solution for you."

"Oh yeah? What's that?"

"Just don't turn it on!"

Beautiful.

So What's the Point?

I started thinking about our business, and especially about the choices we offered to our customers in terms of product or service and why.

What could we offer that traditional banks weren't? If people want a bank that provided financial advice, a full-range of services, monthly statements, and all kinds of added features and fees—the air conditioning—that's fine. It's a free market place. They can stay with their bank. But how about offering a choice. Fewer buttons on the remote? In other words, a real and authentic alternative.

Think about who you are: air conditioner guy? Or a fewer buttons guy?

I do it all the time. What always fascinated me about the story of David and Goliath was not that David outwitted and outmatched a physically superior opponent. It's that his genius was that when Saul offered him his own sword and armor, he road tested it before the match and decided, no dice. The fit was all wrong. If Goliath was so much bigger, he reasoned, why fight him in the conventional manner with someone else's strategy and equipment?

Be unconventional. David rocked then rolled.

How to Think about Innovation

Successful innovations fall into two categories.

Innovation versus Stagnation: Rock or Be Rolled Over

The first deals with the *scope* of the innovation. If you're going to innovate, which means to improve, enhance, or make a product or service better in some way, you need to look at how broad or how narrow that scope is.

In terms of most businesses, and certainly this is true in the financial services business, the broader you make that scope the more opportunities there are because you're not really sure what you can accomplish in what kind of timeframe. For instance, reengineering the product, the process, or the customer is a pretty broad way of doing things. What I mean by reengineering the customer is making sure that the customer is buying what he or she actually needs and not just what they think they need. The process is to streamline the steps that are involved in obtaining the product, and in different industries you see this in different ways. You build a different car, you sell the car in a different way, and consumers use it in a different way. You've seen that in all types of other industries in terms of how it gets done.

The second part of the innovation puzzle is a mindset, and the mindset is, quite simply, *curiosity.*

I'm always amazed that so many CEOs actually believe innovation can be accomplished in a premeditated way in a department or by some technicians cordoned off in a room. The reality is, the leader himself has to not only see the vision but also have an idea and a curiosity about innovation— about how to make the vision better.

Leaders of businesses often look forward to improve and grow their businesses. First order of business? They hire consultants, do research and hold brainstorming sessions and come up with the best ideas. At some point the question comes to the table: "Has anyone done this before?" Usually the answer is no.

This is when Rock then Roll culture should kick in. But more often it doesn't. The idea is innovative and it's new. That's good. It also makes it risky. The default "move it forward" move for those kinds of leaders is to decide to wait until someone else—probably your competition—discovers it and implements it first. "We will be the smart follower. It's the pioneers who get the arrows in the back," they think. "It's the settlers who lay down stakes on the land."

Leaders need to take risks were no one else has tried. You have to risk failure. That's real leadership.

If you and I are going to conquer a mountain, for instance, it's not just the question of do we go up the mountain? The big question is *how* are we going to get there? You have to find the best way to do it. You, as CEO, have two mandates. One: eliminate doubt about getting there. Two: figuring out the best way to do it. That's innovation.

I've spent a lot of time agonizing over the question, how can we do this better? Good CEOs, aside from eliminating doubt, are always thinking about ways to make things better. The trick to making things better is to improve the fundamental ability to achieve your vision or goal. In America, leaders that stepped forward thought about how to execute a business and make it better, but somewhere along the line profit became a terrible substitute for that vision or mission to innovate. Why are we not celebrating CEOs that are innovating, doing things differently, more efficiently, and helping not only their share-holders and investors, but society as well?

Why is the only measure *profitability*—who makes the most amount of dough? We have to get back to the things that made this country great, like innovation and the desire to make things better in a sustainable way.

Think about this, every time we improve or make something better, we have an ability to reallocate that one thing into the next thing. If this helps us in our industry, can't it be more inclusive for *all* of society? Doesn't this, in fact, get us back to the heart of what our leadership in the world should be all about? Shouldn't it be about our ability to innovate and move society forward as opposed to being satisfied with the notion that "we're just bloody big?"

A Definition

Creative destruction is breaking things down or apart even when they are working well. No matter how good something works, it can always work better.

———◁◦▷———

CEO Message II
THE STARTING LINE

It's amazing how simple starting a revolution can be.

Some revolutions start with a bang; others begin almost anonymously and inconspicuously, accumulating momentum over time and then just continuing. Compare the Russian Revolution to the current wave of democratic revolts in the Middle East. Business is similar. Some businesses just grow in a steady way; some storm out of the gate. On occasion it can seem this way because it takes time and it's hard to get noticed in the marketplace. But they all have something in common. Key is, something happens to get the business noticed. To rock the status quo is a great way to get noticed. Then you can roll. Then you can make a difference.

Starting something brand new in the banking industry struck a lot of people as nuts. First, it was a highly regulated industry. Second, no one had ever created a model like ING Direct.

How could we get around the regulatory straightjacket? Well, we could create ourselves in the image of all the other banks and, like good workers, labor for our tiny piece of the pie. Then maybe we could hook up with the other banks and use their combined market muscle to maybe change or relax the rules. Or, we could accept the rules and regulations and focus the illuminating beam of the innovation lantern elsewhere: on the products and services themselves. For instance, all banks pay interest on deposits. Is there any rule that prevents a bank from paying higher interest rates than the other guys? No. So we figured out how to do that. It's called redesigning the product.

Another useful concept is customer reengineering. It simply means identifying the gap between what a customer wants and what you provide, then figuring out how to narrow that gap to zero. Both are increasingly useful tools when talking about innovation.

For instance, I wanted to do commodity-standardized products for the mass market. Others may want to provide customized goods and services. That's great. But that wasn't my vision. For thirty years I had watched the entire banking industry follow the same lemming-like parade of all the time spending, more and more, and adding more and more: more services, more features, more options, more bells and whistles. Why? Because the biggest more in the equation— the one you didn't hear about as a customer—was more fees.

So my idea was to reverse direction. If everyone is traveling south why can't I head north? Let's do the exact opposite of what they are doing. Instead of adding things on and charging the customer for services they aren't sure they need, let's strip things out. Let's reduce our menu of services and pass along the savings to the customer. Take stuff out. Strip it back down to the chassis. Go back to roll up windows as opposed to electric windows. Why not? Make the company's vision the customer's vision! Rock then Roll.

CEO Message 299
ADDRESSING—AND REDRESSING—THE IMBALANCE

I am in the banking business. We don't save babies, we don't go to the moon, we do nothing except deal with the allocation of money over a timeframe composed of borrowers and depositors. We time-allocate to different groups. Who needs a loan today versus who needs to save today? This allocation of time, the oil in the economic machine, makes the machine run more efficiently.

Why should we not do anything but get out of the way? Why should we do anything to slow up the oil in the machine? Why should we take any more than the pure efficiency of running the economic machine, which is American industry?

As a banker, if I can save you time or money, if I can make it easier for you, then you can take that time, take that money, take that energy, and spend it on something you think is important. I'm not allocating your gain, if you will—you are. The empowerment of the people is to do what the people want to do. Remember that old adage: life, liberty, and the pursuit of happiness? Damn right, and bankers should start doing it!

You know the ING Direct story: we wanted to be different than the rest of the industry. How come? Well, let's do the math: there were roughly nine thousand financial institutions in the market place at the time. Would you rather be the one of one? Or one of nine thousand? From a customer perspective, will you take notice of yet another bank in the same model as all the others, or do you want one that's different?

If you want to get into the game and the game is dominated by huge players, and your plan is to play the same way as them, you are going to have to play by their rules. By default, their rules become your rules. The trick is to figure out what you can do to redress that imbalance. How can you tip the balance in your favor? Invent a new set of rules. Invent a new game.

CEO Message 31
TRADITION VERSUS INNOVATION

"We're astonished," wrote the poet Wislawa Szymborska in her 1996 Nobel Prize for Literature acceptance speech, "by things that deviate from some well-known and universally acknowledged norm, from an obviousness to which we have become accustomed." She goes on: "I sometimes dream of situations that can't possibly come true."

The impossible is only impossible if you treat it that way. It is when you look at the impossible as being possible that innovation becomes not a dream or a fantasy but a roadmap to your goal.

CEO Message 45

START SIMPLE; STAY SIMPLE

When we started ING Direct, we had one razor-sharp idea: we were going to be simple, easy with a human touch. Years later we have grown enormously from our starting mark. The business has flourished but one thing hasn't changed. We still have the same idea: be simple, easy and with a human touch. Have a clear vision of what you want done. Never deviate from the vision. Think of the American automobile industry. General Motors, for instance. Cars were invented in America and General Motors used to be the gold standard for quality. They dominated the industry and their market domination appeared unassailable. But competitors started building better cars and, after setbacks like the oil crisis, more consumer-preference oriented cars. It didn't take long for American drivers to change their minds about their own preferences. Foreign car manufacturers were responsive to changes in consumer attitudes and had the flexibility and capacity for adaptation built into their structure—in fact, beating GM at its own game. The lesson is this: GM's focus over time shifted from meeting consumer needs to meeting its own needs; building more cars trumped building better and more consumer-friendly cars. How can you build a better car if you don't know what drivers want and are willing to pay for? Every business has the same challenge.

Hold true to your vision! But never lose sight of your customer either. That is why you have a vision in the first place.

DON'T PRETEND TO BE A GENIUS; BE BOLD AND COMMIT TO A GOAL INSTEAD

Sometimes innovation is the result of truly inspired and original thinking.

Einstein, man. What a genius. His theories of special and general relativity were a breathtaking leap in intellectual history. Einstein improvised a method for thinking about the way the world worked that was both transforming and transcendent.

But as impressive as Einstein was, he was not working inside a vacuum. Progress was being made along similar lines by other intensely gifted scientists working in the same culture. But while their progress was patient and incremental, Einstein, by thinking five or six steps ahead of everyone else, took what the Danish philosopher Soren Kierkegaard called "the imaginative leap across the abyss."

A Rock then Roll rebel!

Most of us are not geniuses. That's the bad news. The good news, however, is this: we don't need to be geniuses. What we need to do, both as innovators and leaders, is to have the courage to take that leap into the unknown. This means trusting our commitments and believing in our goals.

The only leading you can do from the back of the pack is a retreat. If you want to Rock then Roll, approach the edge of the abyss. Do you see a dark deep hole? Or do you see opportunity as the bridge to the other side?

CEO Message 231
THE SOUND OF ONE HAND CLAPPING IN AN INDUSTRY

I'm not trying to win my competitors over to my perspective. This is the platform that I am working. Whether it's Wall Street, Detroit, Silicon Valley or whatever or wherever, isn't it in every industry's interest that someone expresses a different view? I'm tolerant of other views. Should you not be tolerant of mine?

CEO Message 223
THE SOUL OF THE NEW MACHINE

In that same Nobel Prize speech, Wislawa Szymborska wrote that, "Inspiration is not the exclusive privilege of poets or artists. There is—there will always be—a certain group of people whom inspiration visits. It's made up of all those who've consciously chosen their calling and do their jobs with love and imagination.... Their work becomes one continuous adventure as long as they manage to keep discovering new challenges. Difficulties and setbacks never quell their curiosity. A swarm of new questions emerges from every problem they solve. Whatever inspiration is, it's born of a continuous 'I don't know.'"

Always ask questions.

CEO Message 139
CHANGE YOUR MIND? OR CHANGE THE WORLD?

"Philosophers have hitherto interpreted the world in many ways. The purpose is to change it."

Wise words—especially when it comes to innovation. The truth is that we are creatures of habit. We tend to fall into ruts not because we have no choice but because ruts are comfortable and risk-free. Let's face it: we like our ruts. But ruts are walls that we build up around our brain.

Most animals avoid risk. Instinct domesticates us in the art of self-preservation. But in business self-preservation often is the surest path to self-destruction. Business writer Bill Taylor sums it up nicely by explaining that risk comes in two forms. There are the leaders who worry that failing to take action will make them "miss the boat" and leaders who worry that acting impulsively or hastily will "sink the boat."

To an innovative leader there is the third option: rock the boat!

You rock, I roll. *Validate that the vision is in line with what society thinks is good.*

By the way, any guesses about the source of the opening quote above?

Karl Marx. Yes, *that* Karl Marx. The point is, he was right. It isn't about interpreting the world as you find it; it's about changing it. And it is also a nifty reminder about where you should go looking for new ideas. Maybe the million-dollar ideas are out there already.

Are you looking in the right places? And when you do find the right idea, what are you willing to do to make it happen?

CEO Message 73
WINNERS AND LOSERS

Most modern business practices share much in common with the military and its roots in economic conflicts over borders, geography, and resources. Armies are created to forcefully take what one entity desires from another. What the victor gains, the loser loses.

Winners and losers.

Conventional business management looks at the relationship between industry and the marketplace as a zero sum ratio: to grow a business means taking market share away from someone else. You don't have an army, however. What you have is product or service. What you need to do to conquer market share, then, is to come up with something a hell of a lot better than what your competitors out there have come up with—competitors who are probably a lot bigger than you, have been doing it a lot longer than you, and probably are even doing it really well.

Academic research has proven how companies get started, how they mature, how they die, and how they get reformulated in some way. The research seems to support the idea that what is normal for business is an evolutionary growth—the slow but steady climb up the gently inclined plane. The most successful businesses, however, are the ones that have created a *new market*; in other words, those that have come up with a new *big idea* that has created new shelf space in the market. If you look at the marketplace as it exists today, it's hard to see opportunity. The chances of finding success or a way to expand or change the marketplace appear to be very small.

New companies—new industries even—are not necessarily created from huge investments and tons of resources. And this is true more and more today: the most exciting growth industry is created by big ideas—ideas that should be brought to the market. Hewlett-Packard did not come into existence in a lab. It started in a garage. Steve Jobs gave birth to Apple in his basement. Facebook was a humble idea with comically modest expectations that began in a dorm room.

Things happen because individual leaders want them to happen; they will them to happen, they have an idea.

The least original, and most self-defeating, idea you can ever have is thinking that all the good ideas have been taken. You pull up an empty bucket from the well. What do you do? You stare at the bucket—like a batter who stares at his bat at after a strikeout. The bucket is fine, don't blame the bucket! It's time to get your head out of your bucket and dig a new well!

Good ideas do not respect borders, either. They migrate freely from business to business and across one industry to another. The idea is to take an idea from one part of the world and transport it to another, transport it from one side of the country to the other, or from one industry to your industry. People are people and there is a never-ending need for coming up with new ideas—most of all big ideas.

The tendency in any busy company is to focus increasingly on what is immediately ahead of us—all the little things that need to be dealt with or fixed. That is important, but you should also devote quality time to thinking about what is coming down the road. Why not think of a big new idea?

Why is that so important? I look at this way: most people get into business and are satisfied with their slice of the pie. Innovators don't look at it that way. You should be thinking, "How can I use my creativity, energy, and commitment to bake myself my own pie?"

CEO Message 236
THE BABY IN THE BATHWATER

Remember that cliché about how rules are made to be broken? Let's face it, we all live by rules. It's what gives society its shape. Without rules it would be anarchy. At the same time, rules, and a rule-based environment, can be like those steel chutes that cows are forced to walk to slaughter. The cow is just minding his own business, right? He sees the guy ahead of him marching along and since he likes to play by the rules he figures he won't make trouble so he will just follow along in the same direction.

So much for playing by the rules. Convergent thinking and actions are easy to defend but they can lead you astray if not challenged.

Being known as a rebel and an innovator is fun. I won't lie about that. It gives me a rush to think I am breaking the rules. The *old* rules. The rules that just are not working well. I love the collective outrage and universal skepticism that innovations at ING Direct inspired in the banking industry and its apologists. They saw us as upstarts, challenging market dominance. They saw us clinging to their flannel-suited pant leg. They mistakenly assumed we wanted a piece of what they had. See, that is what happens when process completely takes over a business and you forget about what got you into the business in the first place. Passion. Vision. A mission.

Have a clear vision. Stick to the vision. Rock then Roll. Innovation is your key to creating the right culture that will get you to your goal.

But being a rebel or breaking the rules by innovating is not enough. The key to effective rule-breaking is to know exactly which rules to break. Figure out all the things that cannot be changed and ask what is left over that *can be* changed? What *needs* to be changed? It's especially the *needs to be changed* factor that is so rich with innovative opportunities.

If your car's carburetor breaks down, the mechanic automatically replaces it with a new one. Makes sense, right? That's the way the car works. That's the way its system is built and needs to operate. But isn't that just another way of saying we build things we know ahead of time will eventually break down? And that they will break down in the same way, again and again? Who stops to think that maybe a car these days shouldn't need a carburetor?

Think of it this way: as an innovator you can be, one, a revolutionary or, two, an evolutionary. You choose. Figure out what rules or parameters exist that you need to operate within, if any. That is not the end point, but the starting point. Banking is regulated and controlled and that means the innovation model will be evolutionary. But look at Apple. The iPod strikes me as an example of the revolutionary innovation.

Ten commandants—great rules. But the innovator wonders: maybe I could get away with five.

CEO Message 318
REALITY IS OVERRATED

"All great works of literature either dissolve a genre or invent one." —Walter Benjamin

We tend to look at our ideas and compare them to reality. Reality tends to win. Why? All new things come from someone dreaming or imagining—whether it was that we could fly, or that we could instantly communicate with people around the world, or travel to the moon. Nothing is impossible.

Your business is neither more nor less than a genre—a way of doing things. A habit. What can you think of to create a new genre for your company?

CEO Message 81
IMITATOR VERSUS INNOVATOR

Innovation is not a reflex; it is not a response to stimulus.

It isn't a panacea, either.

I remember years ago an American presidential campaign came up with the slogan, "New Ideas; New Generation." The idea of the fresh, new approach sounds appealing. But what is it really saying? Sometimes the issue is not whether a solution is new or old; the issue is whether the proposed solution actually solves the problem in the most effective and efficient way. Maybe there are some old ideas collecting dust in your business that need to be taken off the shelf and re-examined. That an idea is new is no guarantee that it will work. In the long run—in the big scheme of things—the duration of novelty's appeal is five seconds.

In the same way, innovation does not guarantee financial success. Some innovations never pay off. There is a price to be paid by the pioneer. The costs and risks are high. Think of it this way: in any business there is going to be the eagle— the innovator, the loner who takes the great leap and soars the highest. Behind the innovator flies the migrator. The migrator waits to be told when to fly and where to go. His bias to action is to wait for the innovator. Then there are the vultures—the bottom feeders of the industry. They have no new ideas and no interest in the industry. All they want is to make a fast buck and move on.

The cost of innovation can be prohibitive. Most businesses take a *wait and see* approach to success. They watch you take the risk, and if it pays off they fall in line and duplicate your initiatives, but at much lower costs. It's fantastic to be out front and all alone and rewarded by one hundred percent market share. Obviously, the drawback of being an innovator is that a new idea will only put you out front as long as it takes for everyone else to copy you. Look at Sony, or RIM. Timing can be a killer.

It is *much* easier to imitate than innovate.

For me, it wasn't important to be the first out there with a new model of banking. It's no news flash that banking is not an industry known for the breathless speed by which it innovates. Fine. I knew we had a good idea. That was my greatest innovation. We measured our bottom line not by the numbers on the balance sheet but by customer sign-ups.

Of course, the whole time the industry was saying that we were not a threat they had ripped off most of our ads, copied our color, copied our logo, strategy, and just about anything else they could get their hands on. Was I angry? No. As far as I was concerned, they could plow the ING Direct field as much as they wanted. I didn't care. It was a compliment. As long as they were content to *copy* us I knew that they did not have the right stuff to better us.

At the time the banking industry was worth 1.6 trillion deposits. We didn't need that much. I figured we'd be happy with a few hundred billion.

CEO Message 53
WOULD YOU RECOGNIZE INNOVATION IF YOU SAW IT?

Aristotle said that science was the domain of the new; art, however, was the domain of the unexpected.

In my experience, innovation is almost always an ally of the unexpected.

That being the case, how do you approach a new idea? How do you respond to a radical suggestion? Do you see it as new and exciting? As unexpected and intriguing? Or do you dismiss it out of hand as too unorthodox or nontraditional?

If you saw the billion-dollar innovation coming down the highway, would you know what you were seeing? Chances are, you would want to find out what your boss saw *before* you committed to what you saw.

A Rock then Roll rule is: commit to the vision. Heart and soul. Sell the vision.

Trust your eyes!

———◄○►———

Thinking Small is Not Small Thinking: Innovation to Scale

It's vital that you remember that innovation is less an act of creativity than it is a creative act of thinking.

Everyone can do it. It does not require genius or eccentricity. Some of the most clever and important innovations have been way below the radar. Also, innovation should be like a muscle that is exercised regularly. It can't be a *one and done* mindset.

———◄○►———

CEO Message 125
CHANGE THE MARKET

You cannot change the market if you do not defy conventional wisdom. You are always taking a risk by being unconventional. Your effort should look strange, difficult, and unusual to your peers. But, your point of view should be sound and the customer should see it as a great idea. Listen to the right voices.

Most industries are lorded over by the gurus of conventional wisdom—mandarins of the traditional way of thinking. Trust me, they're everywhere. And they will always find it easier to dump on you than to change and adapt. So what do you do? Let them dump on you?

Why not buy a hat instead?

For me, it's cowboy boots. Whatever works for you.

CEO Message 64
THAT GREAT IDEA

Ideas are like weeds: they're all over the place and nobody pays any attention to them because they don't think they're worth much.

I am asked all the time how I came up with the ING Direct idea. Well, I use banks. Do you? If you do, have you really been that happy with the experience? I wasn't.

Think of the source of all innovation as a transaction. It doesn't matter what it is, how complex or how simple. If the transaction was good then the opportunity for innovation may be poor. However, if the transaction was bad the opportunities for innovation rise exponentially.

I looked at the banking industry and decided it was bust; the consumer generally loses. So the obvious questions were, "How would we do it better? How could we do something radically different?"

CEO Message 95
CURIOSITY

Inspiration comes with imagination. We are all in possession of passion, love, and imagination. To search and find the natural flow of thinking is the door to new ideas and to building your business.

Think about what your company does and take it up a notch. Try looking at your company from a completely new angle. Re-conceive it. Re-imagine it. One of the hardest aspects of innovative thinking is getting beyond the hurdle of thinking that because people do something a certain way they cannot do the same thing a *different* way. The key to innovation is defining exactly what it is that is innovative about your idea and what that value or benefit is.

"What's in it for me?" your customer will ask. Exactly, what *is* in it for them? Innovation is a zero-to-sixty leap to perceived value.

It takes practice, but you, as a leader, will be better for it. Everyone looks to the leader to point the way. Bring a new idea into work today.

Remember me saying we had the idea to take away paper checks from ING Direct's checking product, Electric Orange? Some colleagues thought we were nuts. How would we do this? Why not, I thought, print the check and mail it for the customer? The idea was, if we could get a customer to only use the computer to fill in data then we could slowly move customers off of the idea that they need traditional checkbooks. The trick was to start and try it. ING Direct did.

Yes, it added to our overhead. But that was a short-term cost we believed would be compensated for in cost savings long-term.

CEO Message 191
WHY NOT?

It seems healthy to question what we work on every day.

One of the great privileges of working at ING Direct was the freedom to look at what we did with a fresh set of eyes. The principles of the Orange Code created the context for all of us to commit to a vision: Rock then Roll. But, just as important, it allowed us to be ourselves and created the incentives to always think about what we were doing with the goal of improving both our performance and ourselves.

I asked managers, "What can you do?" Most important: allow the associates you work with the freedom to challenge what is done. Allow yourself to be open to ideas. The positive energy that gets created is to everyone's benefit.

Innovation starts with open-ended inquiry—endless questioning and a quenchless curiosity—and ends with a moment of powerful clarity. Looking at something old and familiar and then re-conceiving it requires focus and creativity. As I said, it takes a lot of practice. What is important is that you put your mind to it.

CEO Message 120
GO INTUITIVE

It seems to me that our society is becoming less and less intuitive. Doubt has crept into the most routine activities. Nothing is simple anymore. Everything is charged with complexity. Experts pop up from everywhere to warn us how dangerous life is or advise us on how to perform even the simplest procedures. We can't trust anything anyone says and yet we seek out advice from strangers on TV, the radio, or the Internet. Young parents waste money on the newest parenting guides, consultants are hired to second-guess every decision we make, we wonder how reliable or trustworthy our mechanic is, we don't trust what we buy, or the person or place we bought it from, we worry where our food comes from, and how come gas costs so much. When our phones die or our computer freezes, we sit there like helpless babies.

Weren't all these tools created to make our lives easier? The truth is that we are the tools of our tools. Who's in charge here?

It's *Planet of the Apes* times, man!

Put Consumers Back in Control

These are exactly the trends ING Direct was created to address. Put control of consumers' financial, long-term well-being back in their hands—back in their control. Our phrase "Leading Americans Back to Savings" was created at ING Direct to encourage consumers to adopt a more conservative, fundamental, and long-term approach to financial behavior. I deeply believed that most consumers—if they were asked—would tell you they were happy and comfortable with their financial goals but who were being told—often by traditional banks—that they should not be comfortable or happy with those plans and needed to buy more advice. Saving more and spending less, however, does not require a lot of advice or services. Most banks would tell you that your needs are special and you need a lot of help. "We will be there for you!" Really? But for how much extra?

The ING Direct innovation was creating a simple tool that actually helped consumers do what they wanted to do and without the inflated fees.

I don't want a hammer that doubles as a microwave, okay? Just build me a hammer I am happy with that does the job it was intended to do.

Don't challenge your customer. Don't create products or processes that collide with your customer. Make your business intuitive.

CEO Message 218
AHEAD OF THE HERD

The best place to be is ahead of the herd. It's tough; you have to figure out where to go and you have to run fast. It's still better than behind the herd. It's dusty and the scenery never changes there. That's retail bank innovation in a nutshell.

CEO Message 99
REENGINEERING: DOES IT WORK?

As we have seen, reengineering is taking a process, breaking it down into its component pieces, and finding a way to make it more efficient, faster, cheaper, less prone to error, and any number of criteria that you want to attach to it. However, what's most important about reengineering is setting the scope: are you going to reengineer a process from the front to the back; are you going to redesign the overall process and change the business fundamentals of that task; are you going to continue to make individual improvements in the various steps involved in that product to service?

The important thing about reengineering is breaking down and documenting the current steps of the process and understanding how that process will achieve your goal. Or flip it around: find out why the current sequence of processes is not achieving your goal. It is then the task to think in a creative and disciplined way about new, and ideally more efficient, methods for what can be done to meet those same objectives.

Easier Said than Done

Successful reengineering is just like making things simple: it's easy to say but hard to do. Being successful at it means measuring the results and clearly communicating them to the task at hand. Never underestimate the power of reengineering and never underestimate the amount of work involved. Is it time for you to tackle reengineering a product? At ING Direct we took the account opening process and started by looking at the application form. How easy is it to read? How much space is there to fill in data? How logical is the order of the information asked? Standard process review so far. Then we asked, "Why do we need to have date of birth?" The answer was: everyone asks this information. But why? Do we use it somehow? No. So why collect it and store it? Can't we automate the way we collect data-scan? Most important we are making customers fill out more data than what is needed. We left information about birthdates off the account opening form.

The fact is, to break a product or a process down and rebuild it is an excellent way for you to discover new ideas and uncover fresh approaches to old processes. Disassemble and then reassembling will give you ideas on how to make your product simpler or improve its performance.

Interestingly, it's usually people outside the business that bring new ideas, which should not be a surprise because as much as we are the creators of the products we make, we are also their consequences. Often what is most in need of reengineering is our own perspective. It isn't that people outside your business are smarter; it's that they don't know they are supposed to do something in a specific way.

There is no reason why the innovative thinking done in the outside world cannot be done inside a business. You can get ideas from anywhere, but the most direct way is to tackle it yourself. Take charge. Rock then Roll!

CEO Message 63
DON'T BE AFRAID TO GET YOUR HANDS DIRTY

There is a show on TV now about bosses who go undercover and work with their employees. Generally they end up doing a lousy job. The conceit of the show, of course, is that most bosses are ivory tower dilettantes who are completely out of touch with their employees.

Well, that is mostly true—most bosses are out of touch. And I will go a step further—most CEOs wouldn't know one of her own customers if she camped on his front step for a week.

Let's face it, if you never leave your penthouse on the fifty-third floor you will never have any idea what is happening on the ground. If you don't know your business inside and out, if you don't know what each and every one of your employees does and what their contribution means to the overall goals of the company, how can you expect to innovate?

To be innovative you need to get a tour of the shop floor. You need to research your customers, understand their challenges and then figure out how you can makes things more simple, standard, and easy to use. ING Direct believes a key to innovation is asking yourself the following question again and again: how could we provide more value to our customer?

I laugh when I hear or read about struggling companies calling in outrageously expensive consultants to lecture the executives on what has gone wrong and what needs to be done to improve business. If you are an executive of a failing company shouldn't you already know why you are failing? Why do you need to bring in outsiders to tell you what is going wrong inside your own company? Nine times out of ten a company fails because they never knew who their customers were in the first place, or, they knew at the beginning but then lost touch.

Try it some time: get up from your desk and walk around. Or how about this: talk to your customers. What if one day you were at home and your phone rang and it was the president of your bank?

"There's no problem. You're a good customer and I was just wondering if there was anything we could do to improve our service?"

Wow! Now think about it: a five-minute conversation. Cheap and ridiculously low-tech. But I bet you become a customer for life. Why? That bank president did something that bank presidents *never do*. Your business's culture *is what your customers think of you*. Make it personal. Every day.

You say you want a revolution?

CEO Message 49
WHERE YOU *SHOULD* BE BUILDING A BUSINESS

The best chance of you getting run over by the competition is to stay in the middle of the road. So if you are looking for an opportunity, try to find out what your real competitive advantage is.

CEOs speak too much about scale, size, distribution, and market share. We are like the Wizard of Oz hiding behind our quantitative curtains. Look, that can postpone the truth only so long. Every business has its Toto tugging on the curtain hem. The *real* truth is that we need to find out what our advantage is because that's the edge we should be honing;

Thinking
Small is
Not Small
Thinking:
Innovation
to Scale

unfortunately, that edge is never found in the middle of the road.

Competition is always on the move. It's always moving in one direction, too, and that is right up your backside. The more predictable your products and services are, the more your product development can be predicted. And that means the easier it is for competitors to find a way to overtake you. The irony, of course, is that for the marketplace to know you well you must be completely transparent and that exposes you to your competition. That can put you in the middle of the road and very vulnerable. What to do?

Zig then zag.

At the back of the pack, middle of the pack, or even if you find yourself sitting pretty on that market leader perch, come up with new ideas that are unexpected and that will make you a constant challenge. If the competition has the ammunition they need to kill you, they will.

CEO Message 7
IDEAS AND TIMING

Had a good idea recently and was told to forget about it and just get on with things? Or maybe you have been the manager who shot down an idea from an associate. Maybe you had good reasons.

One of the least admired skills, I have found, among managers and executives is authentic receptivity. And by that I don't mean simply being polite and flashing the teeth as you escort the associate out your office door. I mean being open and receptive to new ideas. Remember, a secret of culture-driven leadership is that leaders come from anywhere. Same is true for ideas. The better leader you are the more open you will be to new ideas and new leadership. Look, you don't find cut diamonds lying around in the dirt. Ideas are like diamonds that are harvested from deep underground and require an incredible amount of patient work to acquire their brilliance.

Acknowledging and respecting one another's ideas and opinions are, at the end of the day, what gives us break-throughs.

Sure, timing is an important factor in the process. Often an idea needs to mature a bit. It might need to have the rough edges planed and polished. But you are kidding yourself if you think your business can survive on breathing the same air all the time. You need fresh air. Fresh ideas.

Does this sound familiar: "What's your policy on this?" Or, "We have a procedure for that." Okay. Again, no business can survive without some rules. We all get that. But rules should be created to encourage and shape innovation, not destroy it.

Ideas Come from People, Not Titles

Innovative breakthroughs are the key to finding fresh or alternative ways of doing things cheaper, simpler and more efficiently. The more complex and layered, or hidebound a procedure is, the more difficult it is for innovation to occur. Innovation cannot move up a crowded ladder. The more flexible and responsive the team—the culture—the more receptive it will be to embracing and implementing innovation. New ideas and fresh ways of doing things can come from anyone at any time. Real innovation occurs and takes shape within a horizontal environment. It has no pedigree and no provenance. It's not important who came up with the idea or implemented it. What matters is that every member of the team—every employee in the business—knows he or she has the permission and the respect to bounce ideas around and find a winning breakthrough, together, for the team.

- Reengineering
- Innovating
- Communicating
- Being receptive

Making things better and striving to make the best product or service is a job for everyone at every level. It needs to be part of the company's culture if it is to be effective. How do you know if it's working?

Watch ... listen ... ask. Do some observing and testing throughout the company; try to determine what the focus of the work is. Ask yourself, *is* there a focus? You may be surprised by what you see.

CEO Message 230
IMITATION AS FLATTERY? OR JUST STEALING IDEAS?

I have to laugh every time I hear some rival bank crowing about a new product or service that we at ING Direct pioneered.

Too many businesses copy each other's programs. It's a herd mentality that kicks in. No one wants to be left behind. Conventional wisdom dictates that it's easier to copy and follow, especially since most business are always trying to catch up. In this *me too* mentality you commit tons of money and resources to replicating and duplicating shiny new offers, products, or services and even more time, energy, and money servicing those new programs and trying to keep the customers you have attracted, but all the while waiting with dread for the inevitable moment when your competitor launches yet another new offer and the whole crazy cycle starts over.

How come no one in this situation thinks about *leap-frogging* the competition?

The goal should be to make the initial acquisition and subsequent retention of customers cheaper—not more expensive!

In an ideal world the customer would wise up to the simple fact that all these new offers and reward programs are promotional gimmicks and come-ons to entice and manipulate him. No free lunches, right? We all pay for it in the end.

But we don't live in an ideal world. You have that choice: join the pack, hunt in groups, settle for whatever you can get and keep paying more and more for it.

Or, learn how to hunt alone.

CEO Message 143
SO WHERE'S THE COFFEE?

In our ING Direct cafés, we made a conscious decision to standardize the pricing of our beverages. Pricing should be simple; no endless add on for different flavors, cups, sizes. Just one simple great price. Our brand promoted the message that we are for everyone.

However, not everyone would be for us. And that was okay. In fact, it was perfect.

The principle was straightforward: at ING Direct we have a great product at an affordable price. We offer great customer service. We treat everyone the same. A great bank and a great cup of coffee: the values behind both are the same. If you like one, you'll like the other. If you want something different, something more fancy or exotic, well, there probably will be a Citibank or Bank of America down the block. Or a Starbucks.

Have an enemy! Always have a strategy at hand to keep your enemy on the defensive. It comes down to this: the more they are looking over their shoulder the better. Better to be the one gaining then the one gained. Us and Them, man!

Now, the obvious collateral benefit is that by making yourself the good guy you make your customer a good guy, too. Maybe they don't even know it. But they know they are part of something new and different and that gets back to the culture-driven business principle of your business—vision validating a social good.

It is the same reason why we operated with no personal offices and no titles on our business cards, and why we tried to keep the same informal, relaxed way of working with each other as we do with our customers. The principle was based on integrity and honesty. The social good. *Validate the vision by making it good for society.* We didn't create integrity. We didn't invent honesty. But by making values an authentic centerpiece of our business culture we tapped into its universal power.

CEO Message 88
OUT IN FRONT? OR ON YOUR OWN?

It still amazes me how convinced conventional wisdom was—especially amongst my industry colleagues—that the ING Direct model could not succeed.

They talked as if they actually had first-hand experience with alternative models. But all of them were conventional bankers from traditional banks. Where had they earned their stripes as innovators? What had they rocked?

Zilch, as far as I could tell. But that didn't stop them. Our low-cost model would never work, they said. What we were attempting was foolhardy and reckless. But we believed we had the right idea. Look, it was nuts. Who did we think we were? We *had to believe* that the low-cost model was the best approach. Otherwise we were that skunk on the road with the tire tracks across its belly.

Cutting costs was the first step; redesigning the work-flow, marketing programs, and products was the second. Third, being able to fully take advantage of automation had a huge impact on the timeliness and quality of delivery to the ING Direct customer, and also to the type of selling we did. Being a low-cost provider meant we must have and maintain, always and everywhere, a low-cost mindset. In our case, that meant putting a high emphasis on core competency in critical areas like marketing and IT as the surest and most reliable way to finding and maintaining lower unit costs. The savings represented competitive advantage and in turn increased value to the customer.

The Bottom Line

We had to believe when no one else did. Have a clear vision of what you want to get done and sell the vision. We seem to have done okay.

CEO Message 135
DIFFERENTIATE

Remember that TV show Star Trek? Okay, I used to wonder why the crew wore those outfits. I guess in the late sixties that is what TV producers thought the future would look like?

Isn't it interesting that so many visions of the future come to feel dated? Could it be because we keep conceiving of the future in conventional terms? Why do we always think the future will look so conspicuously different?

Whether it is a company, your brand or product, or you as a leader, you must differentiate. But how? How far do you go before you have gone too far? How do you stand out? What are you known for? What do you wish to accomplish? For instance, think of that product of yours that has been around for a while and has done well but might need a refresh. The temptation generally is to think of new as necessitating different. That means breaking links and boldly leaping into the future.

"Warp factor ten!"

Okay, but don't let yourself get carried away by the shiny sparkle of novelty. Sometimes the real source of inspiration and innovation is the past. Who were you when you started? Do you remember the mission and the vision? If you can't, then you need to revisit the past and dust off that original template. Here's a rule of thumb: novelty works when it conforms to the mission. If novelty changes the mission, it's the wrong way to go. Always innovate in the direction of clarifying the original mission.

Going back to basics—remembering the old—is not nostalgia. It's a way of hooking into your business's real power: the mission.

CEO Message 208
WHAT ARE CUSTOMERS LOOKING FOR?

The chicken and the egg question: do we have an answer—i.e., our product—out in the marketplace looking for a question that no one has asked? Or do we wait for the question to be asked and then fit our product or service—our answer—to the question? For instance, does anyone need the Apple iPad? Is it the answer to a legitimate consumer question? Or, is it possible that Apple is structured in such a way that its main commercial product—innovation—has moved faster than the market can absorb? Meaning, the company's problem now is not coming up with new ideas but convincing consumers they need those new ideas.

In other words, are we asking the right questions and from the right perspective? This occurs frequently. In fact, it happens more and more today especially in the high-tech areas where the pace of innovation seems to be way out in front of consumer demand. But, no matter how much the landscape changes, one thing remains constant: products need to be matched to consumers. Managing that simple but formidable equation is key to success.

Keep in Touch

Don't let innovation get in the way of staying in touch with your customer. Innovation is not the product; innovation is the path to the customer.

There are only two scenarios. One, consumers are out there already waiting for your product or service. They won't need convincing but they will need to know you are for real. Or, two, consumers are out there but don't know they need your product and service and you have to convince them.

As an example, our belief was that traditional banking institutions were not meeting the needs of all consumers. ING Direct products were standard commodity products—no exceptions, no changes. We came up with a product that met the needs of consumers. Not *all* consumers. That was key. We had no intention of staging a palace coup to overthrow the old banking industry. We came up with a product that was an authentic alternative for the consumer who wanted exactly that alternative and no more.

If a consumer came to us with a broader need than what we provided, then we passed that customer on to a full-service provider. Not all innovations can address the needs of *all* consumers. For ING Direct the magic formula was high volume, commodity products, and standardized processes. Back to the iPad: was this product targeted to the average Apple consumer? Or was it designed to meet the pre-determined needs of a consumer with limited or specialized needs in mind? Or was it delivered to the market open-ended? The point is, innovation comes in many colors and flavors. As important as the *what* is in the innovation equation, just as important are the questions *who* is it for? and *why*?

You have to decide what kind and what level of innovation works for you. Return to the mission. What is it telling you?

CEO Message 209
"YOU CAN'T FIRE ME! I'M A CUSTOMER!"

Everyone was shocked. Our critics were appalled. No one had ever heard of such a thing. Even our directors had a hard time coming to terms with it: we fire our customers.

And you know what? I am quite proud of that.

Here's why: we created ING Direct to be different. By being different we meant not doing things the as traditional banks. When a customer cannot use one of our accounts in the way it was designed, or if a customer has too much trouble with the web and telephone banking, or insists on having monthly statements mailed out, then we respectfully close the account.

Tough Love is the Best Love

We love our customers. But we love them *all the same*. We don't play favorites. That is not fair, and it destroys our bottom line.

For any account the reasons could be different. We do not explain the reasons to anyone or any customer. Why? There are complicated legal, regulatory, and liability reasons not to do so. The banking industry is not like baking biscuits. It is a hugely regulated industry and there were rules that we were compelled to follow. Fine. Frankly, we could deal with that. The real reason comes down to our mission. *Do it differently. Keep it simple. Be fair.* Those values work for us. To our customers we ask, "Do those same values work for you?" If so, welcome to the ING Direct family. If not, well, that is a shame but we know you will find what you are looking for elsewhere.

Another reason has to do with human psychology. We human beings are social animals. We're joiners; we like to feel like we belong. Basically, it's not easy learning that something is not right for you in some way. A business needs customers so a customer has every right to expect to be wanted. So I am telling this customer he or she isn't right for us? To take their business elsewhere?

Sounds nuts, right? Kuhlmann has lost it again! You are insulting your customer.

It isn't nuts, and, no, I am not insulting my customer. It is all about protecting the integrity of the brand and how the business gets done. Again, an innovation ceases to be innovative if immediately the brand begins to accommodate alterations that return it to the mainstream. If you start to make allowances or exceptions you dilute that integrity and your brand loses power. No one argues with an ATM machine. It just works one way. As leaders and managers you need to be tuned into this. Our whole approach was, we need to be sensitive about this *but* strong in our resolve. We needed to be seen as even-handed, consistent and, above all, fair.

Was closing customer accounts a cheap stunt to attract attention? Absolutely not. We never closed an account impulsively without reason or without weighing the decision carefully.

From the beginning we decided we had a new idea. But we also knew we would not be the solution for everyone. So we made it a policy never to pretend we would be. An important innovation in our evolution was making sure our customer fit our model. That is so easy to ignore.

The Bottom Line

Again and again I make the point: it isn't enough for your business to say who you are. You have to be seen *being who you are*. Even if that means risking offending a few customers by being seen as who you aren't.

CEO Message 239
PERCEPTION IS EVERYTHING

Often in newspaper or magazine profiles I am described as a palm-reading, Harley-riding, highly unconventional CEO of a rebel bank. I was even christened by my own banking colleagues as the Bad Boy of the industry. Why? ING Direct disdains fees and heavily promotes savings. From the beginning my philosophy was to take a retail approach to banking. Our focus was on saving customers money so in turn they could save more of their own money. Remember the slogan: Leading Americans back to savings.

Okay, here is what is so funny about that: can you think of anything less radical than promoting the idea of people saving money?

Reckless? Risky?

Really?

Think about the difference next time you get yet another credit card application in the mail. Ask yourself, whose side is your bank on?

A Brief Biographical Digression

As I've said, my grandmother used to reuse tea bags. She understood the value of things and disdained waste. She—like a lot of her generation—shunned charity and prided herself on hard work. What they could not afford they did without.

The point is that innovation can be confused with novelty. Innovation in not necessarily a different way of doing things; it can be a better way of doing things. Think of it as a way of retrofitting the proven ways and methods of the past to meet the needs of the present. Innovation can be a way of reminding yourself of why something worked well in the past and questioning where it went wrong and why. What you might find is this: it wasn't wrong. We just lost touch.

CEO Message 128
COMMUNICATING YOUR INNOVATION TO THE CUSTOMER

For ING Direct, our biggest advantage was standing out in the financial service market from all other players. Our message was in our name: Direct. Our innovation was that by going directly to consumers we cut out the middleman. That saved us money, but most importantly it saved the customer money.

Adopting a retail strategy—being simple, focused, and direct—added up to good value. This is a retail trend that consumers know and we emphasized it in everything we did. We still do.

A Word Is Just a Word ... Until It Isn't

It amazed me, however, how many people saw that ING Direct was *direct*, and, yet, they still expected to use our products *in all the traditional ways*. Our innovation was in our name—we are direct—but clearly for some customers the meaning of the innovation was not as immediate. They saw *direct* but heard *traditional bank* and brought to our bank all the conventions and biases associated with the industry norms and traditions. So the lesson here is that you need to make the *what* of your innovation immediately understandable to your customer.

Our job was to steer them towards our business as a real retail store so that they would know how we worked. In a business such as retail banking, it takes longer to reengineer the customer.

Depending on where you are in the evolution of your business, what you do may be less important than what you don't do.

CEO Message 224
STOP THE ACRONYMS!

The ING Direct brand was targeted for Main Street America.

To me, Main Street was busy people with busy lives and not a whole lot of spare time to devote to mind-numbing details. I decided none of our customers needed to learn acronyms, so we stopped using them. No PIN, APY, CIF, etc. It's the name in full. Your Personal Identification Number. We decided to simplify our website and our sales and marketing material to accommodate these changes. Our war chant was, "Nuke the acronyms!"

Was it a game changer? No. But customer-directed inno-

vations or improvements don't always have to be game chang-
ers. The race to acquire market share is never over.

Think about what is convenient for the customer, not
what is convenient for you. If there is something your business is doing, no matter how trivial or inconsequential it may
appear, that the customer does not understand or would
rather not do, don't do it!

Don't create barriers.

CEO Message 130
GETTING BACK TO BASICS

I talk about customer service. I talk about customer service a
lot. But what does it mean?

For me and everyone at ING Direct, it meant direct,
short, simple, friendly, honest, one-on-one, and, most of all,
consistent—the same message. The same message from everyone, every day. Think of it as the way you would speak to a
friendly neighbor if you were in a hurry.

Tune in to the Right Tone

Setting the tone that fits the brand image is a constant
struggle for any business. It's much like tuning a musical
instrument. Constant use stresses the strings—even though
the music is the same and you are playing the same notes, it
sounds a bit off. So periodically it needs to be retuned.

No different in business. Periodically your message needs
to be tightened up a bit to get it back into tune.

At one point we had developed a series of commercials
and advertisements titled the "Road to Happiness." The imagery looked good and the concept was sound but somehow the
tone, the words, were not on the mark—it was not what we

thought a customer would expect from ING Direct. We needed to tune the words. The tune sounded remote. We thought our brand voice should be like talking to a neighbor across the backyard fence—friendly and straightforward. We adjusted the script to sound more conversational and friendlier.

It was a matter of tuning into the right tone or voice.

But don't think fine-tuning the company message only applies to your ad campaigns or to lower-echelon employees. It starts with you and runs up and down the company and across the board. Remember the idea that culture dilutes from the center out? Everyone needs to be playing the same tune—all the time.

When it comes to customer service, it's a symphony performance and not a solo act.

CEO Message 2
HOW TO REENGINEER THE CUSTOMER

No matter the business, not every customer will fit the way the business needs or wants to operate. For most businesses, the majority of customers have a sense of the frame. They generally know what a business does, what it offers, what they expect, and how to get it.

But there are always exceptions. Like the customer who wants, and even expects, the exceptions. It's that guy in the restaurant booth next to you who wants to change every item on the menu in some way. Probably he read somewhere that chefs would do this if asked.

Well, it's your business and your kitchen. So no. It drives everyone crazy and drives costs through the roof. Make one exception and you are on a slippery slope. Just say no to exceptions and reengineer the customer.

Okay, an admittedly silly example: a customer demands to stand up in an airplane on take off. He is accommodated and then next time maybe two would want to do it. Before you know it we will have subway handrails on the roof of airplanes.

Your business shouldn't be about inventing procedures for not accommodating your customer or being obstructionist. It is about matching your customer's needs to the services you provide. When what you provide makes the customer happy, Hallelujah! When a customer wants something you do not provide? You have to say no politely. In this case, it's about reengineering expectations. That's how you stay true to your mission.

---<o>---

The Art of Business; the Business of Art

In an earlier section I talked about the appeal of thinking more like an artist than an accountant. But I think it's so important that I hope you will indulge me if we revisit it for a few more turns.

The consequences could be profound.

It's a familiar syndrome: it begins with an idea and leads to a question. I have a great idea for this or that. That leads to questions like, is there a market? How do I do that? How can I accomplish this?

Good questions. All knowledge begins in ignorance. If you're lucky and you work hard, you and your business will be a success. For a while.

The problem, of course, is when you stop asking the questions. Curiosity morphs into complacency. You stop thinking about the basics—the how's and the why's. A common—much too common—problem in business is the belief that we know more than we actually do. We treat every problem, opportunity, or process the same way every time. It's worked before so it will work again. It's like stimulus and response. Pavlov's dog, right?

Well, the hell with that. I'm not happy being a dog pushing a button for a biscuit. Are you?

That's why I have brought up the analogy of art in business time and again. It's simple: artists never assume they are finished asking the questions. Face it: there is no innovation without first the question. The blank canvas is always an excuse to ask the same questions again. Why? How? Why not? Or how come?

Art frees the human spirit as it opens the door to the possible.

Shaping our dreams energizes our work, but most of all it reminds us of our place in the universe. The time we spend in life's journey is enriched by the art we create, share, and enjoy. We have a responsibility to fulfill our destiny, and appreciating the beauty of art is a milestone on the road.

Don't let some fancy degree or a corner office fool you into thinking you have insights you don't actually have. Listen to the music in your head! What do you hear? Can you even hear it? Or is just musical wallpaper?

Follow your instincts and intuition. Find a new soundtrack. Rock then roll!

CEO Message 159
A FRESH APPROACH

As we have seen, many seek business insights in the world of sports or organizations like the military. We talk in business about *hitting a home run* or *being in a battle* for total market supremacy. It's a way to frame and shape the effort through metaphor. Metaphor is a kind of narrative or storytelling. But like any overworked metaphor or cliché, the message—the lesson—can become stale through overuse.

A fresh approach, I think, is opening yourself up to the metaphor of art.

Business is a unique blend of humanity and science skills. Creativity is what moves our thinking along and finding new thoughts and approaches is the path.

There is a school of thought that says that there is no such thing as a new idea. What we do is basically select from a big pot of ideas, maybe mix them around a bit, and then dump them all back in. It's a process of endless recycling with only very subtle changes along the way.

Reinhold Niebuhr said that "history repeats itself, but never in exactly the same way."

New and old thoughts can—and do—work together. What is important is that we free ourselves to imagine and see new ways of rearranging and configuring old ways of see-ing and doing things that will improve the managing of our business and, hopefully, improve society.

CEO Messages 37
THE VALUE OF THE BLANK CANVAS
Artists are explorers.

They tend to see a blank canvas as an opportunity.

In business, I think we need to see more blank canvases. The tendency is to look up and down one minute and left and right the other. What is the competition doing? How they do things becomes the model for how you should be doing things. We all agree ahead of time what we are looking for and then pat ourselves on the back for being so smart to find it.

It's called benchmark management and I am not—as they say—a big fan.

For instance, who goes to a flower show to figure out how to make a better cell phone? No one. But maybe we should. Conventional change is incremental; innovation tends to be a leap into the unknown. Change is what happens when we look for solutions only from within. Innovation is what happens when we look outside our zone of comfort and familiarity.

Artists aren't afraid. Creative people who know how to think can create tremendous ideas by coming from a totally different industry and seeing things that we have been looking at forever. They see the forest and can help us see it, even when, at first, we see only the trees.

———◇———

Rock then Roll Your Business: The takeaways

- Chaos is both essential and inevitable.
- Create the right culture and chaos is your ally.
- There are no crystal balls. You need to be preemptive and proactive.
- Innovation is not a thing one does; innovation is how one thinks.
- How can I make my business more intuitive for my customer?

- Break everything down to the basics. Even when it's working.
- An anarchist breaks all the rules. The goal is to use the rules you need and ignore the rest.
- What you already know could be the biggest stumbling block to figuring out what you *should* do next.
- Never let innovation get between you and your customer.
- Being first is better; but being better is best.

CHAPTER 4

ROCK THEN... WHAT?

How to Keep the Rock Rolling

Hiring? Or Casting?
The Culture-Driven Alternative to Team Building

Putting a team together is the single most important job of a leader. If you think of it as casting for a play or putting together an orchestra then you can be more creative in building the best team possible. Most of us directly or indirectly hire in our own image, drawn to characteristics that we are most comfortable with. Being able to assemble a team based on skills and characteristics that work together *but* may not be easy to see or understand is a difficult task. But it's worth the effort and it's a leadership skill that will set you apart.

A key part of shaping the culture of a business is hiring the right people. It may sound counterintuitive, but I believe in hiring people who have made honest mistakes, because they most likely will have learned from them. We are all the products of our experiences, good and bad. Successful people wish to remain successful, while others will do anything to become successful. The way we weather the storms shows true character.

It is true for any industry, but in my case I looked outside the banking establishment for people with broad and unusual backgrounds. People who are too narrowly educated will make the right decisions some of the time, but they won't have the wide scope of knowledge to make the right decisions most of the time.

The ING Direct Experiment

At the beginning of ING Direct we had a simple but audacious idea: change the face of banking. Okay, great start. Great idea. But how? We figured that out. Go direct. Cut out the perks. Keep it clean and simple.

Cool. Now all we have to do is start letting the profits roll in.

Not quite. You have neglected probably the most crucial factor in any business: your team.

Often, the easy decisions come first and the difficult decisions come last. That's a bit counter intuitive: most people might think the hard part is coming up with the idea. Or the business model, or strategy.

In fact, the hard part is not necessarily the *how* or the *what*. It's the who—as in: who are you going to team up with to make this happen? Who do you want to be with you on this journey?

Find the right people. It's crucial.

Crucial Innovation

My thinking came down to this: we were going to change the banking industry, right? Why hire bankers? Yes, I know, there are a lot of good people who work in banks—really smart people. But for the most part they were not people who had any investment in changing the industry. They *were* the industry.

I wanted innovators, not replicators and imitators. Where did we go for our team? Not to other banks. We went to:

- Retail people that had sales experience
- People that had different kinds of marketing experience
- People that came from different walks of life; people who could look at the banking challenges and the challenges of money with clear, fresh eyes—new insights and perspectives

Case Histories

I'm sitting at a car dealership waiting for my car to be serviced and I strike up a conversation with a friendly guy doing the same thing to kill time. He had just graduated from law school and was looking for a job. Not sure what, but looking. I liked his manner and friendliness. I tested him on an idea.

"Look, I'm working on a new project. I'm building a new bank from scratch. Would you be interested in giving it a look?"

Answer: "Sure I would." No hesitation. "When do I start?"

"How about tomorrow?"

"By the way, what does it pay?"

"Oh, about a hundred and fifty thousand."

"You would pay me that much to be head of legal?"

"No. Thirty thousand now until you learn the job."

"Okay. That's great!"

He displayed a willingness to step up, take a chance, and earn his way. These were clear signs that he was not the standard guy looking for a job. He wanted more and this was his chance. A rough diamond but a diamond with potential. He excelled and today he can run any business he chooses. His best strength? He knows how to build the right team.

I met another amazing guy at—of all places—a laser-tag party. His father was a commercial painter. He told me that the school district stopped accepting hand-written invoices for work. He wanted to help his father out, so he hunted down some software for creating invoices. Pretty soon other people were asking about it. He started his own business. Real successful.

I was looking for someone to head up the ING Direct IT department. I asked him if he wanted to take a shot with me and ING Direct. Today he is a CIO with a graduate degree.

By the way, he told me he never finished high school.

Now here's the truth of it: how many of you would even interview a kid who never finished high school?

Some of you may be saying I was taking a huge risk. You know what? I was. But so were they! That's the whole point: for the mission to be real there has to be a real risk of failure.

One time we were looking for someone to lead a hugely important bidding process for currency exchanges in airports across the United States. I asked an associate what we would need.

"Give me two days," she said. Two days later she was back. "Here's what you need."

"Fine. Go do it." She ended up nailing it and has never looked back. She is one of my most valuable and trusted colleagues. Where did I meet her? She was a cashier at Deak International when I worked there.

What do these three have in common? None would have piqued the interest of the traditional business. What most businesses want are people working for them who look and think just like themselves.

You don't lead a business. You lead people.

I find that people who fall outside the traditional comfort zone ask the most direct questions, too. They are the most driven. If you have a lot to lose you also have a lot to prove. They aren't locked into a conventional mindset or indoctrinated into the rules about how the industry is supposed to operate. You want insights into how to do things differently? Why ask the person who has been doing it one, and only one, way for the past ten or fifteen years?

It is a rigid and locked-up mindset that has become routine. It can't handle change or innovation. It's like riding a bike on the autobahn, okay? Cars are just flying by you. What are you doing out there? If you want to win the race you have to surround yourself with people who aren't afraid and who know how to put their foot down hard on the accelerator. Innovation, change—whatever—it's all the same thing.

After all, there are laws against incest for very practical reasons. Breeding from within is the surest way to destroy your DNA. We don't do it in society and we probably should not do it in business. But we do. When it comes to hiring, I have consistently found that managers tend to gravitate towards the safe and familiar criteria: the credential, the excel-

> "The process of hiring employees is like casting for a play." —AK

lent school, the resume, the references. Inevitably, we hire from within our own industry. We keep plucking goldfish out of the same bowl.

Stop hiring based on criteria that are safe and familiar. Hire people who will get the job done.

If everyone is fighting for talent with money, then bring in talent with love. Use a different approach. That's the way to hire people.

Fish Tanks
We all swim in the same ocean, folks. But not in the same tank, okay?

For the same reasons I hire, I've never sent any ING Direct associates to industry conventions. Why would I send a promising retail maverick in my business to an industry trade show? So he or she can be distracted by industry convention?

Frankly, I'd much rather send someone to a good jazz club or an art museum. That way at least I know they will be hearing something or seeing something that is new and fresh and requires some lateral and sideways thinking. Not to mention having an experience from which they might return with a brilliant new idea!

Getting It Right

Once you've made the right hire, it's essential to try to understand the personality of the person working for you. "Understanding personality has become essential for leaders of the complex, knowledge-based companies operating in the global marketplace," writes Michael Maccoby, a leadership consultant and an anthropologist.

Hiring? Or Casting? The Culture-Driven Alternative to Team Building

I agree. Great advice.

This is where a leader's true nature comes into play. If I am prepared to be completely open and honest with you, I am inviting you to be the same. Go beyond the slogans. It's the fireside chat versus the office chat. We team up for the right reason. We believe in the vision and will behave as outlined by the code that defines the company's culture. That's the best chance I have as a leader to empower the culture of the organization, allowing us to win by being on the journey. If we're both honest and open, then we're rocking then rolling on time.

———◄○►———

CEO Message 32
THE CAST

Think about language.

A director assembles a cast. A restaurant manager hires a waiter.

What's the difference?

Well, a cast can help that director realize his dream for the play. A waiter can deliver a food experience. Who do you want the people working for you to be?

You need to put a cast together to create that dream. That's the vision and, in the case of ING Direct, it happens to be leading Americans back to saving. Pretty noble. The mission then is the fulfillment of that vision. Remember the three-part play from earlier?

1. Captivate and stay focused on the outcome.
2. Create strong content.
3. Come to a full and logical conclusion.

Your mission is the play. Finding the right people to help you achieve your company's mission and vision is critical. So who do you look for?

It's all about data and how much you can learn about an individual in a short period of time. Making a decision to hire someone is not about ticking off boxes on questionnaires or making an assumption that if they have the training and the experience then all is okay.

You need to find out what makes people tick. Not to use this knowledge in a negative way but in a positive one. How do you do this? Ask questions that give you clues to failures, successes, and how someone dealt with the personal challenge of life.

What about resumes and references? Forget about them! Resumes and references are too high level. Anyway, who provides a bad reference? So what does one friendly colleague chatting up another friendly colleague reveal? Nothing.

Make It Personal ... Not Personnel

What you need is personal story telling. Getting to know someone the way you get to know a friend. Do you ask a potential friend for a resume? I hope not! You click with someone else based on subjective, but very important, criteria.

Like, what kind of movies do you see? What is your favorite book? These are tests. Picking up on body language and physical appearance—what you wear, how you carry yourself, or what kinds of words you use—can help reveal important insights about who you are.

And if I don't know who you are, how can I be sure that I can work with you?

The cliché in the banking industry is that everyone wears a suit because that inspires confidence and trust in the customer. Really? I wear cowboy boots. Sometimes I wear a tie and sometimes I don't. It's not a sham. That is who I am. Now, who do you think I will feel more comfortable with, the customer who is not happy with who I am or the customer who is? I think this works in reverse too, which is why so many of our customers tell us they really like being with us. I am convinced it is because who they see is who we are and that is what creates trust.

I have a technique I like. Palm reading. Yes, *palm reading*. People who don't know me think I'm nuts. It's something I actually learned from my grandmother. The point is that it doesn't matter if you believe in it. Sitting down with someone you have just met and asking them to give you their hand for a palm reading is a huge zag in the road. I see it as a perfect opportunity to collect important personality data about that person that no resume or reference would ever reveal. How naturally confident is this person? How open? Does he or she offer their hand enthusiastically, possibly meaning they are open to new ideas, or do they withdraw suspiciously, suggesting someone who shuns the unexpected and likes things to stay the way they are? You can find a technique that works for you.

Why Look for What You Need Where You Know You Won't Find It?
If you are launching an innovative new company that puts a premium on innovative thinking and creative problem solving, who do you want along for that ride? Who will you trust more to do the job right? And not just once, but doing it right over and over?

Look, if all you need for the job is a paper clip, well, any paper clip will do. From my perspective, I don't hire paper clips. I hire people. I look for people who I know share my commitment to vision and mission. To find the unusually productive people you need to use unusual techniques. They won't just fall off the tree like ripe pears.

Learn how to read people. The pay off is that any clues you find will help you make a better decision on whether a person will succeed in the job. As a leader your batting average is fundamental to your performance on choosing the right people for the right jobs.

A resume can, at best, tell you if someone has experience for a job.

What you want to know is, does this person fit into the cast for this company?

CEO Message 97
BEHAVIORS VERSUS SKILLS
I created the chart below to put into visual detail the pitfalls of hiring. How it works is this: most businesses hire for skill and fire for behavior. I hire for behavior and fire for skills.

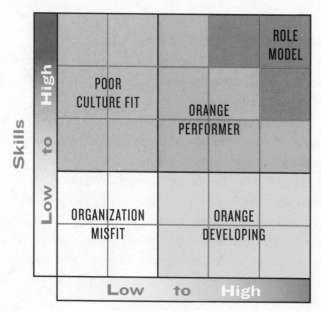

Hiring?
Or Casting?
The Culture-
Driven
Alternative
to Team
Building

As you can see in the illustration, an individual can fall into any one of four categories, plotted here along two axes. The vertical line measures job skills, while the horizontal line measures fidelity to the Code, or behavior.

Someone with topnotch job skills who fully embodies the Orange Code would fall in the top right corner of the graph—these people are the role models for the rest of the organization. They are looked to as leaders. In practice we tend to look at culture first and job skills second. We've found that someone who is a good cultural fit can learn and develop any missing job skills. The reverse is not true. Someone with great job skills who is a poor cultural fit is unlikely to really embrace the Code.

CEO Message 300
UNIQUE APPROACHES TO FINDING A TEAM

A recurring problem I have when it comes to recruitment is finding people mentally equipped with a philosophical view of life and business.

There is no shortage of resumes that cross my desk from seasoned executives or aspiring managers. Some come from outstanding companies or prestigious business schools. The problem is that I need someone who can think in a way that is responsive to today's challenges. Most of these candidates are products of a highly structured environment. Either they have matured in an industry that is comfortable with a business-as-usual model, or they are programmed to approach a problem with a preconceived notion of the solution. Not

"We look for people to fill a specific job skill and then human beings show up"
—AK

because it is the solution but because it is the solution they were taught and that is all they know.

Many managers and executives lack a context that allows them to be reflective, to think, and to be creative.

Business is not an isolated, self-contained environment. You as a business leader and as a human being are a part of the world at large. The problems out there are the same as the problems in here. So why in business do we so seldom look to the world "out there" for answers? It's an outward versus and inward focus.

We have used the comparison many times to building your team as casting for a play. You are the director. An extremely important component of your job as a culture-driven leader is this: *you need to allow people on your team more freedom than you are comfortable with.*

An extremely important dimension of that freedom is delegating. It will be covered elsewhere in more detail (see CEO Message 147), but just to hammer the nail home: delegating is an opportunity for you to create passion and authenticity on your team. Each team member needs to know she is free to develop her skills as she sees fit.

On more than one occasion I have been in my own performance review where this comment was made: I was *too unpredictable.* They were happy with my performance across the board. Except for that: I was *too unpredictable.* Apparently not one of them made the causal link between my so-called unpredictability and the excellent results I had produced. We all want excellent performances but it is so interesting how often we will not allow for those performances because they aren't how we would do it.

More freedom than you are comfortable with. It is a question of both allowing for and building trust.

The Return of the Renaissance CEO

How many leaders in your business do you know who study philosophy, literature, poetry, and the classics? Why not? Is there nothing to be learned from studying what the greatest minds in the history of the world have thought about the human condition?

Oh, come on, you might be thinking. What could the human condition have to do with running a successful business?

Everything. What you know is who you are. The more you know the better equipped you will be to tackle the problems that you will face. I see these books being written about leadership and everywhere I speak I am asked about it. What do I recommend? To be honest, if you want to get some invaluable insight into leadership why not read Machiavelli's *The Prince*. Best leadership book ever written. Or *Macbeth* by Shakespeare. Yes, instinct is important. Instinct is what motivates you to act quickly and decisively. But instinct is never more powerful or successful than when launched from a foundation of knowledge. It's the level and breadth of what you study, learn, and bring as a foundation to a commercial enterprise that is important.

CEO Message 53
FIND PEOPLE WHO ARE MOTIVATED

When I recruit people, I think about the mission.

I say, "Do you want to join me on this ride? Here is who I am." And then the first thing I ask is, "Tell me all about your setbacks. Have you been fired, divorced, or does you dad not think you add up to much?" I want to know that you've had challenges in your life, and I want to know what you've done about them. Because if you think that riding with me on this mission gives you an opportunity to prove to a lot of people and to yourself that you're actually pretty good at something, you're right! If you think you can make something happen, then this is your moment, and I'm giving it to you. I can give you a break, but you've got to get it done.

A lot of successful people look good; they've got degrees, great families, they've got everything. How can you motivate them? You're not going to motivate them. You're going to keep them in the great style they're accustomed to. So you can't be a rebel if you don't have something to prove. You can't be an outlier unless you want to actually turn the tables upside down. And you've got to mean it. One clear sign of an outlier is this: you're difficult. Outliers are, by definition, always difficult. They're difficult to manage, difficult to get along with. The other thing is, you've got to start looking outside the industry. I'm looking for people with new ideas, a new set of eyes, who look at things differently.

I look at the person I'm interviewing and I need to know, what makes this guy tick? I'm trying to find data points, clues to figure out what you are all about. How do I do that? Rock then Roll! How big of an impact did you make on me? Did I find that I wanted to spend more time with you? Would I invite you to my place to meet my friends and family?

CEO Message 81
FIRING

It is the most unpleasant aspect of the job but often someone doesn't work out. I cannot emphasize enough, however, that firing is just the logical conclusion of the decisions you make on hiring. If you hire for the right reasons chances are you will have fewer occasions to regret.

It's the reason I said I hire for behavior and fire for skill. The whole point is that the decision to separate should be mutual. I know that sounds odd.

Think of it this way: I hire you because you have a great resume. Wonderful skills. But it turns out no one can get along with you. I need to fire you but how do I do that without making the process deeply personal? On the other hand, what if I hire you because I see something in you that makes me think that you have the fire and the drive I am looking for? I figure the skills can be learned. If it turns out that you cannot bring your skill set up to par, however, that is an *objective* and not a *subjective* criteria. It's not about you or me, it's about our ability to get to the goal.

My motto is: if you can't fire someone with a handshake or a hug, you are the one who has failed—not the person being fired. The endings need to be as good as the beginnings.

⊰◦⊱

Communication: Did You Understand What I Said?

Most people may have a more intimate or rewarding relationship with their cell phone than their partner or spouse. That's how it seems, anyway. Welcome to the era of mass communication. In the old days it was the eccentric standing on the corner yelling at the sky. Now it's the guy walking down the street yelling into his Bluetooth.

Has there ever been a time when communication seemed easier or more convenient? So then how come communication seems to be the root of so many problems that afflict business? I think the answer is simple: we have the tools we need to communicate. More than enough. My god, there have been days when I have sat down to deal with a string of emails and realized the guy who wrote them is just down the hall. Hours wasted when I could have just talked to him directly.

We need to work harder on the basic communication skills that make those tools—all our devices—so valuable.

Don't think the tools will communicate for you. Tools can only roll after you've figured out how to rock.

WHO NEEDS TO COMMUNICATE?

We've all heard the comment, "We need to communicate better."

So where do we begin? Do we communicate down, sideways, or up in an organizational structure? You probably already know that you need to communicate in all directions, slightly adjusting the communication when necessary, listening for the message's effectiveness, and checking that what you've actually communicated is understood the way you meant it to be. In many ways, communicating is hard work because it usually means repeating the same things over and over again, but often in minutely differentiated ways.

Effective communicating requires you to be open and direct. It requires you to be willing to share data even when many of us know that filtering, or even withholding, data is a powerful tool in interpersonal relationships. Never forget that overall teamwork and collaboration is predicated on the wide dissemination of information.

An effective leader is as transparent as possible. It is better to be accused of sharing too much information than not sharing enough. If you want to be completely mercenary about it, think of it this way: if you don't tell people what they need to know you will be blamed for whatever failures result. If, however, you tell them what they need to know, the focus is once again aligned with the mission. It becomes an issue, then, of how that person uses the information.

Never let blame filter up to conflict with the mission.

Communication needs a lot of focus and attention. It's hard work and many times we drop the ball. It's a bit like exercise; just keep at it.

CEO Message 283
CAN YOU HEAR ME NOW?

Getting the details right. Jeez, again with that? The paradox of a cliché is that its familiarity tends to dilute its truth. Why is that? When we talk about getting the details right we tend to think about the details as they relate to the product, not as they relate to us as communicators. So ask yourself, am I getting my details right? Here are three rules to live by when it comes to communication:

- Be clear about what is the truth.
- Be willing to communicate the truth.
- Have the courage to say the truth.

For instance, what is the best way to communicate bad news to a boss? Best way is to say it straight and say it quick. Too much beating around the issue just confuses the message. There is never a right time to bring bad news but any delay always complicates things.

CEO Message 22
COMMUNICATING UP

Another cliché is that communicating down and to everyone around you is important, but what's often overlooked is communicating up. There are a couple of very important dimensions to it:

- It gives a clear signal of what's going on and what has a

high priority—whether there's a problem or something that requires attention.

- It clearly indicates what your own view of the position is.

Solid Foundations

The saying goes, "You cannot build a foundation unless you know where to place the pillars." As a leader, your opinions and views are the pillars upon which the whole enterprise is built. The sum total of those views is the consensus opinion that tells everyone in which direction to go, where the priorities are, and where the resources should be applied to achieve them.

The ultimate value of that strategy is that effective communication depends on everyone having opportunities to communicate up! You stand to be counted, the message reads. It builds a powerful culture that will serve you well over the long run. Your views *do* matter and you do influence the success of where the company is headed and those views are well known to the people you report to.

At the same time, too much communication can create a white noise problem that adversely affects communication. It's like always having the radio on in the background. After awhile you forget what you are hearing. A leader needs to encourage communication. Here's the caveat: you must impose limits. Communication must be directed and focused.

CEO Message 74
WITH RESPONSIBILITY COMES COMMUNICATION

One of the greatest virtues in management is clarity.

Whether you are sending a message, making a decision, or having a conversation, you must be conscious of how people are interpreting what you are communicating and be sure your message is clearly understood—that the recipient really understands your point, your opinion, the factual information that underpins the message, and the full context of your decision.

First, use direct clear communication. I stress discipline—the more rigorous the better. Remember the old adage, "Think first before you put your mouth in gear"? Good advice.

Once the salt is in the broth you can't get it out. Think of everything you say no matter how trivial or profound as a message that will be out in the universe for all time.

Next, size up what you consider might be potential objections from colleagues or bosses and prepare a rebuttal. Have the facts and details you need to undermine those objections and strengthen your argument. The most important ingredient is thoroughness and rigor. Never allow your message to be co-opted or misinterpreted. Effective communication is hard work. The rigor and discipline you bring to that hard work is what makes the difference. Clearly, the object of effective communication is to reach the objective in as direct a line as possible. Whether that objective is introducing a fact into a conversation, persuading someone to accept a point or proposal, delivering a decision, or instructing someone to carry out an action based on your request, the words you use must be measured and exactly appropriate to the situation. A rigorous and disciplined approach is the best way to ensure that whatever directive or responsibility is cargoed within the message is clearly understood and carried out as directly as possible.

A lot of times we need to get something done because we have a responsibility to get it done and we haven't the time or luxury for crafting our message with care. We're rushed and we think there is no time for finessing the message. The reality is, the more you work at effective communication the more it will become second nature. It is always more time- and cost-effective to clearly explain a directive than being forced to waste time and money fixing the problem. None of us are mind readers. Creating reliable ways for communicating effectively and working at it religiously is the next best thing.

CEO Message 45
WHOSE RESPONSIBILITY IS IT?

How often have I heard something on this order: a manager I have tasked with an important assignment pulls the excuse out of his hat that "I could not meet my deadline because the information I needed was not given to me in time."

You have probably heard this many times yourself. This situation begs the question: who has ownership of a task and who should be proactive and who should be reactive?

Answer: we all do. We all need to take ownership of every- thing we do. Don't let yourself think of your responsibility as only within some self-defined and limited zone where you operate and outside of which you take no interest. Successful teamwork is a spider's web of linked and overlapping inter- ests and responsibilities.

To get results everyone has to work as a team and be able to depend on one another. This sounds easy, so then why does it happen so often and why do we use it as an ex- cuse for not delivering on time? It might seem self-evident that the discipline needed for managing deadlines is solely an individual responsibility. That might be true if instead of a component production system, where each aspect of a job depended upon and influenced other aspects of the job, we each followed through on a job from beginning to end. But we don't. We each have our domains of expertise and we trust that when we hand something off that person will oversee his or her domain with the same care and attention. The truth is, I have my own deadlines. And she has her deadlines. And so does he. If he misses his, it means that she will have less time to do her job. And so will I.

It is critical that deadlines be thought through comprehensively and critically. They need to be mutually agreed upon so that potential delays can be communicated well in advance. As a manager, make sure everyone on the team knows what the deadlines are. Not just in your domain but throughout. Remember, we are all fully invested in the outcome—every one of us. Not just of our *personal* outcomes. But the outcome that matters most: achieving the goal as efficiently as possible.

We're All in This Together

No pointing fingers. No blame game. At some point we could all find ourselves reluctantly playing the part of the weakest link. What you need in place is a response strategy that quickly bridges that failure and puts the project back on track. Communication is key. You know, we all tend to build walls around us—both literal and metaphorical. What you want to do as a good manager is take the walls down as far as you can. Walls send the message that you don't trust the people who work for you. You want the opposite message to come through: we need to trust each other. We are all in this together. The focus should always be on the mission—not on privatized agendas or defensive *my space* work habits. So, to make sure we all understand what the mission is and how we expect it to be achieved we periodically need to peek over the walls just to make sure we're all on the same page.

Who's to Blame for Missed Deadlines?

Poor or inconsistent communication is often cited as the biggest management weakness when it comes to missed deadlines. Certainly there is no excuse for that, so make sure you know how to communicate. But what might be in order is a moment of reckoning: take a look in the mirror. Do your own work habits and management style set the tone for everyone around you? Look, the *how* of how we measure performance is a much-discussed metric. But from where I sit, achieving excellence in a highly competitive high-performance environment can only be accomplished by meeting deadlines. How those deadlines are routinely met is a good portrait of leadership in action.

It is your responsibility!

The more team players take responsibility, the less friction and more ownership. It's the best thing that could happen.

CEO Message 215
REMOTE IS NOT JUST A PLACE; IT CAN BE A STATE OF MIND

It's a paradox, but as electronic technologies bring us together we are becoming more remote. Cell phones, Blackberries, and laptops have freed us to work from just about anywhere, anytime. We all notice that working together is getting harder. Sharing information is easier but collaborating is much more complex. Here are a few ideas to make working together better in today's environment.

- Communicate more often with all members of your virtual team.
- Have a clear understanding of the goals and tasks you are working on.
- Set out clear ground rules for working, such as timelines and deliverables.
- Spend some time to meet and get to know your team members face-to-face. Openly talk about how to work together; it's the only way.

Good management has always stressed the importance of planning. Few do it and many do it half way. Planning how you and your team will work together is time well spent. Why roll that rock uphill, man! If your plan rocks, then you can roll a lot more easily.

CEO Message 271
"PLEASE" AND "THANK YOU, MADAM!"

Being polite is never out of style and even more appropriate in tough times and tough circumstances. Manners are like the sugar on the social cake that fosters respect for one another. The key to good manners is that we recognize and pay respect to everyone we encounter—not only customers but also the person right next to you. It's not easy to say thank you, smile, or give recognition. We are, at many times, extremely preoccupied with just getting the job done and we forget that what motivates us is a little recognition and a thank you. You probably agree with me that a smile and a thank you can be infectious, and sometimes there is hesitancy about who says it first. Take the initiative. Smile, say thank you or that you hope things are going well and you will be surprised with the response; you will probably get a smile back and it will make your day, and mine, just a little better. Isn't it nice to know that among all the problems we are facing, just making the day a little bit better is a pretty good thing!

Mom always said to be polite, be courteous. She was the original Rock then Roll rebel!

Culture-
Management
Is Messy:
What Culture-
Driven Leaders
Must Do
Well

---◦---

Culture-Management Is Messy: What Culture-Driven Leaders Must Do Well

We all have expectations—about everything. Even if we are not aware of them. There is virtually nothing we can do for which we do not have some vague expectation of the result. How we respond to something is a comment on that expectation.

How often have you been surprised by something and said, "Wow, I didn't expect that!" How come? We all have expectations—even when we say we don't.

What a Leader Does

A leader has to manage expectations. It's a life statement. You have to consciously work at it. You have to think about what impact you are having and you have to do it with commitment and purpose. Most people know how to do that for a job interview. They rehearse a scenario in which they meet and exceed the interviewer's *expectations*. What if we adopted that same attitude—that same approach—for everything?

A good leader is always on and knows that everything counts—all the time.

Managing expectations, sadly, is often overlooked; especially when designing a new service or product for a customer or when something needs to get done in a hurry. It is overlooked in planning and it is certainly overlooked when the time comes to analyze what went wrong—the so-called *post mortems*.

What Are the Expectations?

Managing expectations can be like herding cats into a sack. Expectations already in place need to be compared to expectations of what can be done versus what is actually going to be done. How do you get the cats into the sack?

Expectations need to be made realistic. The question needs to be asked: can they be accomplished?

For instance, my expectation was that the book you are reading *could be* done. That was a very realistic expectation with high certainty. Was it realistic that it *would* be done? Well, that was less certain but still of a fairly high probability. Would it be done on the timeline I had projected? Suddenly the uncertainty percentage increases. How good would it be? Even less certainty. Will it sell? The highest level of uncertainty.

So when I am talking about the book with, say, colleagues or friends, I never say, "I am working on a *New York Times* bestseller." I say, "I am working on a book I hope to have finished soon." That is an expectation I can deliver on with credibility.

If you can anticipate the gap between the *can* and the *will* and deal with it up front you have a better chance of avoiding failure. "I'm writing a book" leads people to believe that I am a writer, but since they have never heard of me they might assume I am no good. I say instead, "I am thinking of giving writing a book a shot." The expectations in place are immediately adjusted.

It's been my experience that being realistic about expectations and being very explicit about expectations is something that is fundamental to good results. Extremely focused managers will drive at any expense to get the job done. People get carried away. They lose perspective and it's not unusual to get so involved that they overdo it.

The challenge for a leader is to make sure that the damage that sometimes results in pushing for results too hard can be mitigated by aggressively managing expectations and getting those expectations out in the open. Be aware of what others expect and manage the result to your best advantage.

———◄○►———

CEO Message 108
MANAGING GROWTH

Knowing what is the right speed of growing a business is complicated. The rush to have the first mover advantage is often considered as critical. Building the largest market share in a product category is powerful because it puts all other competitors on the defensive. The assumption is, if you are undergoing rapid growth, then that growth is itself market proof of the value and demand for your product or service. That gives you some pricing power and will make your company more profit. Generally these aspects are true.

The reality is, the benefits of rapid growth are more often illusory. Fast growth can put dramatic strain on service and quality control, and generally requires substantial increases in investments—investments that may not pay off. It's a gamble. Growth is addictive. It's a rush. Leaders like it. It's focused action and everyone sees quick results. Most of the time it's a high-risk strategy.

CEO Message 89
WHAT COUNTS IN MANAGEMENT?

You need a plan; you need motivation to execute the plan; you need commitment; and you need a team that understands the plan and how to get the end result.

You need to keep track, but most of all you need to measure the progress. You cannot manage what you cannot measure. Reconciling economic results for a business against the accounting treatment of the financials has become very difficult in the financial world. Numbers are the way we evaluate business performance, but how do we interpret the numbers? In today's accounting world we are in a transition. The fair value basis of accounting does not always line up with economic reality, namely cash flow today and tomorrow. Today it is often overlooked that a balance sheet is a picture at one point in time and not very accurate a day later. The differences that arise force a real dilemma on managers. Do you improve the accounting results or stay focused on the underlying cash flows? This challenge will stay with us for many years since the world is more interconnected, and valuations can be made in more ways by more stakeholders. What is a company worth? What is someone willing to pay for it? Or to invest in its stock?

Measure performance to understand what is going on. It's done in sports. It's done in science. Every leader needs to do it. The numbers do not do the business; they show what is happening. The numbers also do not provide solutions any more than a medical diagnosis is a treatment.

A History Lesson

When financial results started going negative for ING Direct in 2008, the reaction was to study the numbers. It's what we all do, right? Okay, but the solutions should have been found by focusing on the business, not on making balance sheet adjustments that improved the numbers. Huge gaps have forced management to solve a dilemma: look at improving accounting results or improve the underlying business. This issue will be a challenge for many years to come.

CEO Message 93
RETAIL AS THE THREE-ACT PLAY

We have often heard this phrase *retail is detail*, and I think most of us think that it means focusing on all of the details if you're selling directly to a customer. As a manager, however, I would like you to think of this more as a piece of drama—a movie or a play. If you were putting on a play, you need to focus on all of the details to make sure that the execution is flawless, that it flows the way it is intended, and that nothing really upsets the overall objectives. We talked about the three-act play briefly already. A business is a lot like a play. Think of a service solution with a customer or a retail experience. It should:

1. Captivate the audience—have a solid opening and keep us focused on the outcome.
2. Have and maintain strong content.
3. Come to a logical, full conclusion.

The three-act play! We all learned about in school and probably thought that, like most things, we would never have any need for it. But the three-act play has an awful lot to do with retail interactions in a culture-driven market and business. If we focus on the details and look at every selling opportunity as a three-act play, we can make sure that we are not missing any of the main ingredients. Remember, in any transaction there are likely to be things left out and things that are missed. The customer, much like the viewer of the play, can't fill in some of the empty spaces. However, keeping the entertainment strong and keeping the threads of the message tied together well is what's really important. A customer will forget a little slip here or a little mistake there if

"Everything is a three-act play. Yes, everything." —AK

the overall program is basically successful and captivating. So, next time you, as a manager, use the *retail is detail* slogan, think of the implications. Are you ready to direct the three-act play?

CEO Message 110
LEAKS IN THE PIPE

Managing costs is never easy.

For me at ING Direct, keeping costs down in a direct banking model—fighting *cost creep*—was a real challenge and a constant battle. Always hunting for new and innovative ways to lower overhead and become more efficient and making the best use of resources was tough. And it's a job that never ends. Every day a new problem appeared like a burst pipe. In the creation and execution of your business model, it is imperative you have strategies in place to ensure that your business is cost effective and stays cost effective. When the pipe bursts, will you be ready with a plan of action or will you stand there and watch your basement flood?

No strategy is perfect; nothing is one hundred percent and there is no insurance policy you can take out against the chaos that is inevitable in the marketplace. A certain amount of chaos is to be expected. But always know exactly what you can control and don't lose control over it. Disaster is what happens when a leader stops managing his options and trusts fate. Focus on the main issues; concentrate on the drivers to reach the vision and the mission. Stay true to your principles and your mission. All else will follow.

CEO Message 92
STILL WAITING FOR THE EPIPHANY?

Answers do not put up their hands or wear pink tights and shout, "We're here!"

If you think you have an answer to a problem, you have to be certain. That is the first thing. But the second thing can be just as difficult: don't forget you have to sell it. It is a curious fact that in my experience so many problems have been created not by failing to come to a decision but by failing to properly implement the decision.

Making a decision is just the beginning. The key is to stay on track and all the way down the track; you have to communicate progress to your team and thereby confirm the wisdom of the choice. The same is true for a wrong choice.

Communicate the failure. If the error was made in good faith and based on sound judgment then more than likely it is redeemable. But delay is fatal. Never let a mistake take root. The point is to stay on track. Keep moving. The track is what is taking you to the goal. Every leader is up to judgment. By definition it is a high wire act.

You need to rock. You need to roll. The in-between is often overlooked: you need to sell your solutions, and make sure your solutions are implemented.

CEO Message 255
WHO *WAS* THAT GUY?

Surprise all who you work with.

- Speak your mind.
- Make a difference.
- Fight to get the business right.

CEO Message 86
ACTIONS SPEAK LOUDER THAN WORDS

Integrity, one of the corporate values at ING Direct, was often referred to as honesty, but it was more than that. Integrity is uniting thinking and action together. I used to ask myself this question about a product or service of ours: how easy is it to follow? What is clear to us, for instance, may not be viewed the same way by others. In fact, it seldom is.

How often have you spoken up merely for effect or to test someone else's idea? It's a temptation but best resisted. The best manager knows when saying less is saying more. You need to be critical but your criticism should always feel objective and not subjective. It's part of culture-driven thinking that discipline shapes our approach. The more disciplined you are the more those positive habits will filter outwards and become adopted. Speak when you need to and when it will have the most impact. A huge part of creating the right culture is building your credibility. The most direct path to credibility is consistency. It is the cornerstone of credibility.

Culture-
Management
Is Messy:
What Culture-
Driven Leaders
Must Do
Well

Try This at Home, Kids

Here's an experiment: today when you get home, write down every action you took and review them all. How do you think about them now? The value of retrospection is that it can sharpen our introspection: most of us would decide that we could have done things differently. That usually means we could have done them better.

That is the point. It focuses you on doing things more purposefully tomorrow.

CEO Message 50
STYLE VERSUS RESULTS

We all have ideas about our ideal work environment: flexible hours, casual clothes, easy and stimulating conversation with interesting colleagues, good coffee, a relaxed atmosphere with lots of opportunity to share comments and observations with the bosses ... all in all a friendly, creative, and positive environment.

On the flip side, a successful business requires a great amount of precision, tireless devotion, discipline, flawless execution, respect for deadlines, accuracy, and a very militaristic execution for steady, positive results—twenty-four hours a day seven days a week. So the question that comes to mind is how do managers deal—how do they balance—those competitive orientations? Call it the qualitative versus the quantitative.

On a See-Saw

Here's the problem: lean too far in the direction of the quantitative by emphasizing the structure required to execute the daily requirements and the business becomes extremely—perhaps overly—bureaucratic. This can result in a very rigid and formal environment. Lean too far in the direction of the casual and the qualitative, however, and the discipline required for quantitative results suffers. That can result in increased breakdowns, gaps, execution mistakes, and lack of follow through.

Obviously neither extreme is desired; neither extreme can do the whole job. Is it really possible to manage to the middle? When we look at other industries such as entertainment or sports we see that personalities can operate in two different modes; an athlete is extremely focused and rigid in the execution of a specific task, but once that is accomplished there is a break period where the warmth, personality, and charm is shared and things are more relaxed. We do find it in our own life; there is work time, study time, relaxing time.

I think it is important that we do not lose those thoughts and be conscious of what mode we are in. To achieve all we want to achieve requires the right balance between a rigid environment focused on execution and a warm environment focused on personal satisfaction.

A leader needs to understand what mode his team is in and why. The idea is not to sacrifice one for the other but to use them creatively as a blend.

CEO Message 153
LET'S SCHEDULE A MEETING TO DISCUSS A MEETING

The key to the management kingdom when it comes to meetings is always have an outcome at the outset. A distressingly familiar error made by many managers, however, is using a meeting to acquaint oneself with or review an issue or problem instead of to solve it.

Meetings are a part of life. It is important that we plan for and execute a successful meeting. For every meeting you participate in, set aside the same amount of time preparing for the meeting (one hour meeting = one hour preparation) and half the amount of time planning (one hour meeting = half an hour planning).

Have an Agenda and Stick to It

What will occur at the meeting? How will you conclude it? A meeting is like any other production; it involves people, a subject, has a clear beginning, middle, and an end. The better you can plan for and participate in a meeting, the more successful the outcome. If a meeting can't be done properly, then it shouldn't be done at all. Remember, a lot of things get done informally—one way or another! Often meetings become the most boring and least productive thing to do.

The way to change that is to look at meetings with a different set of eyes; make meetings one of the most important things you do, and plan and prepare for it as you would for a class you are about to teach, a play you are about to act in, or a social event you are about to participate in. Meetings are designed to be more effective in managing the work.

Everyone complains about meetings. The best thing is to have a good balance between the number of meetings and the importance of the subject that needs to be discussed. Just remember two words when it comes to meetings: fewer and better.

CEO Message 84

ON VACATION AND NOW YOU ARE BACK

It's good to get away and recharge those batteries and get to the things you have been planning with family and friends. Is it important? Yes.

Too simple an idea? No.

The first day you are back, you find yourself in the thick of things and you are thinking, "So much to catch up on!" Was it worth it being away?

Making the Easy Transition

A good manager does a few simple things to ease the vacation time in and out of the job.

First, clearly set out who, in your absence, is carrying on the work. Not just the "go to" when there is a problem, but who can keep things moving.

Two, communicate this to everyone; yes, the when, what, why, and who! Second, stick to the vacation and the plan. You need to take a mental and a physical break. It's good to rely on your fellow workers to pitch in so that they can do it, too.

Third, make a plan for when you come back. Set priorities and schedule enough time to catch up on projects and issues. You cannot do it in a day and if you charge in, you will be far too stretched by the end of the first day back.

Fourth, remember that it's your responsibility to get caught up on decisions and progress. Read the minutes and check on things before you draw conclusions.

Who is Running Whom?

You cannot expect to control the things that went on while you were away. You were away—not the business!

Want to test a business for its management strength? See how well it operates during the vacation breaks.

A good leader can manage vacations without losing the benefits. If you have created the right culture it will keep the business up and afloat. I have seen CEOs who have succumbed to the ego-driven model where they confuse their presence as leadership. I mean, think about it in terms of how we parent our children. The goal is to produce people who have the skills to act and think on their own. As a leader you need to lead by example so that your example filters through the company. Were you the kind of kid in school who loved having a substitute teacher because you thought you could get away with things? Well, doesn't that say something about your teacher?

You need to make sure that as leader your influence will be felt in your absence. If not, you have some great feedback about how good a leader you are.

CEO Message 182
USE YOUR SIXTH SENSE

Can you read the mood of a meeting? Do you know which way the wind is blowing when a client or competitor calls? Can you sense at any given time the atmosphere at your company?

Are you aware of what other members of you team think of you?

The point is that you can have in your hands the best idea since sliced bread. But if you are tone deaf to the condition of the soil where that idea is going to be planted, you are wasting your time. You need to know how to read people. You need to tap into your sixth sense.

You do have a sixth sense. You probably have just never used it.

Reading Signals

A good manager can read the signals. How do you develop this ability? Focus, ask questions, and visualize. Remember as children we played pretend? Learn to see the world from different perspectives. It's the same when managing relationships at work. It's called intuition. If you have it, use it. If you don't, learn. The best way to start is to observe. Study your surroundings like a detective over a crime scene. Be conscious of yourself and the situation you are in. Practice the way you used to memorize facts. Ever try to find *Waldo*? It's the same process except you are studying everyone around you and what is going on. Looking for clues.

Think like a detective! Hunt like a hound dog!

CEO Message 116
COMPETITION IS EVERYTHING

What captures the attention of a good manager? Typically, managers like to keep themselves focused on efficiency measures, organizational models, product pricing, assessing capital requirements, assessing customer satisfaction, etc. However, what usually takes a back seat is studying and keeping a very close eye on the competition.

Competition is the measure that tells us how successful we are in the market place. Accurately measuring who amongst our competitors is getting the best responses from the customers, who amongst the competition is applying their business model the best, is a good place to figure out a company's strength.

A focus on competitive rankings is the key because it forces us to redeploy our resources, allows us to measure where we can find the best business opportunity, and helps us to balance our value proposition to the customer.

You will find in your business that each year more and more focus will have to be given to watching the competition, both in each community and in each market footprint that we operate. Not only studying our competitors' strengths and weaknesses, but also their responses to our own activities.

Study Your Enemy

Elsewhere in this book I talked about *benchmark comparisons*—using other businesses to measure your own. I said I was not a fan. So how is this different? The point is, don't focus on your competition because you want to be just like them. What you want to do is always do better than your competition. Always be different. Always be better. Always be more responsive to your customer. Never settle. Benchmarkers are happy when they settle in with the mean. I never felt comfortable sitting safely in the middle of the pack.

Remember, competition is an interactive process. Anticipating what your competitors will do next is the mark of a good manager.

"The enemy is out there." So says the slogan on the shop floor. No sense fighting among ourselves. Competition is what drives a lot of good thinking, passion, and a desire to be the best. A big focus on competitors is good as long as the idea is to beat them and avoid becoming like them.

If you are small company challenging the big dogs, always think small. Make sure you keep that chip on your shoulder about your competitors. And if you are a big company, force yourself to think yourself into the challenger role.

The proverbial underdog. David and Goliath, man!

David had attitude. A huge challenge, a sling, and a pair of big rocks!

CEO Message 14
PRIORITIES AND THE TWO WORKING STYLES

There are two types of working styles when it comes to priorities: the type that makes a list and the type that doesn't.

We are all familiar with those to-do lists that sit on desks at businesses all over North America. The attempt to put a priority on things that need to be done and things that need to be remembered? These people tend to be overly rational and organized and regular in their habits. They deal with tasks in succession and experience a thrill of delight when they can cross an item off the list. *Next!*

Then there are the ones who basically work without a list and rely on the pressure of events unfolding around them to dictate what needs to be done. These folks tend to be less organized, more impulsive and like to imagine they are quick on their feet. They are the fly-by-the-seat-of-your-pants people.

So between the to-do-list people and the seat-of-your-pants people, which one are you?

It's not an idle question. Imagine you are working closely with your team. If all of them were either to-do-listers or seat-of-your-pantsers, all would be harmony and sunshine.

Alas, most work environments are composed of a mix of both types plus a generous helping of any number of in-betweeners, all of which can create tension and stress and even induce destabilizing resentments.

What to do to defuse the tension?

Effective communication. It works; it is essential. But it is a daily challenge for all of us. Figure out what style you have and why. Is it the optimal style for who you are, your skill sets, and what you need to get done? If so, hone that skill on a daily basis. If not, find a new style that works. Never stop thinking about how your style can be most effective with those around you.

Look, during those dark days of the Battle of Britain, Churchill could have said to those heroic RAF pilots, "Hey, thanks you guys. You were great." But instead he adopted a high rhetorical *style* that perfectly matched the gravity of the events. "Never was so much owed by so many to so few."

Oh man. Legendary! Lincoln? Washington? Roosevelt? Leaders? Oh yeah. Style? Absolutely!

Style makes a difference. You have a communication style. Work hard to understand it and master it.

CEO Message 72
DOES YOUR MANAGEMENT STYLE FIT?
One size fits all hardly works for anything.

Each business situation, much like all situations in life, can be best evaluated by the management style that is most effective. In some businesses, strategy is the most important factor; in some it is tactics and in others it is follow-through. For ING Direct, for example, it was execution. Success required a tremendous focus on detail, close coordination between all facets, divisions, and practices throughout the company, and demanded that every activity and feature be performed in a consistent and proper manner. Our contact-style with clients, how we communicated, and our commitment to providing accurate information all were indicative of having had adopted and enforced a management style that valued flawless execution above all else.

Of course there were many managers within ING Direct—just like at any business—whose responsibilities and accountabilities fell outside the execution domain. But I thought of it as I would a well-balanced team composed of talented players with different styles for different tasks. However, across the board, day in and day out, the style I found most reliable was from the manager who was deliberate and efficient.

In the long run, nothing beats effective.

Tortoise or the Hare? They Both Make Lousy CEOs

It's an unforgivable waste of valuable resources when one person accomplishes a job in twice the time it takes someone else. It's just as frustrating when a process breaks down in the middle of a job and the project has to start over. Remember the fairy tale about the tortoise and the hare? Okay, I have no time for either one. The hare burns out halfway through and the tortoise is too damn slow. But I do reward the steady and the effective. That person that has a reliable style that doesn't roller coaster from beginning to end but who still knows how to press down on the accelerator to get there first. The person who earns trust by producing results.

A leader has to identify the people who have that style, and who can adapt their everyday—their so-called default— style to one that emphasizes execution. A manager can drill his players and review playbooks and the fundamentals of strategy until hell freezes over. On paper, every team looks like a winner. It's what happens once the game starts, however, that makes the difference. Some players rise to the challenge; some players don't. What separates the winner from the loser is execution.

Look at the player who comes up to the plate in the bottom of the ninth with a chance to win the game, and strikes out.

What do you think he's thinking? Maybe that he can't wait for another opportunity to take another crack at it? Yeah, sure. And maybe he will. But a CEO doesn't have a next time to correct a mistake.

The Stakes

We play for keeps. The stakes are high and the losers eat gravel. Every day it's a new game and a new moment with you at the plate and everything to win or lose. This is the challenge business is faced with every day. Unless all ten of ten aspects of the business are successfully completed, no way you can hope to make the break-through achievements in record time. Take a hard look at your management team; celebrate those managers who are clearly focused on whatever style you have endorsed, the managers who clearly make getting the detail right a priority, and who are relentless in their pursuit of completing activities on a specific time schedule. Make sure everyone on your team understands who she is; acknowledge their contribution to the business model and learn as much as possible to adopt their style.

And the ones who don't? Well, like they say, there's always next season. Only there isn't.

CEO Message 68
GETTING THE BEST RESULTS

I have often been asked, "How should a manager make decisions? How can a manager get the best results?"

No crystal balls, right? It doesn't get any less true the more you hear it. We will, at best, only have limited information to deal with. If we had perfect information there would not be much skill or experience required in decision-making. Read the signs; figure out what the odds are of getting the desired outcome. Review and consider carefully the information you do have. When there is doubt there is no doubt.

There is a type of manager with a bias to inaction and he defends this by pleading "not enough information to act." A manager with a bias to action, however, has a heightened attention to information that is reliable and against information that is suspect or irrelevant. Call it intuition. Doubt also brings into focus accountability and the consequences of a wrong decision. Doubt can be an agent for clarifying the equation. Here it comes again: your job is to eliminate doubt. Doubt is not the goal. Action, as in effective decision-making, is the goal.

We learn from mistakes; small mistakes can easily be tolerated and corrected, major mistakes can be fatal. Making good decisions over the long run is the key to being successful. So you ask yourself: when should I make a decision? What level of confidence do I have in the outcome? How should I make it?

Focus on the scope of the decision and decide if you can live with the consequences. You need to understand your own bias and that of the team you are on.

Personality—your own, one another's, the team's, and the business'—is an often-overlooked factor in how you will deal with a decision. How I decide is as much a consequence of who I am, as who you are and how that will affect the way you decide. One is not better than the other. The trick is to understand what your personality bias is and make sure it works to the advantage of the culture you are building. The essence of culture-driven business is removing the subjective from the objective. You are the subjective. That doesn't mean you want everyone to act like robots. But think of your mission—the culture you are building—as the objective. It means that we are all individuals and that who we are can sometimes be a distraction. The right culture is like beautiful music: thousands of *different* notes all arranged in a gorgeous harmony, not thousands of the *same* note all played one after the other.

We are all in business. Break it down and we all pretty much do the same things and confront the same things. We

> "Management without chaos is like peanut butter without jam." —AK

all live with the same circumstances. The unaccountable and uncontrollable x-factor is personality. Be conscious of both—circumstances and personality. Use both.

Focus on the scope of the decision and decide if you can live with the consequences. You need to understand your own bias and that of the team you are on.

CEO Message 161
IF YOU HAVE DOUBTS

The next time you are faced with a decision, consider your doubts. Think about the consequences and the trade off between a successful result and a negative one. Come to grips with how much doubt you have as a result. If, after careful deliberation, you feel in your gut certainty about the decision, best make it and see it through. On the other hand, if the doubt persists—if your intuition waffles—you may want to keep working on it until you get all the right factors in play.

Intuition is like any other muscle. The more it is exercised the stronger it becomes. A good manager—the great leader—needs to have a strong and reliable intuition. The higher up you are in the decision-making hierarchy, and this may seem counterintuitive, the less you will have in terms of reliable information. Decisions are critical and the consequences monumental and there often is not very much time to deliberate.

Intuition is your finger in the breeze; it will tell you which way the wind is blowing.

CEO Message 98
MANAGING YOUR BOSS

I've often been asked, "What is the most important thing in making your own career and job a success?"

The first is, effectively managing your boss. No kidding. By making your boss effective, you, in turn, make yourself influential. When you are asked to do something, follow it up and report on the progress that's being made: confirm that things are getting done, anticipate questions and problems, do the work to the best of your ability, and communicate any surprises that may go on. The first thing to ask is, "What would I do if I was in my boss's shoes? What do I need and how do I get my job done?"

The second key is to understand that it's all about perception. It's not about who is right or wrong; it's not about what you think, but the perception your boss has. This is a general sense that's very challenging but most effective when you begin to learn how to master it.

A third is learning that you cannot effectively manage a situation, change an outcome, or get a business result unless you can effectively manage your boss. For those of us who have been in management many years, we begin to learn this over time by the hard experience of days passing. As a new manager, this could be one of the most powerful tools and insights that you can apply early in your career.

Remember: it does not matter whether your boss is good or bad, or whether he is successful or not; you will have a boss, so do the best you can. This shows professionalism and a commitment to getting results.

CEO Message 102
BOUNDARIES AND LIMITS

In our personal lives, we prefer to be liked. It isn't possible to be everybody's friend, of course. But it would be nice.

Business is different. How often have you heard something like this: "I'm not here to be your friend. I'm your boss." We want to be liked of course; we want to be respected. But we also want people to do what we ask them to do. We are focused on results.

What can happen, and what often does happen, in daily management of any business is that a manager's style can shift from objective to subjective. It shifts from a goal-focused approach to a personality-focused approach. That creates huge problems.

However, setting boundaries and limits on what you will do, can do, and insist on doing, is a critical step in shifting the management focus from the subjective back to the objective. You cannot have integrity without boundaries. You cannot achieve excellent performance without others knowing your personal capabilities—including incapabilities. For instance, saying, "I cannot do public speaking, so let me do the follow up questions." Others need to know what you are good at and what you are not. You need to explain this in a positive way.

Limits are helpful. It forces you and those you work with to establish respect.

CEO Message 121
GOOD NEWS/BAD NEWS

Who doesn't like good news?

One of the most challenging things for a manager to do, however, is deliver bad news to the team.

As leaders, we should always be eager to champion and reward hard-working teams by bringing good news, such as recognition, raises, and good assignments, to team members for a rewarding experience. However, delivering bad news is difficult because it forces you to put the message into a broader context, and, psychologically, you must then represent the larger organization in implementing decisions, such as a rejected bonus, demotion, or difficult assignment.

These are not easy, and you as a leader must stay objective and remember your responsibility is to earn the respect of the team and not get caught up in making everyone happy or being liked. When delivering good or bad news, limit the emotions involved and make sure that the underlying reason is well communicated.

Culture-
Management
Is Messy:
What Culture-
Driven Leaders
Must Do
Well

CEO Message 132
IF ONLY I HAD KNOWN

Later on in life you realize the importance of the decisions you made early on. A good manager always thinks about the impact of today's decisions.

CEO Message 71
GOOD TO GREAT

A key metric for performance is how well your business reacts and responds to management issues. I have a three-step plan for measuring success:

1. Identify the problem or problems.
2. Resolve them as quickly as possible.
3. Move on as quickly as possible to the next issue.

In my experience, following this plan results in creating a positive sense of urgency (not panic) and a sense of accomplishment (decisive action taken in a timely fashion). However, if the goal is to reduce stress and get a better handle on how to get results with less effort and better coordination, you need to adopt a proactive management perspective. This, of course, includes such things as planning and forecasting and, at the same time, anticipating problems and putting the right amount of resources in place early enough so no one is scrambling to meet deadlines.

It is an acquired art, frankly, learning how to decide how much planning and work should be done ahead of time, especially since most of us just want to get on with it.

A More Ecological Approach

If we are not to waste resources, however, and if we want to reduce the amount of pressure to meet deadlines, it is imperative to focus on proactive management—getting all your organizational and management ducks in a row. You want to be in a responsive position: look at what is coming at you down the road and do what needs to be done. The alternative, of course, is being forced into a reactive position: what was coming down the road at a safe distance suddenly is about to crash into you head on. It's intense, for sure. And every once in a while it can't be avoided. A crisis is a real test of character; but there is nothing so powerless as confronting a problem and having no options at your disposal *except the worst and most expensive* option. It's a huge waste of money, resources, time, and leadership capital. Believe me, nothing is more destructive to your reputation than creating more crises than you solve.

CEO Message III
TIME TO THINK

An article asks, "Are managers spending enough time thinking and working through the problems they are faced with to do the business they need to do?"

Most of our days are filled with meetings, transactions, emails, telephones and teleconferences, travel, conferences—a whole lot of activity and not a whole lot of good time to think. It is important that you find the time during the day, depending on your own style, whether it is early in the morning, early in the afternoon, or later in the day, to reflect on the challenges and big issues ahead.

Remember, if you spend all your day in activities dealing with the small things, the most important things never get the due consideration and never get properly managed.

The most important thing a manager can do is think of how you are attacking the work, meeting the challenges, and especially staying in touch with how you feel about the progress being made. Usually your intuition will tell you if you have thought the issue through well enough and have come to a conclusion that will find the conviction and commitment that is necessary to see it through.

Find time to think!

CEO Message 47
WHEN IT DOESN'T WORK, GO BACK TO BASICS

Not long ago two things crossed my desk: one was a copy of *Fortune* magazine. The other was a bestselling book by Jim Collins called *Good to Great*. In the *Fortune* article, Ram Charan, whom I have known for more than twenty-five years, wrote a fascinating piece on why companies fail.

One characteristic was the, conscious or unconscious, fostering of a dangerous culture. Basically, a blanket term or description of any habit or practice that could prove destructive to a business environment. The other was being softened by success. I agree. No business is immune. Nor is any leader— not even the most conscientious leader who tries with the best of intentions to create a unique and positive culture in an organization and has a track record of seeing steady and good success. Sooner or later we all inhale the virus.

A rule of thumb is, success keeps you doing what you have been doing and makes adaptation more difficult; success can make you risk-averse. The paradox, of course, is that it is often the risk that created the success in the first place. Destructive behaviors that are contradictory to the ones you profess to live by, your culture, creep into your business; the result is an overall malaise.

Collins writes that great companies focus not only on what they have to do to become great but also on what not to do and what to stop doing; equal time should be given to both activities.

Find Out What It Is You Do Not Do Well, and Do Not Do That Thing! Sage advice and absolutely true.

Sadly, this is seldom done. In my experience, companies devote too little effort and time to managing change, motivating people, and creating patterns of alignment. It means making sure that people are in sync. Leaders talk about alignment of interests and activity but mistakenly impose that definition on people and assume it means that everyone thinks the same. It's seldom done right, and most simply pay lip service to it.

For instance, consider the military. They spend a lot of time on alignment. If done right, it has a big positive impact on coordination and improves communication. *If done right*, of course. Under the wrong conditions and the wrong culture, however, the potential positive benefits of commitment, alignment, and motivation disappear.

If you have a good group of friends and you know each other very well, everything becomes automatic and you are in sync. If something happens that puts a wedge into that alignment, the bonds unravel.

All companies need a positive culture to survive and thrive, and the first and most important step is always putting the right people in the right jobs and then setting up the right vision and goals. In most cases we tend to reverse that process by trying to set strategy and plans first and then trying to put the right people in place.

Great companies find and assemble great people, and only then do they set out what the right vision is and transform the culture by what they are doing. It's too easy to rest on last year's success or just good enough results. If everyone has round heads you don't create a vision based on square hats. If you have to tell people to be disciplined in execution, you have probably already lost the battle. You have to have a disciplined culture to execute well. To do that you need to select people by their inclination. People who are disciplined by nature.

Don't Look For Miracles

I've always said that resurrection has only been done once well in history and for most of us to be truly transformed or changed is not an option.

What does a business do?

Rethink the basis on which you want to lead in business and focus on the fundamental questions. Who are we? What do we really want to achieve? How can we be great at doing it? Acquisitions probably won't be the answer. Doing what we did last year won't work either. Exposing ourselves to risk, however, and becoming ruthlessly brutal in making decisions about the right team to get the job done is a step in the right direction.

The next time you're confronted with a situation that just doesn't seem to fit or work right, ask yourself, is the culture right or is it dangerous? Does it *feel* positive? Are the people around the table the right people? Is there really a spark that could make the business mission great or will it be just average?

It Happens in Every Business

In more than ten years of ING Direct existence, we have had to face the Big Question a number of times—the moments when we hit a snag or a pothole in the road. It could be external or internal. The economy sinks into a recession, say, or a wholesale price rise jacks up your costs or a key person on the team decides suddenly to leave. It is the same for every business sooner or later. You will face the inevitable question: Now what?

Are you prepared for your own "now what?" Are you prepared to do what it takes to make those critical and necessary adjustments and then do them?

CEO Message 147
DELEGATING

In an earlier message I had mentioned the importance of delegating as a key leadership tool. One of the most difficult things for anyone to do is to delegate a task to someone else. Managers accept this as a key requirement to organize work and effectively get things done; however, delegating is a much more difficult task than just asking someone to do something.

I return to the idea of you as leader, *as director*. The mission is your play and your team is the cast. Remember, each and every cast member must be chosen specifically with a role in mind. It is important that the distinction is not only understood but embraced. It is absolutely crucial to making culture-driven leadership work. Remember this mantra: always surrender a bit more freedom than you are comfortable with. Yes, it is generally easier to demand that people who work for us execute a task exactly as we would. I have outlined already that, even within a culture-driven business, the leader needs to establish clear parameters. Always focused on the goal, okay? The mission. But you do not want to dictate the details of the performance. The great director is the one whose suggestions and encouragement frees the excellent performance from inside the actor. By conceding more freedom than you are comfortable with, you are allowing your team to create its own sense of authenticity. That ability to create the authentic performance fully invests team members in the outcome of the play: in your case, the mission.

It isn't easy to learn how to become comfortable with other people's freedom, especially when you have the power to compel compliance—the "do it my way" strategy. Remember how my bosses were critical of my unpredictable behavior? It is a good example of leaders not being comfortable with authenticity. I was doing my job as authentically as I could and doing an excellent job. They were happy I was doing an excellent job, of course, but not with how I was doing it. They had their own idea on how it should be done. In a culture-driven business, excellence and authenticity are inseparable. That forces you onto a steep learning curve in terms of your own ideas about authority. As I said, it is not easy.

You worry that by delegating too early in the process, there is a real danger for failure. Someone will not be up to or lack the skills to accomplish the task. Or by delegating too late you will be criticized for micromanaging or not making decisions fast enough and slowing the process down. It's a classic dilemma; handling the problem efficiently and cleanly is imperative. In general, process does not produce results. People produce results.

A culture-driven approach, as we have seen, begins with making the right hiring decision. Hiring for behavior and training for skills. I always want to know how people I work with have handled the problems of their lives. To be honest, those data points of your life are crucial clues to me about how you will perform under stress. I have hired people who did not come to the party with the requisite skill set or experience, but they always had the behavior. I knew I could always send an inexperienced team member off to learn a skill. But I could never send them off anywhere to learn life skills—that is what they need to bring to the table. So if you find yourself unwilling to delegate, you might need to rethink who you have hired and why you hired him or her.

A second critical component of delegating is making sure that while the mission is clearly understood objectively, the method for achieving that mission is understood subjectively. Mistakes will be made; that is inevitable. But if everyone is fully committed to the goal and understands why it is so important the risk of huge mistakes is far less. Think of it this way: I cast an actor in my play to be Hamlet. He memorizes his lines. I tell him who I think Hamlet is. He has his own idea of who Hamlet is. We might argue back and forth about it. In the end, however, we both know how it will turn out. The plot has not changed. But the interpretation probably has. Ultimately, it is the actor, not me, who steps onto the stage. That is his moment to create his authenticity. If he succeeds, the audience will give him a standing ovation.

Your responsibility as a director is to have supplied your actor with all the tools he needs to succeed. As leader, you need to create opportunities for your team to find its own moments for creating authentic performances. You must learn how to delegate creatively.

How?

- Make sure you have a complete understanding of the scenario.
- Get a good read on where the indicators are pointing.

Listen to the Force, Luke

How large is the cry for autonomy and freedom to get on with it, while on the other hand, how many positive indicators can easily be seen that the enterprise and the day-to-day work is pointing in the right direction? It is imperative that you read the signs right; gather as much information as possible in a timely way. In the end, a successful leader is one that consciously delegates, not too early and not too late.

For instance, I have learned that a lot of the time things work a lot better if you surrender some space. And I learned that, actually, from my two young boys. Like a typical dad, I play with them, and then they have something they're working on, and I try to help them. And then I go away because I'm off running an errand or doing something else. I come back, and they've done it, actually quite well, on their own. And the light bulb goes on, saying, well, sometimes you've just got to let people do their own thing. And they will get it done.

Delegating requires a clear discussion of the goals, objectives, timelines, and projected results that need to be accomplished. If one doesn't delegate well, the consequences are serious. The damage is much wider than one normally would expect, and includes poor results, task ineffectiveness, and critical relationships becoming stressed.

Remember: agree upon the process, negotiate what is involved, and verify to see that you are both on the same page.

Make delegating work for you, not against you.

There is also a personal risk to delegate. I had to give up some of the things I enjoyed doing. I loved to work on new products, but with other responsibilities I had to delegate and then not put my finger in all the time. Things may not go the way you want them to, but that's a part of the process.

It's not easy.

CEO Message 31
WHO SAYS SO?

Do you remember when you were a kid playing outside and your brother or sister yelled out to you, "Come in for dinner" and you would say, "Says who?" and their response was, "Mom says"?

It's interesting. We still do this when we want to get employees to pay attention. We invoke our title or someone else's more impressive title as if it alone were the magic wand that could make everything happen. Lots of managers still feel that titles convey authority and that getting things done means using that authority to compel compliance. Look, no business can survive without hierarchies and chains of command. The issue is how those hierarchies and chains of command are created, structured, and operated.

One rule of thumb: authority should never collide with corporate values and culture. It may work in the short run, but it creates a train of really heavy baggage in its wake that always derails the mission.

A History Lesson

My approach was always to manage in the spirit consistent with ING Direct's corporate values and culture. For me, that was always about being direct, respectful, friendly, and supportive. I think it's basic human nature to feel some kind of meaningful investment in whatever we are trying to accomplish. At ING Direct, I wanted my authority to emerge not from the so-called weight of my title, but, naturally, as a shared consequence of my convictions and commitments to the overall goals. If I took the trouble to explain the *why* and the *how* of what I wanted done, my hope was that the person tasked with carrying it out would share my investment.

If you want to see a portrait of frustration, just look into the face of someone who is working on something but who has no idea why it is important or necessary. We all want to feel that the contributions we are making are valuable to the overall success of the business. The smartest thing you can do as a manager or CEO is to create as many opportunities for shared investments as possible. It isn't always the easiest thing in the world to take the extra time that is necessary to explain the why and the how each and every time. What you will find, too, is this: the effort you make now will carry over to every other task that comes down the line. Think of the process as a kind of positive indoctrination for your team in effective work habits.

Know the Walk; Know the Talk

Managers that can explain why and what needs to be done, and who can suggest how it should be done, in a conceptual framework that is consistent with the company's vision, culture, and mission will gain power and, in the end, will be much more effective. It also reinforces the team's commitment to the company's culture. Over time the system can even achieve a capability for spontaneous self-correction. A task that may be headed off the rail suddenly will steer itself back in line and the right path will be restored. Why? Not because your employees have been told that is how it must be done. It's because they believe your way is the best way to get it done.

The power to influence your company's future is at your fingertips.

CEO Message 91
ARE YOUR FAULTS FORGIVEN?

I'm sure you have had bosses who have had that clichéd, domineering management style. Maybe she thought that to be thought strong and effective she had to be strong and effective all the time. No humility or weakness. Take no prisoners.

Let me ask you something: in your role as leader, how do you think people around you see you? Be honest.

From my perch, the key to good people management is for people to perceive the leader as admirable and likeable. It's funny because in my experience I have too often come across the opposite idea: that to be an effective leader you need to be feared. It's a cop out. Any jerk can throw his weight around. No one admires that. Managers and leaders who are able to communicate a certain humanness, a certain vulnerability, and, above all, are willing to admit to mistakes and show frailty earn respect. That respect can be a powerful tool for supporting your team.

Look, we all tend to admire people for their strengths. But what makes our admiration soar is when that same person is willing to confess his weaknesses. And trust me, we all have them. We generally have a sense of why people do what they do.

We understand that the way they act shows:

- A vulnerability that begs forgiveness
- A selfishness that is at the core of people's desire to succeed
- A balance of greed or control that makes others uneasy

Think of that individual whose faults are always forgiven. Think about your own faults and ask yourself if they're forgiven. Not accepted—forgiven. For me, there is a huge difference. We seldom forgive faults in others—especially if they impact us. Mostly we move on and it's sometimes easiest or most practical to do so. If they're not forgiven, then perhaps you can think about what you could do. Change the way people see you. Start with acting humble and vulnerable. Be open to criticism and wear it well.

Strive to have your faults forgiven.

CEO Message 78
SUCCESS IS NEVER A FLUKE

If you want to change, be more effective, or get something done, set a goal and create a ritual. Plan quiet time; plan concentration time; plan e-mail time, but most important, do it on a set schedule and stick to it.

The thing that impacts management success the most is consistency. The best way to demonstrate it is through the use of rituals.

A Fish Tail, or, a Tale about Fish

In Seattle there is a fish market called The Pike Place Market.

The vendors are a wild bunch of seemingly free spirits who inject some novelty into their business routine by tossing fish to each other. Sometimes they throw them to customers. This ritual has made them famous. Customers gather and cluster just to watch the show. They're a lot of fun.

A great ritual.

Oh, and they sell *a hell of a lot* of fish.

CEO Messages 108
THE RIGHT LEADER FOR THE RIGHT MISSION

Growth is a normal, and desired, consequence for any business. Making business plans for an upcoming year is well understood, for instance, but the consequences are seldom discussed. Usually it's, "Can we make the plan?" "What do we need to make the plan a success?" "What do we want to change?" "What do we want to stop doing?" "Any new big ideas?"

Managing scale and growth creates perceptual as well as operational challenges. Waking up to the realization that you are now larger, face new and perhaps more deadly risks, and many more points of failure is not what most leaders want to think about.

At ING Direct we knew that we were a good start-up entrepreneurial company. Then came the threshold moment when we had reached a size where we knew we needed to talk about the transition to a mature business. The hard work continues to be to address the challenges of being a larger company. It means spending more time discussing processes and how things should get done. It's a gradual but difficult adjustment. For most leaders it feels more like homework than getting things done.

Be Ready, Freddy

You have to be ready. You need to ask yourself some questions. How about some Rock then Roll questions?

First, do you have the ability and talent to manage a mature business in a more traditional, formal way? At ING, truth was, we were not sure. We would give it a try. Second, do you have the courage to step away when things are going very well and the time is up for pure growth? Third, is the current state worth risking things that are going well for what is unknown?

A business culture that has a foundation of growth needs a leader with a growth orientation—a leader who knows when the company will shift to a new growth priority.

It applied to ING Direct directly. But it is relevant to any business. The right leader for the right mission. The key here is being self-aware and realistic about accepting the mission that is right for you. It's just not always true in business that this happens. I see the wrong leaders in the wrong positions all the time. Business just tends to think that anyone can do anything and that is just not true.

CEO Message 26
LEARNING HOW TO STEER

If a company is growing too fast or too slow, it is easy to over-react as a leader. A bias to action is central for any leader.

But over-steering in a car or a boat has the same effect in a company.

Instead of a steering-focused approach, it may be more important to refocus on the company mission. Instead of dodging what you see as obstacles flying right at you, try looking at the horizon to bring the business back to steady. In practice this means going back to basics. Ask yourself: what creates value for my customer?

CEO Message 15
THERE MUST BE A BETTER WAY

Saving money has a bad reputation. It's not hard to explain. We live in the most consumer-friendly economy in history. Being thrifty used to be a virtue. Now we call thrifty people cheap. The clichés abound: you get what you pay for; a penny wise and pound foolish; shop till you drop; retail therapy. Whatever.

In business, cost savings is not a fad. It's a reality that cannot be swept aside with a cute cliché. Each and every day we need to create value for our products and services, and we only create value when we use our energy and creativeness to reduce costs without sacrificing quality.

There's No Place Like Home ...

You should always be thinking that there must be a better way. There must be a faster, more reliable way of doing this product or service. Getting costs out means rethinking the work.

Pricing the input components and determining what revenue you can command are the first steps. But the only sure and reliable way to consistently beat the competition is to have more cost savings, and that means more efficiency.

For instance, at ING Direct we looked at our account opening procedures. Pretty basic, right? I mean, how much savings could there be in that? Well, by some clever tinkering we managed to cut out a few steps. It wasn't without risk. There was the huge concern that consumers might rebel. But they didn't, and overall we managed to save twenty percent on our costs.

A huge cost and efficiency improvement!

Every company talks about cost savings. But often the tone is punitive. They broadcast a message that cutting costs is not something that should be a fundamental part of their company's DNA but an act of desperation. "The company is plunging over a cliff and we will all lose our jobs if we don't cut costs by whatever percent."

Make the Strategy Work for You ... Not Against You

Cutting costs is not a strategy in a box on the top shelf that is pulled down and dusted off in moments of panic and crisis. It should be a feature of everyone's daily routine. What do we do and how do we do it? How can we do it better? And by better we mean more efficiently and cheaper.

It's absolutely a key that the cost savings strategy is communicated up, down, and all around the company as a positive, and not a punitive, value. Cost-savings initiatives need to become incentives propelling your company forward. Remember, most people who hear "cost saving" immediately hit panic mode. Who wants to waste time peeling employees off the ceiling? My preference is to incorporate cost savings as a core value in my business culture.

Make every day a cost savings day. Incentivize.

Performance: Free to Choose

It's about building your track record.

Managers are often faced with a critical choice. Tough choices by definition are always shades of gray; we need to find a way to make the right decision. Sometimes it's better to make a decision than to not make one; that, in itself, is a decision. The obvious risk is that delay can be interpreted as confusion or lack of nerve. Always make sure that when a decision needs to be postponed the reasons are convincing and airtight, and consistent with company culture and values. Frankly, nothing is more dispiriting in my experience than an enthusiastic or spirited discussion being neutered by a manager who either is unprepared, incapable, or simply unwilling to make a decision.

It is always much better to be prepared to make a decision. Otherwise the process is running ahead of you and it needs to be reined in. You will appear to be in over your head. Don't jump into the pool if you don't know how to swim. No one wants to see you flailing for your life and don't expect anyone to jump in and save you. When you make a decision, be totally committed to the outcome. No backing into a decision and then being frustrated with the outcome. In other words, take control of the choice. At the same time, if people see you being backed into a decision, leadership credit for having achieved the desired outcome will not be yours. It is possible your fuzzy decision-making leadership could even be interpreted as an obstacle to success.

The Choices: a Boot Camp Approach

It seems obvious, but a manager needs to clearly understand
what the choice being made actually is. There is the everyday
fact of the choice before you. Like, apples or oranges. Okay, the
choice seems simple. But there is generally a complex universe
of qualifying factors that make the decision more complicated.
Maybe bad weather has raised the cost of apples. Maybe half
of your customer base is allergic to oranges. Who knows? The
point is, you, as leader, need to know how to frame the choice.
And that needs to be communicated to the team.

Breaking problems down to the basics often reveals components you may have overlooked or just not imagined. That
will affect how you approach your choices. It may even rede-
fine what your choices are.

If conducted properly, a good communication process
can liberate hidden or disguised problems or can help raise
new questions or enable a radically different characterization
of the original choice. Ultimately, it's a process that encour-
ages everyone who is involved to become fully committed
and vested in the outcome.

It would be wonderful if we could see all our decision-
making with the clarity of twenty-twenty vision. But that is
unrealistic. So the most protective thing a manager can do
is be consistent, and consistently good, about approaching
choices. This means managing the choice within the corporate structure, and then standing foursquare behind that
choice. It is very helpful to keep a record of choices that have
worked well, and, especially, of those that did not and why. It
shows wisdom and a sense of awareness that is appreciated
by other team members.

But most of all, remember that choices define the outcome, and that choices, and the will of a manager, are what build a great company. You are building a legacy of choices made. Think of it as a blackboard that you cannot erase, with every choice marked on a scorecard.

Don't Fog It Up!

Be clear on how choices are made. Identify who makes them.

At Deak International we started to matrix responsibilities with the idea that it would help get the best results and encourage more teamwork. The idea was that everyone would have more than one person to report to and multiple responsibilities to more than one person.

Well, the concept was right. But in execution, the matrix framework resulted in more and, ultimately, too many meetings, overlapping dialogues, and bad compromises. So much for the matrix of responsibilities experiment. The reality for a leader is simple: someone has to make the final call; someone has to be accountable.

No structure is perfect. There is no one-size-fits all solution to the decision-making structure. Some preferences are national. In the USA and Canada the top-down decision-making approach is familiar and well understood. In the Netherlands it is not. More often choices are made collectively in a spirit of determining what is best for the group. Decisions are by consensus among the team so that accountability is collective. There are no Big Winners. But no Big Losers either.

As with so many questions today, the answer probably is having the flexibility and willingness to adopt whichever approach works best at any given time under any given sets of circumstances.

Nothing is written in stone! No Moses with his Ten Commandments!

CEO Message 85
STILL TRYING TO PLEASE EVERYONE?

Well, it cannot be done. No matter what you do, no matter how you try, you cannot make everyone happy. You just can't. You will drive yourself crazy if you think it's achievable.

Do what you think is right. To be liked is easily given or received; respect is much different and must be earned. If you go too far trying to please, you will end up frustrated or with hurt feelings; others will not be happy and will initially react poorly, but this generally fades over time. The facts always come to the surface; however it is you who is left to look in the mirror.

A Digression by Way of Example

It is Thursday morning and I'm in for a long day at work. I am not happy with the things that were left unfinished last night. That alone puts me in a bad mood since I know that two of my deadlines are going to get missed. I want to blow off some steam, bitch and moan but know that this will not do much and will not really make me feel any better.

God how I want to be a crazy teenager again!

But I'm a decent guy and instead of having a tantrum I play nice and end up placating and pleasing the very person who has let me down. "How are you? Did you have a pleasant evening? Dog walk was okay this morning?" This goes on for some time. The point is, I am unhappy with yesterday's performance. But I keep grinning.

This pleasing approach sounds nice. Remember that chestnut about "catching more flies with honey than vinegar"? Good advice if you're catching flies, but not so effective if you're leading a company. The problem with that approach is that it creates the wrong incentive and has just as good a chance of permitting a repeat of yesterday's unacceptable performance! *Why* I did that was a puzzle but it was not good leadership and I should have known better. What I should have said was this: "Yesterday was bad and here's why." Have a specific list of points about who failed and how, and why the system broke down. The key feature is that we face up to our mistakes and get it done right today.

No More Mr. Nice Guy!

Straight up and direct. No pleasing! To err is human. To err repeatedly is guillotine time.

Trade offs with people you work with are always a challenge. You need to be close but at the same time keep some distance. I have tried to buy time with people because I did not want to deal with a situation right then and there. It has to be done so I am not saying procrastinate. I'm saying find the right time and soon. How much depends on the situation and how well you can read the people involved.

CEO Message 219
GET BACK TO ME ON THIS!

Want to make things simpler for you and me? Looking for ways to save time and money? Best thing is ask for something in a clear and concise manner. Be specific. Always say the date and time you need something. The most important is when you have finished something. Complete the task, then go back and confirm that it's done.

Close the loop. Good execution. It builds confidence.

CEO Message 105
DETAILS

We've talked a lot about execution and how it makes a real difference with the success of any business. The right strategy, tactics, resources, and timing are the common factors that impact execution. The leadership qualities of agility and flexibility are at the cutting edge. So where do the details come into play? Focus! You need to see, act, and be relentless on the details. An execution of a good plan can only happen if all the details are looked after.

In retail banking—in all retailing for that matter—it can be summed up as *retail is detail*. Little things make the difference for a great performance.

For customers it's the "wow!" experience.

CEO Message 12
SLOW DOWN AND DO IT FASTER

There is a story that Ernest Hemingway, at the end of the day, would stop writing in the middle of a sentence. The idea was that he could much more easily pick up the thread of his sentence the next day.

Sometimes doing something right takes too long and sometimes doing things too fast means you can't get it right. A good manager knows that he has to find the right balance between doing something fast and doing it right the first time. At the end of the day, if we are going to simplify and keep our cost down, this is probably the most difficult challenge you will face.

An Explanatory Digression

Let's say I am dealing with a new product or implementing some new services or initiatives. I am tasked with creating a blueprint of business specifications. Okay, whatever needs doing from a project basis, identify the business requirements quickly, write them down and in very short order on your first draft. By end of day it may be eighty or ninety percent right. Have this reviewed by the people on your team to get critical early feedback and input. That way, when you revisit the next morning, you can easily and precisely finish the last ten or twenty percent of the business specifications as quickly as possible.

When that is done, off it goes to operations or marketing and whoever else is involved. You need to budget enough time to put those plans in place because they do require the selection and allocation of the correct resources at the right period of time.

So if you want to shrink your implémentation horizon and be both fast off the mark and build a quality organization at record speed, you have to practice finding the right balance between slowing down and doing it faster.

Coordination is key. There is no magic bullet. No two companies do it the same way or have found a magic formula. Keeping the overall business objective in mind is the best method that can be used to focus the effort.

———◁○▷———

For the Culture-Driven Leader It's Not the What; It's the How

Effective leaders know that many times they must ask others to do difficult or unpleasant tasks; the most effective leaders measure the tone and how they set the direction of the request that appeals to the rational response.

An emotional response tends to be defensive, especially if it's in response to a perceived threat. Defensive action separates the person from the desired goal. An appeal that produces a rational decision preserves that commitment.

That you clearly understand and feel the difficulty or unpleasantness as the leader and share it across the board will ensure the necessary result is achieved. In developing the skills we use for dealing with difficult situations, let's focus on the *how* as much as we focus on the *what*.

It is ironic that we talk a lot about the *what* but the success of most decisions rests on the *how*. It's a good subject to consider.

Remember the story about telling someone with no carpentry skills or knowledge to put up a fence? That's the *what*. But without a hammer and nails they don't have the *how*. That creates tension and resentment. It's also a huge distraction from achieving the goal and increases the likelihood that even if the task is done it could be done wrong. If you focus forward on the *how* of how the work needs to get done, however, everyone will pick up on that focus and become immediately invested in the process, resulting in a lot less friction generated.

Chasing That Bottom Line

I know managers who trust everyone to trundle off to figure it out for themselves.

Don't get me wrong: trusting initiative is hugely important. Initiative is an important component of innovation, as is discipline. But you need a leader in the room to clearly define the problem or task that needs to be solved and the outline for achieving it. "Let's do this and here is how I think we should handle it." That way, at the very least you know that the task will get done. If someone comes back and says, "I can take two steps off this process and here's how ..." well, that's innovation. And now you *all know* what the innovation is, how it came to be, and how it will work.

Of course, results are the bottom line. But routinely overlooked by too many managers is the critical question how it gets accomplished. The *how* of the process also speaks to the way everyone works together as a team. If the coordination is good, you can get the results you want efficiently. It makes success reliable and repeatable, and further strengthens the team's ability and capacity to perform.

You have the tools you need to build that fence today!

CEO Message 80
JUST DO IT RIGHT

It was getting late. Everyone wanted to get the meeting over with and finally I said: "Look, let's just get this project underway. Everyone is expecting us to move forward so we will figure the rest out later."

Have I said that we all make mistakes? Well, that was mine. And it was huge.

Conventional business thinking suggests that execution is more important than strategy. Basically, it doesn't matter why or how something is done as long as, in the end, it gets done.

There is limited truth to that. Or rather, it's true but it doesn't go far enough. It's like always hitting deadlines. In business, the job has to get done. But what really matters, and this is known and understood by the successful leader, is getting it done *right*. That means creating a working environment where the probabilities of success are maximized in both the long and short terms. It is not enough to succeed once. You want to succeed over and over and over. The alternative is like saying that every time you need a wheel you have to go to the trouble of inventing one.

The mistake I made? I was impatient and frustrated, so I hastily decided we could improvise a strategy after the decision was made to move forward.

Strategy is the mechanism for reducing the overall cost of success and is a key factor in getting a job done right. It is hugely important. It has to be a part—a critical component—of any job. It cannot be improvised or imposed onto a job.

But strategy is not just a plan. It can be a state of mind inside the culture of your business that can be relied upon again and again to produce the right results.

CEO Message 217
SPEED IS KEY TO EXECUTION

"Time is money!"

Who hasn't heard that, right? Well, it's true. One and done, man. We need to do things right. But they need to be done efficiently and in a timely fashion. When you are looking at ways to cut costs—and no great manager should ever not be looking at ways to reduce costs—how often are you looking at speed? The difference between what is great and what is okay execution is generally the speed of solving issues

Maintaining a sense of urgency is important. Urgency, not panic—huge difference. Urgency is what keeps the team focused. Panic is what happens when the wings come off the plane. Always keep your foot gently on the accelerator. Apply the right pressure to move things forward. You want to slide? Go to the park. Otherwise, keep it moving and make sure it's done right.

The Three Rs
Right place, right time, with the right answer. Speed is a sense of urgency and a willingness to make something work better. Identify what is not working and put a fix in fast. Set realistic but clear deadlines. And reinforce them.

It's a *how* that makes a huge difference.

CEO Message 26
DISCIPLINE AND PEOPLE
I'm watching the news and it seems yet another Middle Eastern dictatorship has fallen to an outbreak of democracy. It makes me think of business.

Let's face it: most business models *can* work—just like most governments *can* work. The question becomes, what is ultimately meant by *work*? And for how long? If all that matters to you as president, or business leader, is the end result—let's say a stable society, for instance—it may not matter whether your country operates as a democracy or an authoritarian regime. You've got your mandate: stability. So whatever gets the job done, right? In fact, that's the way some CEOs like to run their companies.

But it does make a huge difference to the individual citizen whose liberties are being crushed trying to "just get it done." Just ask the Egyptians or the Libyans or the Tunisians!

Finding the Right Combination

Long-term success (and what other kind matters?) does depend on how, and how well, the business is conducted or managed. This brings to mind two issues: discipline and creativity. Or, authoritarianism versus anarchy.

When it comes to getting the result you want at the time you want it, I seek out people who share a combination of the following characteristics: an entrepreneurial or opportunistic perspective and outlook, creativity, passion, and discipline. These are the agents of change who will have the flexibility you need—people that bring the intuitive flexibility required to get the job done right. You need people who can enthusiastically embrace a sense of urgency combined with a taste for winning. Of the four, discipline is the trickiest. How many of us have had million-dollar ideas? Probably more than one. Okay, how many of us have actually made a million dollars? Exactly.

In my experience the corporate environment and its structure can be responsible for, at most, twenty percent of the overall discipline of the business—not that much. Rules cannot make people believe and excel. Rules can only compel compliance. But I have been in businesses where rules and structure prevail. The ratio can become inversely proportional: the more corporate discipline the lower personal discipline.

rock then ... what? 29I

I run a business, not a reform school. I want creative and passionate people who can focus and who can self-motivate. Those who bring their own discipline to the task are the ones who are that much freer to take advantage of a creative and supportive corporate environment.

Is it a bit schizophrenic to be creative and disciplined at the same time? Some find it so. They are the ones who tend to drop out. From my perspective, no loss. The drones. Easily replaced. The creative person, on the one hand, is comfortable with chaos and is ever on the lookout for new opportunities or ideas. On the other hand, without the discipline required to put a frame around a new idea, what do you have? Air. An empty abstraction. Discipline is what restrains the centrifugal force of chaos. As I said, think of discipline as the frame around the picture: it holds the picture together and allows you to see the scene as a whole.

It's catching and holding onto the tail of a tiger! Chaos requires a leader to use deductive as well as inductive logic, the same way a person may be ambidextrous. Both hands!

Positive versus Negative Frustration

At ING Direct head office, we used a disciplined control approach but we encouraged a flexible approach at the business unit level. This structural tension was what I like to call positively frustrating but highly effective. Frustration can be good because it focuses the mind on the task at hand—the process—and is a springboard for innovation. Frustration is bad when nothing in the structure of management allows the breakthroughs to surface and take shape. Positive frustration keeps people on their toes. It keeps them always guessing.

So whatever you think about execution—not just the getting it done but the *how* of how it gets done—understand not only what you are doing but also what is being done to you. It's always a feedback loop. Acting and acted upon. The difference will help you figure out how to get the job done.

Keep in mind too that people are not robots that can be programmed to obey. We are all about doing things in a way that makes sense to us. Again, this is how and when company culture comes into play and why it plays such a critical role in business. Company culture dictates the way people become oriented and organized within a system and how they are expected to act. If it's easy to adapt to a culture then it's going to function better, and the ability to execute becomes much easier.

Lots of imposed rules and regulations generally require a lot of top-down reinforcement and pressure to conform. It can be—and usually is—a complete waste of leadership energy and resources. A rule-based business is not a business with a disciplined culture. When your company's discipline and its business culture feel natural to everyone, however, it's a habit.

CEO Message 39
ASKING FOR THE IMPOSSIBLE ... AND THEN SOME

What does it mean to set goals? For yourself and your team?

At ING Direct, we set very high corporate targets. Back in 2002, for instance, it was simple: we would double deposits at the bank.

Whew! Are you serious? That's nuts.

For me, the rush was challenging my team to a goal that seemed impossible!

It'll never happen, we were told. I suppose there were even a few team members who may have doubted my sanity. But "Let's prove them wrong!" became our battle cry. It was our Rock then Roll gesture to the marketplace: tell us it can't be done and we'll do it. And on an even larger scale!

It required teamwork, conviction, and commitment. At the end of the day, however, you realize a successful achievement gives everyone the personal satisfaction that we are as good as we think we are, and we can really make a difference when we can bring a worthwhile goal to realization. But it could not have happened on energy and passion alone. We needed that strategy and a commitment from every team member to stay focused. This type of *stretch goal* should appeal to any leader or entrepreneur. In fact, a great manager should always be thinking of challenges to keep the team in shape.

Rock then Roll, baby! The sky's the limit!

Setting Personal Goals

At the same time all this was going on, I asked each and every member of our growing team to set five personal goals for himself which would help us collectively achieve our corporate targets.

Three of the five goals were to be quantitative in scope and two qualitative; they should clearly identify what results you would like to achieve over and above your job description or what your basic function on the team is. I wanted each associate to feel personally invested in his or her own personal growth. That would very much improve the likelihood of reaching our corporate target goals.

I recommended that associates discuss the progress they were making on a quarterly basis with our managers to make sure they were on track and not faced with any surprises at the end of the year.

To make sure the personal goals fit with our corporate results, we took a percentage of our corporate results achieved and compared that percentage to the achievement of personal goals. The philosophy was to see what we as a team could accomplish, and then use that percentage to measure our individual accomplishments. This created a uniform system for measuring performance throughout the company, irrespective of job description.

The target was 100 percent. The threshold for receiving a bonus corporately was 75 percent and the maximum was 125 percent.

The point is: don't establish goals you know your team can reach. Set the bar where you know they cannot go and then ask them to go there.

If you are a real leader, they will try.

CEO Message 201
HOW TO STAY FOCUSED ON PRIORITIES

As any business grows, it's inevitable that we all lose touch with our own as well as our company's priorities. After all, priorities change. But what you should never lose touch with are the values that you embraced from the beginning. This was my list that I shared with colleagues at ING Direct, but it will work anywhere, for anyone, at any time.

- Work smart.
- Collaborate and work as a team.
- Get the priorities right.

ZERO TOLERANCE

Earlier, I mentioned the impossible growth-goal we had set for ING Direct to double its deposits in one year. There is another factor in that equation that needs to be addressed: distraction.

When it comes to growth, expansion, or even a major change, it can be really difficult to focus on anything but that growth and higher profitability.

The challenge we faced was a hugely ambitious goal but that was not what concerned me. Nothing is more stimulating to me than an impossible challenge. No, my fear was not that it could not be done. My fear was that we could do it but only at the cost of our principles. The real danger was failing to maintain and/or jeopardizing quality. What if we doubled profits but, in so doing, lost our edge, and our customers soured on us and walked away? Win the battle but lose the war?

In a sense any growing business is tempting fate. The thinking can be, if you are growing too fast, just like when running too fast, you run the risk of a serious fall. It takes time to do things well and think them through, so the challenge for us was to prove that we could achieve growth at a fast pace and, at the same time, that we could maintain one hundred percent quality in the organization.

Growth Strategies

So we came up with a set of strategies to guide our thinking through the year. Think of them as our growth mantras:

- We needed to adopt an overall business attitude that was very conscious of being on guard, proactive, and always alert to situations that could be symptoms or signs of future problems;

- We would have to be super-vigilant when it came to pacing the resources: we could not afford to fall behind when it came to issues like staff, systems, applications, or processes procedures. We could not allow for sudden shortages or gaps. The right resources needed to be in place at the right pace of growth;
- We scheduled problem-modeling exercises to simulate situations where things could go wrong and worked on coming up with creative and efficient ways for dealing with those eventualities. (An excellent method for discovering how your business works is creating scenarios where it doesn't work and figuring out why.)

It was hard work. It was stomach-churning and exhilarating. And we succeeded.

When you set out to do the impossible, everything becomes possible.

―――――◄○►―――――

Culture-Driven Teamwork: You Can't Lead if No One Follows

We talk about teamwork but we don't always function like a team.

For instance, it is so interesting to examine how consistent the mindset is that judges successful leadership from the top down.

I wonder, what does a board of directors know about me that one of our café associates doesn't? The answer? Zilch. That associate knows what I do and how well I do it much better than any director does. Mostly what that director has is information summarized in reports.

The Feedback Hierarchy: Touch-points that Matter

Every CEO needs to know that their customers love the company, that they love what the company does, and hopefully that they respect the company's leadership.

Generally speaking, a leader gets some feedback filtered up and some kind of rough sense of what your customers think of you. You certainly know what your shareholders or your board thinks of you, and in the case of ING Direct, what our regulators thought as well. You have some touch points.

Interestingly, the one touchpoint that is routinely ignored is comprehensive feedback from the people and the employees that you work with. They're the ones that actually create the interface, after all—the twenty thousand moments of truth every day. They're the ones who actually run the company.

Why wouldn't the CEO, as a leader, then be responsible to say, I'm accountable to my fellow employees and I need their endorsement?

Are You a True Leader or Just a Title?

This may seem a roundabout introduction to teamwork.

But as a leader—as a CEO or manager or teacher or coach—you need to know just one thing from your team: will you follow me?

Just because you're on the horse and at the front of the parade, doesn't mean you're leading anything—it just says you're at the front. You need that commitment—that endorsement. Remember, as a leader you have one job: eliminate doubt. They are only saying two things: I commit to the mission; I commit to you. You need them to commit to you. As a leader, if you cannot eliminate doubt you have failed. You have not fulfilled the main plank of leadership.

A leader who does not have the full support and commitment of his team cannot eliminate doubt—he is the biggest source of doubt!

Chosen, Not Anointed; Privileged, Not Entitled

The reason why I can probably say this is because I believe, like most of us, that we're here by some divine grace. I do not know whether I will be here tomorrow. I hope I am. I earn it every day. And, I'm going to go home tonight and say, I've had a great day. I've added value. I'm going to ask the Lord to give me one more day tomorrow. And that's the way I hope the employees think about the culture we created. That's the way I owe it to the culture. I'm not anointed. I'm not bequeathed. I have no more right to anything in the company than *tomorrow*.

It's them—the team. Not me.

CEO Message 131
TEAMWORK

The most important aspect of teamwork is, no surprise here, working *as a team*, which means sacrificing individual priorities and accomplishments, and working hard to support the shortcomings of our fellow team members. More can be accomplished when working as a team; a team is a balance of strengths and weaknesses.

Look, we all hear about it: work hard and get ahead. That's great. Nothing wrong with success. But real leadership requires selfless commitments and a willingness to support others. The competition out there in the real world is fierce. So don't make a focus of your work criticizing fellow team members; support them with their challenges and struggles. So set a good example as a team player, and come up with ways of helping those you are working with by supporting them with their responsibilities and challenges, to do their part for the team.

You have to like the people you work with.

CEO Message II
OPEN FAUCETS

Good teamwork is a measurement of how well a company can execute its business model. Much is written about teamwork. To me, the critical components of effective teamwork are open communication and the free flow of ideas. Keep the taps open; let the water flow. That means welcoming suggestions from all levels and departments and receiving them with no strings attached.

I know what you're thinking: "Easier said than done."

However, we all operate like that with our close friends; wouldn't it be great if you could do this with your work colleagues as well. So just for today give it a try and see what response you get. It's a first step. You may be pleasantly surprised!

Nothing ventured, nothing gained. The actual level of effort required to build good relationships with a work team is both underestimated and not appreciated enough by most leaders. It takes time and a lot of practice. There will always be some risks and failures. In the next entry, I discuss a few.

But when it works, it's worth the effort.

CEO Message 60
BRING DOWN THE WALLS

The culture and the environment where you work are two important factors that determine success. Be attentive and alert to their nuances. It's like keeping the room constantly in tune to the ideal temperature.

Culture-Driven Teamwork: You Can't Lead if No One Follows

Trapped in Our Roles

Part of ING Direct's decision to bring down the walls at our offices was designed to enhance communications, to talk more casually to one another, and to limit hierarchical-based decision-making to a minimum.

We all have different roles and responsibilities. The problem is, we can find ourselves trapped in our respective roles; we can become complacent and complacency leads to redundant thinking. It's important to encourage a free flow of ideas, discussion, and debate up and down as well as left and right in your business.

The paradox, however, is that keeping the channels of communication open and free can create an incomprehensible buzz of undirected or conflicting chatter that actually limits and stifles creative thinking. The key is open but focused dialogue. Causal dress and a relaxed atmosphere, for instance, do not necessarily mean sloppy thinking or indifferent commitments.

If you understand the difference, it will lead to productive cooperation and excellent team morale.

CEO Message 3
THAT'S NOT MY JOB

It's normal for many of us to feel the need to focus on whatever our duties are and basically ignore everything else. After all, that's what they pay me to do, right? My job? The thinking is, if I do my job and everyone else does his or her job then everything will be all right.

Ghettos

I call it creating ghettos. You look at your desk and chair and the area immediately around it and decide that's where you live. Something happens in another area of work? Not my neighborhood. Not my problem.

To make things work smoothly, the approach and attitude to take is to be supportive. If someone is asked to do something, no matter how insignificant or small, or if it's in another work area, wouldn't it be better to just quickly lend a helping hand, and establish some good rapport? If something is wrong, wouldn't it be better to help fix it? Lending a hand is a key to teamwork and conveys an attitude of commitment and support. So next time you have the temptation to say, "It's not my job," try pitching in and lending a helping hand. You'll feel better for it and you will have made a difference today.

I know. Sounds like motherhood and apple pie.

It is amazing to me how quickly negative-boundary-type thinking creeps into a business. Size does impact this but if unchallenged it will take over. We would all be better off, and so would the business, if we made a commitment to look beyond the particular job and tasks and think in a broader way. Encourage others to make suggestions. Even better: ask others what they think. You might be pleasantly surprised.

You let more light into your yard when you lower the fences.

CEO Message 200
TEAMWORK AND DEADLINES

In everything we do, we have deadlines. Some are easily managed and some are one hundred-meter dashes in bare feet on a track of broken glass. There is a genuine need from the business to respect and honor deadlines. While deadlines need to be accurately established, every once in a while a deadline has to be reset. It should be reset with thought and care as to the impact on other parts of the business.

There is nothing more positive for morale than to know that a deadline has been met, that a project has been successfully completed, and the business has moved forward. We get a great sense of satisfaction when it happens. If you are responsible for a deadline, or have leadership on a project or a specific delivery, and for some reason that deadline cannot be met, you have a real obligation to not only explain it, but also find a way to lessen the impact on your colleagues and co-workers. A true measure of leadership is the commitment and respect that goes into meeting deadlines. The interconnection of overlapping deadlines is often forgotten. A delay here impacts another delay somewhere else in a business.

Are deadlines a high priority for you and your team? Rock your deadlines and you will be rolling it in!

CEO Message 20
REVIEW TIME

It is important that on a periodic but regular basis you and your associates review performance. One, discuss if you have met or exceeded the goals you had established for yourselves. Two, establish new goals for both yourself and your employees. But don't forget that in setting goals and laying out plans to meet those goals, we need to think about how we want to improve as human beings.

CEO Message III
THE ELASTIC FINISH LINE

Teamwork is crucial to any successful business.

The burden on a leader, however, is also to inspire.

Moving the Finish Line

At ING Direct, for instance, I knew that we were not going to convert every North American into a saver. But that was the goal. Reality tells you it won't happen; your leadership and inspiration, however, needs to communicate to your team that it *will* happen. And you need to task them to make it happen. Every team member has to be made to feel personally invested in your company's success.

If you set the bar of achievement too low you won't get the best out of people. You do not want to indoctrinate your team into the habits of mediocrity. You want them to achieve and reach the goal, absolutely. But you don't necessarily want them feel relief when they cross that finish line.

As a leader, you have to—creatively—keep moving the finish line.

If you ask the impossible, you break the rules and force team members to improvise. When they test their own limits people tend to excel. It is also a priceless laboratory for emerging leadership and innovation.

Call it creative disequilibrium.

CEO Message 317
IT'S A TWO-WAY STREET

We look for people to work and human beings show up.

The fact is, people are not robots with the capacity to focus obsessively on a problem or project to exclusion of all else. We are people. We have our own agendas. We come into every situation with our own baggage. As managers we are supposed to show sensitivity. We do that because a company's greatest investment is its people.

But investment is a two-way street.

Try this experiment. Look at yourself in the mirror. Ask yourself, what is my contribution to productivity? What am I doing to keep myself updated and informed?

Do I have anything that actually refreshes the base upon which my knowledge stands, or am I basically a Blackberry brain during the week who watches football all weekend?

Ask your boss or the members of your team in a polite way to do the same thing.

There Are Setbacks, Too

I'll be honest, there have been times over the years that as a manager and then CEO I have concluded that it's not a fair exchange. There were times when I felt that I had to waste *my time* basically teaching people how to do fundamental tasks, like reading, writing, and arithmetic. I asked people to write a page. They went out and got a consultant.

It was, and is, extremely frustrating.

Every day the bar gets set a little higher than the day before. That's business, right? That's life. Okay, so that means every day you have to be a bit better too. And so do you and you and you. We all do. How are you meeting that challenge? How are you inspiring your employees to meet the challenge?

Remember what Benjamin Franklin told the squabbling members of the Continental Congress? "If we don't hang together surely we will hang separately"?

Can you look each member of your team in the eye and say, "I am doing my best"? "I am making the best contribution I can make"?

The mirror don't lie, my friend.

CEO Message 180
VALUE THE IDEA

"Money never starts an idea; it is the idea that starts the money." —W.J. Cameron.

The greatest value for every organization is the people who bring new ideas and listen to the ideas of others. As a leader, you should always welcome employees up and down the organization to propose ideas, to invent, simplify, and improve.

As a CEO I encourage everyone to take part and share ideas with our managers, as well as taking advantage of whatever tools that might exist to make the process of submitting ideas simpler. We created a system called *The Innovation Pipeline.*

Employees are encouraged to submit ideas. Whether that idea is implemented or not, it receives careful and considered feedback. Ideas are not necessarily like shoes, where each one fits on only one foot. Sometimes ideas that may not be exactly quite right for one problem may be just the thing for another problem in some other areas that no one had ever thought of. Or maybe an idea is close enough that all it needs is some refinement.

As leader you need to be constantly alert to the streams of innovation that exist in your company. Employees at every level of your company are like the small tributaries that feed huge and powerful rivers.

A commandment at ING Direct was this: We will listen. We will invent. We will simplify.

CEO Message 76
FINDING THE FIT AS A TEAM

A value is only an aspiration if it is not practiced.

In building a team, the identification and agreement of values and team norms is important. Sometimes it takes time to find the right fit—the ones that will stick and be natural for the team. A leader can, however, start the process by identifying the non-value statements; the negatives are generally easier to identify and isolate than the positives. Most people can more easily tell you why they dislike something than why they like it, right?

Finding and identifying the key attitudes that you clearly do not want in your workplace is a valuable start. This can be an early warning bell, too, for identifying the individuals who will not fit. Deal with them first.

Nothing is more poisonous to the morale of a good team than endless challenges. Remember, questioning the goals or processes is not the same thing as challenging them. The former speeds you to your goal while the latter slows you down and takes you away from it. The values that get created and practiced as a result of good team-building will endure and begin to strengthen the performance of the whole team, and yes, you as leader also!

CEO Message 112
POOR PERFORMANCE

Honest assessment of performance and the right attitude needs to take place if teamwork is to happen. As a manager, you cannot afford to carry poor performers. You cannot make exceptions.

Breaking it Down

Our mantra at ING Direct was that execution is the hallmark of our success. We have emphasized teamwork as one of our key corporate values.

Even so, and especially as we confronted rapid growth, we stumbled. It's inevitable. Often times it was the left hand having difficulty working with the right hand, primarily due to lack of communication, misunderstandings and a lack of attention to detail and process.

As a company matures, it is easy to lose focus. You feel that you need to rein the chaos in.

Most managers tend to resolve problems by applying new or revised policies and procedures. Always adding layer upon layer. Truth is, a positive spirit and expressions of goodwill might be all that is really needed to resolve these gaps and allow for better collaboration and a more fruitful working environment.

Your answer may be breaking down traditional business roles.

Finding a New Wardrobe

Most managers have difficulty being part of a team that lacks traditional roles, mandates, and channels of authority. But most situations that arise in business can be better resolved through flexible and fluid responses. What you want to do from a problem-solving framework is remove what can be imposing or intimidating layers of bureaucratic protocol.

In philosophy the term is Ockham's razor. Simply put, it means having a bias towards the simplest answer or explanation. Moving from following or supporting to taking initiative should be as easy as switching a jacket you are wearing.

Ideally, as a leader or CEO you will have many opportunities to practice switching jackets seamlessly and moving between supporting and seizing an initiative, when the situation calls for it.

The chance to switch an advertising campaign for a new one, for instance, is risky. But if it's simpler and resonates better, do it. The thinking is, the current campaign is good enough so let's wait until it runs out. Bad move.

CEO Message 58
SITUATIONAL LOYALTY

A great piece of the folklore that captures the essence of situational loyalty is: "Remember who brought you to the party. That is the one you should go home with."

The days of blind loyalty to companies, people, or an organization are gone. Nothing is forever and the new loyalty is generally limited to a specific goal or cause. People and companies change so much and in so many ways that it makes building strong bonds very difficult, maybe impossible. That does not mean that loyalty is irrelevant. What it means is, we have to rethink—as leaders—what loyalty means. Loyalty used to mean a job for life. A leader could depend on that. Now it means *this* job until I find a *better* job. The objective view gets lost in subjective feelings. We're not sworn blood brothers. All that had happened was a job change. Nothing personal, right?

Personal loyalty is hard to establish and requires a lot of effort. Nothing can be taken for granted.

CEO Message 8
A TITLE IS JUST A TITLE UNLESS YOU'VE EARNED IT

"So, what do you do?"

It's a familiar question at any gathering. What the question means is, who are you? We live in a world where what you do is code for who you are.

It isn't true. Not by a long shot. But we tend to live in shorthand.

"You can be a jack of all things but you better know how to do something."
—AK

A title is what we have to describe what we do in an organization—the particular rung we occupy in the great vertical hierarchy. A title describes the role. That's it. The value of the role comes from the sum total of all that knowledge, ability and hard work you have put in along the way. Sure, we should respect lines of communication. For decision-making purposes it's important.

From the standpoint of effective teamwork, however,

titles are worthless. What you are looking for is the ability to influence decisions and actions.

When in Rome

There is a common practice in many Dutch companies, for example, that decision-making is organized on a consensus *polder* basis with a lot of people involved and having maximum input on a certain issue. A final consensus decision is then made, but there is always some period of time after the decision is made to further reflect on the merits of the decision. It's the so-called "does the decision stick?" interlude. To managers unfamiliar with the technique, it can be a little frustrating. But the value to morale is priceless. Simply, it allows everyone to feel fully vested in the process. It allows them to make a true commitment to the final outcome or result.

Everyone will feel inspired to action all along the way. We all share in a success, but likewise we all take a share of the blame if it fails. But that is a valuable learning tool.

Communal- or company-based decision-making is like a neighborhood watch. Your house is much safer being monitored by a thousand sets of eyes, not just one.

The tricky part, of course, is being clear about what and when you seek consensus. Not every decision merits such technique. Basically, seek consensus on issues whose outcome has interest to the broadest cross-section of your company.

When Is It Right for You?

It would be ludicrous to poll your team on choices for the expensive new artwork in your renovated private office. That would, and should, inspire a rebellion. However, if you need to impose draconian cost savings in the company, why not seek suggestions from your employees and task them with making final recommendations? You may be surprised what happens.

It is an important point to make clear that when a decision has to be made, it will be made. You need to be clear about what constitutes making a decision. Frankly, job titles by themselves should very seldom play a role in any decision. Rank may have its privileges but at the end of the day your company will not be better or worse for it. What will make the difference is *what* decision is made—not who made it.

We all have our talents and areas of expertise. A job title is like a label on a box. The label tells you what is inside but you won't really know until you open it up. As a manager or leader, you must be aware that there are people all around you who may have talents and expertise even they are unaware of. They may be like boxes with no labels.

A wise leader looks for raw talent. The secret is to focus on the work you are doing—the culture-driven goal—and not the title. Be observant to the not-so-obvious. Read their stories!

CEO Message 56
THE PROTOCOL LIST

As ING Direct continued to grow, I created a list of norms that I wanted to be a part of the air we breathed. Here is the list to date:

- Simplicity
- You must know and exhibit the Corporate Values
- You must know and explain the brand values
- You must understand the Code of Ethics
- You must understand the hiring, probation, and bonus policy

- You should achieve the corporate and personal goals
- No one can just say "No"
- Performance is the top goal for both ING Direct and each employee
- No cell phones, laptops; know the security structure and values
- Cost centers in budget, on time for managers
- The CEO monthly report must be on time and the source of all official numbers
- Keep private and corporate activities separate and transparent
- We build an "NCL" (not customer list) for all banned individuals
- The originator of a document is required to store it
- Clean desk policy—get a clue from the CEO's desk at the end of the day
- No Surprises—tell it immediately; tell it to everyone; tell it often

CEO Message 281
MUDDY RUT-BASED THINKING

It's amazing how we can let ourselves slip into conventional habits or patterns and then are surprised to discover the impact they have on thinking. None of us are immune. We all have our comfort zones.

But maybe you want to escape that comfort zone and drop a few standard conventions; try something new.

Are You Too Soft in Your Comfort Zone?

As you know, at ING Direct we had no titles, no offices. Casual attire if you wanted. We tried holding meetings at a café or work on a park bench—a real departure from the industry standard, and not the ideal work environment for everyone.

But ask yourself, how come? Sure, doing it different is a challenge. But changing the *what you do* can mean changing the *how you do it*. If you really want to position yourself as a company that is something different in the marketplace, don't you actually have to be different?

I figured it was worth a try. What did we have to lose? Or, look at it this way: if you aren't willing to lose, do you deserve to win?

Method in the Madness

Like any principle, it sounds simple. No offices. No titles. Great. Blah blah blah. It's putting principles into practice that separates a manager from a leader.

You know how I feel about titles. They get in the way. Okay, that was a pragmatic lesson I learned after many years of corporate life. Titles get in the way of effective management. Then why do we still cling to them so desperately? It's madness. So why not get rid of offices, too?

What else did we do that didn't work?

I wanted to drop the *employee* label and start referring to everyone as *associates*. As I have asked before in a similar context, was it a game changer? No, but it did make a difference. True, no one had forgotten what salary bands we had or what our basic job descriptions and responsibilities were. It isn't as if my associates suddenly didn't know who I was when I walked in the door. We all understand who we were and what we were hired to do. What dropping the titles meant was that everyone was working together. It meant finding people outside the traditional decision-making hierarchy who showed real skills and talent; it meant a focus on who could make something happen as opposed to who had the authority to make it happen.

A Title is Like Heavy Luggage. You Can Get Farther by Traveling Lighter

Years ago I worked in the development division of a large bank. To get a project approved and funded, I was promoted to vice president. Basically, all the promotion meant was that the bank took the project seriously enough to have a prestige title attached to it. I took the bait, as they say, hook, line, and sinker. I soon found myself mentioning my title more often. "As vice president," I would say, "I suggest we do the following."

What I meant, of course, was that my suggestion should be accepted not because it was the best idea but because my title was a source of power. My title was the leverage, not the value or integrity of the idea.

Don't allow yourself to step onto the wrong scale. What are you measuring as a leader? Your own weight as defined by your title? Or the heft of a really great idea or solution? Trust me, it is an easy trap to fall into. To a degree we are all peacocks. We all want to display our feathers—the glorious rainbow of our brilliance. It's ego. Let it go. Ego and the title are like the con man who gets the mark to look away and switch his focus.

It took me ten long years to try to unlearn the title habit. Best thing to do is think of a title as a convenient way for looking someone up in a company directory. And that's it.

CEO Message 33
WORKING TOGETHER

Synergy is like watering a plant, you can pour water over the whole plant but it's the roots that absorb the water.

Sounds a bit spiritual and, possibly, a bit out there, but you have to really like someone to work well together. People who have interviewed me often seem surprised that I insist that a huge factor in being a great leader is the ability to like people. I find their surprise, on the other hand, illuminating. I like what I do. But how could I like what I do if I didn't like the people I do it with?

You can read all the management books you want. Study all the charts or graphs or case studies that attempt to "quantify" the business relationship. Why? Why deliberately complicate a simple reality?

It's people who walk through the front door of your business, not machines.

CEO Message 2
SAYING "NO"

One of the working principles at ING Direct was that no one had the right to say no. If something is up for discussion or a new policy is being considered or you simply have a suggestion about how you think things might work better, none of the managers can simply say no. They have to provide that person with a reason, an explanation, or even an alternative. The purpose of this is to acknowledge the value and intent of anyone making a suggestion or wanting to do things better, and that there is an acknowledgement and a commitment to participate in finding the best solution possible.

It didn't matter what one's rank was: it was understanding the ING Direct way of doing things, making sure that the solution we adopt is the best solution. It's not important who has ownership of that solution, or who invented it, or who implemented it. What was important was that together we came up with the best solution. For me as a CEO, the practical advantage of having multiple channels for input to solutions was that no one ever knows where the next Big Idea will come from. So why create unnecessarily narrow channels in your organization that choke off new or innovative thinking?

The obvious risk is confusing a dynamic conversation about solutions with a challenge to authority. "I said No!" It's the easiest power tool for a leader. But it is destructive and in a business culture it's toxic. Pushing against the easy use of *no* is an exciting opportunity to change and open up possibilities. A premature or preemptive "no" kills curiosity, creates resentments, and drains interest and investment in the culture very quickly.

CEO Message 17
CHAMPIONS

Every business needs a leader. Every business position needs an advocate.

Champions are your advocates.

Truth is, if you are a leader, you are a champion.

But you cannot do it alone. You will need more champions to move a business forward. Find them, appoint them, and promote them to the business and to the customers so they know you are committed to making something happen. Don't look for your champions in the obvious places. Leaders can emerge from unexpected places at unusual moments and circumstances.

One leader that stood out at ING Direct was the head of IT. He was a champion because he continually looked for ways to improve the business. He came up with new ideas, but more importantly he followed through to see if they could be improved or how they could be used. A champion that ends up being the "go to" guy is invaluable on any team.

Are you seeking out ideas from your team or your associates? Do they feel free to share ideas or innovations with you? If they are heard, will their ideas or innovations be acted on or implemented?

Business is no longer a top-down environment built on four solid pillars. We live in a world of open architectures where ideas fly and the real estate under our feet shifts and shakes. No CEO can feel safe standing still.

You always need to be looking for the leaders of the future. Find and nurture your corporate champions. No leader is universal, right? Your future leaders are your richest assets.

Diamonds in the Rough

Being a champion means: leading, creating energy, coming up with ideas, and making sure that projects and implementations get done on time. Champions are leading individuals who can take on multi-functional, multi-dimensional projects, which have implications to the culture and performance of your business.

For instance, one time we tasked employees to find one thousand ways to eliminate paper. Another time the problem was how to shift to electronics for efficiency, productivity, and cost savings. A champion has to spark and try out ideas, marshal initiatives and implement them for concrete results. These results—irrespective of where they come from—energize the whole management process.

The idea is to create a wave of energy and enthusiasm in order to support two key drivers of our business model: the customer experience and the efficiency of our operation.

Timing is everything and good champions, like good planners, know how to organize the sequence of events and lay out action plans on a day-to-day basis to achieve the end objective.

Make it your priority to inspire your associates to step forward and champion a specific initiative. Nothing is more satisfying than imagining and achieving. And for you as your company's leader, nothing is more valuable than associates who are both inspired to achieve and have the skill sets to make that happen.

CEO Message 38
GIVE AND TAKE

As CEO, I always thought that a great way to kick off a new year was to think about how to create positive energy in the work environment by give and take. What are always welcome from a management perspective are not only ideas but also the openness and ease in which ideas and suggestions are made. It was a key ingredient to executing the best plan. It still is.

It takes a bit of courage to make suggestions and one needs to feel free to make those suggestions irrespective of whether you are in charge of that department or function; as long as you are an associate and on the team, any ideas or aspects of the business should be put forward, or, as we sometimes say, "no idea is too small or too big."

On the receiving side, any suggestion or idea requires a degree of openness and willingness to consider other aspects; so whether or not you are responsible for an area or are the originator of an idea, it's really not as important as being receptive and objective about evaluating suggestions and ideas from colleagues. Your enthusiasm in making and receiving suggestions is a key characteristic of a good leader and manager. If we can give and take suggestions and ideas in a direct and simple manner then we have found another way of truly empowering our business model.

Getting the Best From Your Team? Or From You?

All leaders struggle to get the best from their team.

I have struggled to win the trust of my teams. It was my primary responsibility. It's a challenge in today's business environment to know how few tools we have to get this done well. Every day the landscape becomes more diverse and complex and there seem to be fewer shared ideas and values to bring a team together.

For a leader, perhaps the hardest lesson to learn is that to get the best from your team you have to be willing to constantly

> "A house doesn't get dusty overnight. Problems in any business accumulate day to day." —AK

revise and refresh your own leadership skills and approaches. We do not live in a "one size fits all" world anymore.

I believe this is the reason that few leaders last very long in their jobs and that the turnover today is greater than ever.

How does a leader today immunize herself against premature retirement? What is key to staying in the game as a leader? You just Rock and then Roll. No timeline. Could be short or long. The idea here is, once you start talking about leaving something, you are already near the door. If you talk about retirement you are already near the exit. How long you run is never as important as doing something meaningful.

Length is just length.

CEO Message 115
THE SECRET FORMULA

In looking at the direct banking model that we started at ING Direct, many analysts and managers looked almost exclusively at the quantitative aspects, the high-volume and low-margins, and wondered how we could deliver. However, the real strength was in our execution. It was the strength of our brand and its reputation in our customer's mind.

Your Team Drives the Train

Customers built that positive energy by what they heard, saw, and read from our ING Direct associates. And our associates' morale was the spark plug that got everything going. Without that positive morale, freedom, enthusiasm, and excitement generated by our employees, positive energy would not have translated to the customers. Without that positive trickle down we would have lost our word-of-mouth, our referrals, and the positive impression the customers got from the brand.

The secret formula is the positive energy and enthusiasm generated by your employees. From this, our management challenge was clear: as we grew and evolved, how do we maintain that positive enthusiasm and high level of morale measured by both customer and employee satisfaction? How do we basically find and foster the leadership opportunities to make this happen consistently?

——◄◦►——

How to Keep the Rock Rolling: The takeaways

- Hiring a team should be like casting a play.
- If you want to change the way your business is done, don't hire the same familiar faces to do it.
- Great leadership is about managing expectations.
- A manager needs to strike a balance between the quantitative—the structured—and the qualitative—the creative.
- Study your enemy. The goal is to always find ways to be better than the competition.
- No management style is equally effective in all situations.
- When in doubt, don't look for a miracle. Step back. Break it down.
- If you want the best from your team, they have to see you giving it your best.

CHAPTER 5

ROCK THEN ROLL: A LIFETIME JOURNEY?

Or Journey of a Lifetime

Do What You Like. Like What You Do

In my experience I have found that the people I want working with or for me and the people who do the best work are the ones who take their principles home with them.

If you work in a bakery, it won't help if you are allergic to flour; as a flight attendant, you cannot have a fear of flying. I worked in a bank. I wanted people who, in their daily lives, were good with their money. Folks that had good credit and good financial health. It's critical if you work with money. The people who work at ING Direct become good role models in their neighborhood and community. I didn't ask them to proselytize or preach the Orange message. I didn't ask them to wear sandwich boards up and down their street. Truth is, I didn't need to. Our employees are our most effective marketing tool. They believe. Don't we all admire people who lead by example?

At ING Direct, we didn't have one leader. We had thousands.

Sure, having employees who drank the Koolaid was great branding exposure. But you have to be authentic. You can't fake it.

True success only comes with doing what you really like and what you believe in. Rock then Roll!

———◦———

CEO Message 81
YOU HAVE TO LOVE BREAD

Any business, especially a business model like ING Direct, required us to have a product or service that was remarkable. In the eyes of the customer, this definition needs to be proven. The first thing we needed to do was our due diligence. We had to be confident and comfortable that we were delivering a product that was remarkable, had the value we were promoting, and that the customer believed in it—it had to walk the talk.

Baking Bread, My Friend!

So what does this have to do with bread?

A good baker loves his product and eats his own bread; it is the most tangible acceptance you can find. I tasked our people to do the same thing at ING Direct with our Orange products:

Do What You Like. Like What You Do

- We need to like the product to use it ourselves and recommend it to our friends and family.
- We need to work with the product on a regular basis to reaffirm our conviction that the product is valuable and that we are continuing to walk the talk.
- We need to identify with our customers.

As a leader, you need to create a like-minded checklist for your product or service. By talking about and using the product we feel connected, and this is the best thing to help us gauge if we are still on track or whether we are straying from our overall goal, which is to sell a very successful, remarkable product.

Maybe you don't need to bleed orange or evangelize anything, but you do have to be committed and belong to the program. Don't let anyone fool you into thinking that it does not count. It does. Eat the bread and drink the wine.

CEO Message 62
A NEW BEGINNING

We all need our own mirror. It's about looking at yourself in that mirror and being absolutely honest about what and who you see.

Reflecting on your performance should be a regular feature of your personal business profile. The answers to who you are as a leader are built into the questions you are willing to test your own performance to.

Ask yourself, have I measured up to my own standards? Have I identified where I want to improve? Am I sure of the why and the how in dealing with those shortcomings?

Facing Adversity

Our ability to change is closely linked to being objective in our assessment. While it may be painful, the rewards of moving forward are much greater.

Personal potential can truly grow when there is a setback. I am sure there have been times when you have made both a clear decision to change and a commitment to move forward

"The journey is ninety-nine percent of the reward." —AK

corporately and personally. Use that introspection to move forward. Learning as much as you can about yourself is a major step in the right direction.

We all spend so much time in business plans and projections that the months—our months—become as flat and meaningless as a series of columns on a spreadsheet. It's life, and every day counts. Waste not one day. If something feels wrong then stop. If it feels right, charge ahead. Remember: it's got to count in your life.

CEO Message 145
WELLNESS IN ACTION

We all want to change our life for the better. There are many ways to get there, but the best way is to set new expectations that follow a number of easy steps. Start every day—while brushing your teeth—with setting a few daily goals. Walk a bit more, eat a little less, buy a little less, breathe a little more deeply, feel a bit more positive about you being in control, reflect on yesterday's successes. Good savers pay themselves first because saving is a priority. Make yourself a priority, put wellness into action.

I fail with this most days but go to bed every night committed to trying again at sunrise.

CEO Message 77
ENERGY

Energy cannot be expended endlessly. Take a break. Get refreshed. Lift your spirits. Keeping positive energy in a management team is a clear example of how well you can judge the power of the team. Good leaders set an example; do not automatically reward the marathon workaholic. It's not who works the hardest or the longest hours; it's who works the best!

Another balancing act: work hard, play hard, and rest hard.

CEO Message 171
HERE AND NOW

To really be authentic, one needs to live for the moment; all that is past, is past. The future is not here yet. You are alive only now. A sense of awareness is necessary to see the endless potential in the now. To lead—to be powerful—is to master this concept. We all think a lot about yesterday, and worry, even try to control, tomorrow. It gets in the way and distorts our view with fear and wants, and makes us see life, not as it is, but as we wish it to be. To be authentic is to be naturally rooted in the here and now. It makes us as a human being, real.

If you ride a motorcycle then you know what it is that gets you connected to the wheels and the road. The movement is real and in the moment.

Find it.

—◁○▷—

Personal Growth: Understanding the Journey You Are On

Has today mattered?

This is a touchy question for all of us, but for once we can take a simple approach and reflect briefly, as we do in the morning when we figure out what we are going to do today, and at the end of the day when we acknowledge what we've accomplished. Then we can count our blessings and resolve to make things better.

The first question is, did today matter for you? Have you done your best, have you made some progress, have you learned something today, have you made a contribution? Is there something today that you had to get done where you made a difference, and that difference was of value to yourself and to those you work with?

We've talked about a workout of the mind, body, and spirit and the need to be refreshed. Let us also not forget that our spirit needs to be refreshed, and the job we do is a clear expression of the strength of our spirit.

So let today matter!

—◁○▷—

CEO Message 260
WHAT GAME ARE YOU IN?

Today is what we miss when we are too busy making plans for tomorrow. Thinking about tomorrow is important but not as important as getting today right. Don't lose focus.

Money you put into savings is money you cannot afford to lose. Investing is money you can put at risk and can afford to lose. Your own situation will dictate the confidence you can have to make this decision. Health, job, age, and responsibilities are all part of the confidence factor.

How do you get a good handle on this confidence? Well, greed and fear are easy emotions to gauge your track record. Get a good read on this and it will put you in the right game.

CEO Message 251
FORTUNE'S WHEEL

There are no precautions or preemptive strikes against the inevitable.

The world of business, in particular, is a jungle. It's true. No matter how good you are, there are going to be problems, mistakes, and missteps. Sometimes the mistakes are self-correcting. Sometimes they are serious. Just remember: it's inevitable; everyone feels the pain. Small or large it's bound to happen. Here's what you do. Accept it. Learn from it. Take the consequences and move on. Make sure you move on emotionally! It's not easy, but repeat after me: it's a real part of life.

Look, no one is perfect.

At the same time, let's not pretend that our failures aren't real or that they can be casually ignored. Don't run away from those consequences. Admit them, wear them but don't let them wear you.

Regroup. Recommit. Respond.

That's the sign of a good leader and a good team. It's the battle and reward rolled into one.

CEO Message 165
RESPECT

Are you letting respect turn into entitlement? Respect needs to be earned. It's proved with actions, not words. Entitlement issues are the wages of past efforts. Leave them in the past.

It's your job. It's your right. Now you just have to prove it by earning it every day. Prove that you can do it and do it well.

CEO Message 253
A DAY OF SERVICE

Perhaps every day should be thought of as a day of service. An act of giving needs no special day. Wouldn't that be great?

CEO Message 23
VALUES

You'll recall I said that a few years back ING Direct actually doubled in size. That level of exponential growth was a real test of our management skills, in particular how we worked as a team.

One of the most critical things in doubling the number of people working for ING Direct was wondering on what basis we would select and bring people into the organization to help us power this growth.

Like anywhere else, we celebrate each other's differences in terms of background, experience, personality, and interests, but we should have a common understanding of values. What really mattered was that we shared these values clearly and honestly. As a business this was what truly brought us together as a team. It was our diversity that gave us strength and it was our sharing of values that gave us the cohesiveness to work effectively as a team.

What were—what are—those values? Directness, integrity, responsiveness, excellence, creativeness, and teamwork. No surprise that our corporate values also reflected our brand values: honesty and directness nourished integrity because it clearly communicated where we stood and this helped us position our views around independence, freedom, self-reliance, and the types of family values that we all shared.

Customers saw this, not only in the way we spoke with them but in the way we interacted with them, and since these values were clearly on our fingertips as we worked together

> "If you need to ask what the job pays then your looking for the wrong job."
> —AK

as a team, it was easy to translate them into our business model. When you ask if today mattered, think of the values that you share with your colleagues, values that are enduring, passionate, and worth fighting for.

CEO Message 63
CHARACTER MATTERS

The Roman historian Plutarch said that character is "simply habit long continued."

Think of it this way: do you plan on being in business for the long term? If so, do you want people around you to be built for the short term?

Character is all about how we handle adversity, right? Character matters. What do character and habits have in common? And why are habits so hard to break? Your habits are more than the routine of what you do. They make up a large part of who you are. How you act, how you react, and how you interact are all influenced by your habits.

This isn't meant to discourage you from tackling a tough habit, but to show how important habits are to your future. If you are to grow into the person you hope to be, living the life you hope to live, your habits should reflect that idea.

What *is* required is consistency.

Be patient, and don't be discouraged by setbacks. Remember: how you bounce back from failure is a habit itself. It also says something about your character.

CEO Message 101
GIFTS

Many people are sent to us; they are gifts in life's journey. Most of the time we do not see it or want to see it. We want to give gifts—when we want to! We want to be the one giving. There are special people you work with if you look for them. The sign of a powerful leader is one who understands those with whom he interacts and celebrates the nature of the gift.

Aside from all the stereotypical roles that we all perform on a team we are still unique and find the special chemistry that binds us together. Whether you are introverted or extroverted you have unique opportunities to connect.

It's a gift.

CEO Message 127
ARE YOU GROWING?

I remember how excited and proud I was when ING Direct hired its one-thousandth employee.

What an amazing trajectory we were on. It was such an exciting time with so many opportunities and challenges ahead. But it also made me wonder, had I grown as fast as the bank had? Had I encouraged and inspired my fellow associates to grow?

So ask yourself this question, and be honest: "What is my growth rate?"

The challenges ahead were going to be demanding and more complex. So were the pressures. So what was I doing to prepare myself for those new challenges?

What is your growth rate? We often confuse our "selves"—who we are—with the business we are in. We say that we want to be at two thousand employees by year whatever and at so many billion in profit by whenever... Sure, fine.

But where do *you* want to be?

Think about what you do and who you are. What do you wish to accomplish in life? Everyone asks these questions at some point. Maybe we never find the answer but the searching is surely what we are all committed to.

What journey are *you* on?

CEO Message 137
IMPRISONED BY OUR JOBS

A book, *Aware at Work: 35 Practical Buddhist Principles for Discovering Clarity in the Midst of Work Chaos*, is worthy of further study. How we define work and approach it is personal, yet self-illuminating. Is work war? Is it a problem? Is it entertainment? Is it an addiction? Our needs drive our actions, and a manager needs to self-evaluate, not only the energy spent, but the clarity and authenticity of who we are and wish to become.

Maybe the fit is everything.

CEO Message 138
WHAT MOVES YOU?
Life is a journey with no return; your only compass is your spirit, love and reflection.

CEO Message 40
WHOSE STANDARDS?
One measure of performance is how you measure up to your own standard. The more objective it is, the more your true performance will be shared with those you work with. Taking the time to take stock is a real opportunity to move forward and recommit to what you want to accomplish.

CEO Message 140
"ASK NOT"
Ask not, "How have I done?" Offer your testimony instead. Those you work with will want to listen. It's not a negotiation but an opportunity for sharing.

CEO Message 141
PERFORMANCE IS PERCEPTION
Who would you share your annual performance with? Would it matter to you? *How* you are doing is as important as *what* you have done!

CEO Message 148
ORANGE RETRO

Destiny is built upon values, values are built upon habits, habits are built upon actions, actions are built upon words, and words are built upon thoughts.

This powerful ladder is one that should challenge you as a leader to figure out ways to keep alive your commitment to your company's core values. Never stop learning, always keep challenging yourself and your employees about what you are doing and why. Never stop the relentless pursuit of excellence; continue challenging each other in a constructive manner, being honest and direct with one another, as well as being loyal to what you are attempting to do both personally and professionally.

CEO Message 158
BUSINESS VALUES

If business is to be meaningful—not as a business devoted only to its bottom line and shareholders but in its role in society—it must not become desensitized to the human condition and spirit. Corporate values often collide with social responsibility in not only the *what* but the *how* of its goals and aspirations. Corporations must connect to all stakeholders—not just stockholders.

Social issues must be balanced with sacrifices to meet the goals. Customers, employees and corporate stakeholders must put alignment of their interests first if we are to make a difference in the quality of life.

CEO Message 172
SETTING GOALS

Setting goals allows us to focus our energies on a specific task or accomplishment. Merely verbalizing them is not enough. By putting pen to paper and writing them down, it is more likely that you will achieve them. I challenge my employees on a yearly basis to formulate a list of three personal goals for the upcoming year. Write them down and set a plan in action for accomplishing them. At the end of the year, see how you did. What would you have done better? Reflect on this thought: had you not set them, would they have been achieved?

CEO Message 163
PERFORMANCE CULTURE

It starts with sizing up the gap between you and your company; it ends with the statement, "Change begins with me." The middle is an ongoing improvement, which comes all by itself.

CEO Message 169
HOW EASY SHOULD IT BE?

Success, momentum, hard work, good results—all good stuff. Very rewarding.

Yet character, both for a business and for an individual, is built and tested by adversity. It challenges one to identify and test the stuff we are made of. Expectations are critical in judging where we are today. Managing expectations will determine your success for tomorrow. But if you look forward with optimism, the rewards will come. It's not easy!

CEO Message 177

A WINNING CODE

Here are elements of the samurai code that can help you win any business battle, according to Bill Diffenderffer from his illuminating book, *The Samurai Leader: Winning Business Battles with the Wisdom, Honor and Courage of the Samurai Code*:

- Act honorably. Honor isn't negotiable—it's an overarching requirement.
- Act with courage. When you know what needs to be done, do it.
- Act with rectitude. Always do the right thing.
- Be loyal. Without loyalty, there is no trust.
- Be compassionate. To be a leader one must care for others.
- Appreciate the arts. Art is a doorway to understanding and appreciating life.
- Be honest. Without honesty, there is no credibility.
- Be polite. It shows respect and makes getting along with everyone much easier.
- Maintain self-control. To manage others, one must manage oneself.

CEO Message 181

GO FOR IT!

Never be satisfied. Always strive to be better than you are. It's healthy for leaders to take a sigh of relief, and celebrate accomplishments; but remember, every day is a new day. Take full advantage of it. Your legacy will not only be the sum of what you've done in the past, but what we can do in the future.

WHAT IS YOUR GOAL?

It's always a good idea to think about performance.

Think about this: are you good at setting goals?

To have a successful performance, result, or outcome, the right goal is key. So what is right for you? Set a different goal than last year. Make it a big goal—one that excites you and is worth achieving. Set out clear progress markers—steps to get

> "If you love what you do you will never work another day in your life." —AK

you there. Tell your friends, family and your team what your goals are. It helps with your visualization and commitment. Have your goal figured out today before you go to sleep.

We all face challenging personal stories. You may be facing one today, or may face one soon. Tell someone about it. Sharing is a way of validation. It's not who we are; it is who we are becoming.

WHAT DO THESE ITEMS HAVE IN COMMON?

The best place you lived, your best school year, your best family vacation, the best party you ever attended, the best place you worked, and, of course, your happiest memory. Each has one, and only one, thing in common. Here are some clues: it's where you felt most alive, successful, and happy. Your best moments. You can make more if you put your mind to it and help create them.

They don't just happen.

The answer is fundamental to life and business.

CEO Message 38
FAITH

There are many ways to find personal strength to see you through tough challenges and overcome crises. Disappointments are going to find you. Life just works that way. A good leader knows that these are moments of testing character and personal resolve to see them through. How do you do this? It might be your family, your faith, or your best friend. Somewhere we all have someone in our corner. You need to focus on them and how they are the real bonds you can count on. Faith is knowing that there is a way to deal with things we do not understand or cannot see. A good leader knows that making decisions is working with incomplete information. One has to apply judgment and that means taking a risk with the information you have. Making a call with your team members is all about how well you can read the situation, the people involved and the broad and multiple consequences of the decisions you need to make. To lead means to be out front on issues that are uncertain. Your number one task as a leader is to take uncertainty out of every challenge. To take that on every day is to have faith and confidence.

In a diverse culture your leadership actions are going to be judged differently by many people. Style has a lot to do with it. The quiet servant leadership of more reserved society is quite different, for instance, from the stoic leadership style of Asia and the formal style characteristic of Western Europe. America was a much greater melting pot twenty years ago. Tolerance for diversity is greater today, but the cultural norms we use to communicate and effectively lead are just coming into their own. It is interesting that the best result

Personal Growth: Understanding the Journey You Are On

comes from one-on-one contact and building trust and understanding. You must work hard to understand, read the situation and be sensitive to how your personal actions are being interpreted. It's a tall order, but that is where the best are going. You can too.

———◁◇▷———

Zen in the Art of Rock then Roll: The takeaways

- Make today matter.
- Once you have the secrets worked out for yourself, lead.
- Set personal and professional goals for you and your associates.
- Be deliberate in everything you do.
- Remember the ladder of thoughts to values.

CONCLUSION

Lots of ideas can be easily stated or written down, but making them real and active is very hard. By now you have finished this book. Maybe the best way to make it real and active is to put it aside for a few days or a week. Then pick it up again. What stands out for you? Make a point to take one or two ideas and practice with them. Take the principles of the Orange Code. Take the rules of Rock then Roll or the secrets of culture-driven leadership and copy them down. Make it your screensaver. Find a chance to discuss and debate these ideas with someone you work with or trust. Then make them yours. Use them to your advantage. Add your own! If you are faced with a situation or problem, break it down using the Code, or the rules, or the secrets. Find out what the challenge is and then solve it. Much like in sports, everyone needs practical advice and good coaching. But once the buzzer sounds or the bell rings, you have to play your own game.

Remember this too: we all have our own timelines. I have mine.

Here's what I mean:

April 27, 1997. ING Direct debuted. Fifty million dollars in capital. No customers.

June 16, 2011. ING Direct USA sold to Capital One for nine billion dollars. Ten million customers.

What's next? Who knows? But I like to build. That is what I do.

You have your own timeline. It's the same with our successes and failures. It isn't a question of duplicating. It's all about making it true for you. So make it true. Be authentic.

I wish you luck!

FINAL THOUGHT

Life is a journey. We are born naked and after eighty years or so we die naked.

It's the choices we make and how we spend the time that matters. It's worth reminding each other of this obvious fact. Life will pass one way or another. Now this is not meant to be bleak or fearful; it's just a way to look at life and make the most out of it. The bumper sticker cliché is right: you cannot take it with you!

Rock then Roll!

Note to readers: The proceeds from this book are donated to charity and in particular the ING Direct Kids Foundation.

ACKNOWLEDGMENTS

Since the writing of "The Orange Code" with Bruce Philp in 2008, a lot has happened to the economy, businesses, and consumers. A mind shift and a shift in priorities and values has taken place which has shaped the conversations and commentary by the media and, most important, at every family's dinner table. Amid this new volatile environment consumers are reassessing what to buy and how to handle their finances. Could the "Save your Money" slogan after ten years for ING Direct be right in the middle of the new definitions of the marketplace? I believe it is.

The associates at ING Direct are still on the journey to do good. They have a clear conscience in an industry that has lost consumer trust through the economic crisis of 2008. They continue to inspire me with the vision and mission of ING Direct. The support of ING Direct's board members that has been steadfast through the crisis and which had applied sound judgment has been unwavering. My colleagues, some with whom I have served for many years and others for just a short time, have one thing in common: they are good people with energy and passion, the fuel for doing something great. They are Peter Aceto, Scott Gray, Dan Greenshields, Bill Higgins, Jim Kelly, Scott Lugar, Cathy MacFarlane, Rob Middleton, Brian Myres, John Owens, Rick Perles, Margaret Rose, Todd Sandler, Bill Watt, Kristine Wellman, and Rudy Wolfs.

There is a story for each of these leaders that they have not yet realized. The tremendous impact they are having on all associates at ING Direct in the USA and Canada will continue to happen and has yet to be narrated.

The support necessary to get this book done in good order was generously provided by TY Soh, executive advisor, and Carolyn Imparato, my executive assistant, two very abled individuals to whom I'm indebted. And to Eric Kuhlmann, for help with the website.

This book would never have been possible without the team that created it: Sam Hiyate from The Rights Factory for showing the light on how to make this story come alive; Marijke Friesen, who is a gifted designer and whose work will catch the inspired reader; Jonathan Schmidt, who has labored, edited, and created this book out of a pit of words and thoughts to make it readable and, most of all, true to its mission. His hand guided the expression that I was not able to provide. My thank you comes from the heart for his great collaborative effort in bringing this book to life.

The customers that continue to join this movement of savers at ING Direct are continuing! Above all it is their testament to The Orange Code by which ING Direct operates and the inspiration to help leaders "Rock then Roll" the world. I am forever grateful to serve alongside these fine leaders, believers, and champions.

"PAINTING IS A PASSION AND HOBBY THAT REFRESHES THE SPIRIT AND PLANTS THE SEEDS FOR NEW IDEAS." —AK

The illustrations in this book are from original paintings by the author.

Page 8: *Hallliburton High* (March 1996)
Page 89: *Russian Winter* Night (January 1998)
Page 147: *Irises at Sunset* (October 1994)
Page 213: *Golden Mirror* (January 2008)
Page 322: *Algonquin Magic* (November 1993)
Page 340: *Sunset Beach, Oahu.* Heather Titus Photo. (October 2009)
Page 342: *Goblin Bay* (March 2001)
Page 347: *Lebrubuf Lighthouse #2* (July 2005)

To view more artwork by Arkadi Kuhlmann visit: www.arkadikuhlmann.com